The Irish 100

The Irish 100

A Ranking of the Most Influential Irish of All Time

Peter Costello

CITADEL PRESS
Kensington Publishing Corp.
www.kensingtonbooks.com

CITADEL PRESS books are published by
Kensington Publishing Corp.
850 Third Avenue
New York, NY 10022

All Kensington titles, imprints, and distributed lines are available at special quantity
discounts for bulk purchases for sales promotions, premiums, fund raising, educational,
or institutional use. Special book excerpts or customized printings can also be created
to fit specific needs. For details, write or phone the office of the Kensington special
sales manager: Kensington Publishing Corp., 850 Third Avenue, New York, NY 10022,
attn: Special Sales Department, phone 1-800-221-2647.

Citadel Press and the Citadel logo are trademarks of Kensington Publishing Corp.

First printing February 2002

10 9 8 7 6 5 4 3 2 1

Printed in the United States of America

Cataloging data may be obtained from the Library of Congress.

ISBN 0-8065-2344-1

To the memory of my father

James Cormac Costello
Professor Emeritus
University of Michigan

The most influential Irish person
in my life

It is the entitlement and birthright of every person born
in the island of Ireland, which includes its islands and seas,
to be part of the Irish nation . . .

Furthermore, the Irish nation cherishes its special
affinity with people of Irish ancestry living abroad who share
its cultural identity and heritage.

—*Nineteenth Amendment to the Constitution of Ireland,*
May 1998

CONTENTS

ACKNOWLEDGMENTS

I am grateful for those friends and colleagues in the academic world who have advised me, especially Frank Litton of the Institute of Public Administration, social historian and publisher Tony Farmar, and my colleague Ken MacGowan. I am happy to acknowledge the past opportunities for discussion of various subjects with Prof. Leo MacNamara of the University of Michigan and the late Prof. Gus Martin of University College in Dublin, and Dr. Peter van de Kamp and John Wyse Jackson, my friends and coauthors. And also the senior civil servant and historian Henry Boylan, whose own research has proved invaluable; Prof. Robert Hogan for his advice and for the opportunity to work as an assistant editor on the *Dictionary of Irish Literature*; and Teresa Whitington, of the Central Catholic Library. I am also deeply appreciative of the aid provided by the staffs of the libraries of Trinity College, Dublin, and the National Library of Ireland. Many others have also assisted with their advice and information on specifics. I am especially grateful to Steve Palme and Gary Goldstein for their hard work on an often difficult script. They have translated the Irish idioms of the author, making the book accessible to the widest audience possible. They have also helped to make my meaning clear, and detected some errors, much improving the book. My thanks are also due to their successors at Citadel Press.

My thanks to them all. The selection of persons and the comments in this book are mine, however, and not theirs.

INTRODUCTION

Ireland is a small island, with a small population. Yet over the centuries she has exerted an influence in the wider world out of all proportion both to her size and her resources.

This is partly through those Irish people who have lived and worked in Ireland itself, but also through those others, representative of a diaspora of many millions, who have emigrated to Britain, Europe, Australia, and Canada, but most especially to the United States of America. More Irish people live in the United States than anywhere else in the world (including Ireland), and a great many have an intense involvement with the history and culture of their ancestral home, which has molded their lives as Americans.

A recent survey of national pride by the University of Chicago showed that the Irish led the world in their admiration of specific achievements by their countrymen in such areas as the arts, history, the armed forces, the economy, and sports. Americans came in second.

The survey also showed that many young people had less overall pride than their elders. This was thought to reflect the growth of globalism and multilateralism, or perhaps a reaction to the nationalistic extremism of the past. But it may be that the younger generation has simply never heard of the great achievers of the past, whose influence has done so much to shape the world they live in. The Irish and the Irish Americans, as communities, have kept alive that pride, and it is reflected in this book.

The influence of the Irish can be said to be universal, and the contribution of the Irish-born to the development of the modern world has been an important one. Influence, of course, is not a matter of mere fame. The passing notoriety of a celebrity such as a film star (of which there have been many from Ireland) is not the same as the influence exerted by a great patriot, artist, writer, or humanitarian. To be truly influential, the contribution of any of our Irish 100 must be a lasting one.

Yet the persons I have chosen presented a problem. Inevitably, there has to be great difficulty in choosing individuals from such an array of talented people. I may seem to have been somewhat arbitrary in my choices. Personal preference has been restrained, however, in order to collect together as wide and as historic a range of cultural heroes as possible.

Some of the persons included here will be familiar, others almost unknown. In any selection based on a specific ethnic group, as this book is, it has been especially important to chose individuals with no regard to gender or sexuality. Likewise, it is too easy to lead with those who have been public figures in politics over those whose achievements and influence have been in the arts, sciences, or religion.

Influence works in strange ways. Though our newspapers make us aware of the influence which public figures such as politicians or millionaires think they wield in the world, our everyday lives are actually more affected by the activities of scientists, inventors, and trade unionists. We have to be careful not take people at their own estimation.

These days, many people have a great interest in tracing their roots. In the summer of 1998 Newt Gingrich, then speaker of the U.S. House of Representatives, was in Ireland, and after his talks with the various communities in the Ulster conflict, one of his purposes was to search out his family connections in Donegal. Thomas "Tip" O'Neill, one of his predecessors in the office, was an old-style Irish American, but who would have thought Newt Gingrich was too! History is full of surprises, as we shall see.

Perhaps a note on the historical background of Ireland and the Irish may be of use to some readers using this book as a reference tool.

The history of Ireland and of the various peoples who have inhabited the island is a long and complex one. It is also very controversial. The earliest evidence for man in Ireland dates from about 7000 B.C., at Mount Sandel near Coleraine, in Northern Ireland. These people are the original Irish, and would have been followed in time by Neolithic and Bronze Age people. These peoples are the architects of Newgrange, and the dolmens and tombs scattered throughout the country. But they left no written records of their culture or history. We have to appreciate their achievement through the discoveries of archaeologists.

The first evidence of Celtic culture in Ireland dates from about 300 B.C. These invaders wiped out the original language of the island, and imposed their own Gaelic language on the Irish natives. This race would have intermarried with the earlier inhabitants to begin the process of producing the Irish of today. Other waves of invaders followed: Romans in the first centuries, Christian missionaries in the fifth, the Vikings in the eighth. Then the Normans in the twelfth, followed by English, and eventually Scottish settlers (themselves the descendants of the Gaels who had colonized parts of Scotland).

Irish history is not a simple tale of heroic Celtic warriors fighting to the death and brave Celtic women being raped by vicious Englishmen, the caricature that so often passes for history. Much that is admired, and rightly admired in the history and culture of the island, is non-Celtic. Ireland has also shared the religious fortunes of Europe to the full, with perhaps the exception of the ancient classical mystery cults of the Orient (though even that may be doubtful—it may yet be shown that the worship of Mithras reached Ireland).

Many details of Irish history are alluded to in the course of this book, but in such a limited space it is difficult to enlarge upon them. It is hoped that those using this book will also consult the books of historical background listed in "Further Reading." Controversies over the details in the course of Irish history continue, as do disputes about exactly what it is to be Irish, and who the Irish really are.

Though many Irish people today are Roman Catholic, it is not the special destiny of the Irish to be Catholic. The Protestant culture of Ireland is a strong one, and the inhabitants of the island achieved great things when they were pagans, and may well do so again now that Ireland, like the rest of Europe, has passed into a post-Christian phase of history.

These days an Irish person is someone who was born in Ireland, has made a permanent home in Ireland, or who is attached to Irish culture in some way, even though he lives in another country. All these kinds of Irish people are represented in this book. They are people who have been capable of great fortitude, great passion, and great charity. They are also people who have been capable of great evil. They must be taken as you find them.

This book would fail to present a complete view of the influence of the Irish if it were necessary for inclusion that a person must have been born or worked in Ireland, or had Ireland as the main focus of their life. Thus, many emigrants to other countries would have to be excluded. So this book includes Irish people famous in the wider world, such as John F. Kennedy, Ned Kelly, and Bernardo O'Higgins.

At the conclusion of a long process, I am struck not only by the achievements of those who are included here, but even more by the achievements of those for whom there was no space.

It can safely be predicted that the influence which the Irish have had in the past will be as nothing compared to what they will achieve tomorrow, both in Europe, in America, and elsewhere.

It is a matter of controversy whether one of Columbus's crew, when the New World was discovered, was an Irishman from Galway. But certainly when Neil Armstrong landed on the moon in July 1969, that first step on another planet was made by a man of Irish descent. Armstrong's ancestors hailed from Fermanagh in Ulster, and those of James Irwin, the first man to drive on the moon, came from Pomeroy, also in Ulster.

It is only too likely that the first person to land on Mars will also be of Irish blood.

Peter Costello
Dublin, 2001

The Irish 100

1

St. Patrick

c. 385–461

Everywhere the Irish are to be found, they have taken the name of Ireland's patron saint with them. All over the world, schools, churches, and streets in towns and cities are dedicated to St. Patrick. Paddy is everywhere the nickname of Irishmen.

His influence over Ireland was of the first importance. To the ancient civilization of a country which had never been part of the Roman Empire, he added the Christian culture common to Europe. Yet the irony of the matter is that St. Patrick, for all that, was not born in Ireland.

Who he was and where he came from are still matters of mystery. He himself tells us in his *Confessions*, which is really a defense of his life and actions written as an old man, that he was a native of Roman Britain, born in Bannavem Taberniae, and that his father was a deacon of the church called Calpurnius. Where Bannavem Taberniae may have been is not known, though some think it was in the Clyde region of Scotland, others that it was far to the south, perhaps in Somerset. (St. Patrick's name is associated with Glastonbury, where he is even said to be buried.)

His grandfather had been a priest, and his father was not only a deacon, but also a town councilor, all of which suggests a prosperous background and comfortable childhood. At the age of sixteen he was captured by Irish pirates and carried into slavery in Ulster, the northern province of Ireland. For six years he herded sheep and swine on the slopes of Slemish Mountain for a local chief.

In his lonely exile he turned to the faith of his fathers, and prayed for release. After six years, at the age of twenty-two, he escaped and made his way home, leaving Ireland by a boat from somewhere on the south coast. However, he had been marked by his experience. He relates (again in *The Confession*) that he heard the voices of the Irish calling him to be among them again. He took this as a personal mission, which he set out to fulfill.

It seems clear that there were already Christians in Ireland at this time, for there had been a great deal of contact between Roman Britain and Ireland (perhaps even invasion and settlement). Moreover, there had been earlier missions, one by a priest called Palladius, sent by the pope in 431. But this was all in southern Ireland. After training for the priesthood both in Britain and on the Continent, Patrick found that his superiors were reluctant to let him go to Ireland. However, Patrick returned to the north, where he had been held captive, and began his personal missionary journeys from a place called Saul, in County Down. Though his name is linked with County Armagh, where he had his chief church, he is said to be buried in Downpatrick, also in County Down.

Many legends surround his name. One of the most important tells of how he lit the special Paschal fire on the Hill of Slane in direct disobedience of the rule that no fire could be lit on that day before the Druids lit the fire of the High King of Ireland in their own pagan ceremonies. The legend of his encounter with the High King of Ireland at Tara on the Paschal feast took on almost mythical importance. Its meaning for later centuries was that the civil state was inferior to the church.

As there were no real towns in Ireland, Patrick introduced a form of church rule by basing bishops in little monasteries, as was common in the Near East. After Patrick's death, the church in Ireland developed its own peculiar Celtic features, such as the importance of the monasteries and the lesser role of bishops. It also held Easter on a different date from Rome and used a different form of priestly tonsure. But the church was always in union with Rome, and the country, once Christianized, retained the new religion, mingling it with aspects of the old Celtic culture.

Many points about St. Patrick's life and career are disputed. It has even been claimed that there were two different men of the same name. But these are the quarrels of scholars. Patrick reveals himself in his own writings as an unlearned, straightforward man, but a man with a mission. It is not the details of his life that have impressed Irish people over the centuries, but his vivid personality as the apostle of Ireland.

Among the leading figures of the fifth century, he is almost alone in having left us writings in his own hand, in which he speaks for himself. His voice can still be heard in the *Confessions,* which includes a moving defense of his life against accusations of early sin, and his *Letter to the Soldiers of Coroticus,* a British chief who had kidnapped some Irish Christians. In the account of his life, he lays great emphasis on his lack of learning and his own unworthiness, but claims that through the grace God had granted him, he was able to achieve what might have seemed impossible.

It is this voice that still exerts great influence. Many of his characteristics—courage, perseverance, resistance to false authority, a love of nature, a direct appeal to individuals—are still those of the Irish as a whole. To this day the religious outlook of the Irish people affects their ideas about many things. Unhappily, the religion which Patrick brought later led to divisions which are still to be healed.

St. Patrick's Day, March 17, is a day of celebration in Irish communities worldwide. It had always been a Catholic feast day, but the first celebration outside the confines of the church was held in Boston in 1737 by the Charitable Irish Society, which was founded that year. In 1784, in New York, the Friendly Sons of St. Patrick followed the lead of Boston. This New York society was a joint venture of Catholic and Presbyterian Irish, and the first president of the organization was a Presbyterian. It was not until 1852 that a fully organized parade such as we have today was held in New York City. By this time the middle-class Presbyterians had begun to develop an idea of themselves as Scotch Irish to distinguish themselves from the Catholic working-class Irish, and the parade became a vehicle for an outpouring of Irish nationalist Catholic feeling. St. Patrick's Day began to play a special role in the complicated politics of major American cities from this day on (to the extent that it now includes members of the Irish-American gay community—a contentious addition to the festival). The idea of a full-scale civic celebration was imported from America back to Ireland, where St. Patrick's Day only became a public holiday in 1903.

The saint's name is associated with two of the world's great places of religious pilgrimage: Croaghpatrick in Mayo, which is climbed by believers every year on the last Sunday in July, and St. Patrick's Purgatory in Donegal, a place of vision and penance, which has enjoyed fame since the Middle Ages and may have inspired Dante in the writing of *The Divine Comedy.*

To St. Patrick is ascribed the first use of the shamrock to illustrate the Christian dogma of the Holy Trinity—the Father, Son, and Holy Spirit. But over the centuries the little plant became the symbol of Ireland and all things Irish, thanks largely to its legendary association with St. Patrick.

2

Eamon de Valera

1882–1975

By common agreement of his admirers and foes, Eamon de Valera has exercised the greatest influence over modern Ireland, drawing on the past to create a present which he hoped would be cherished by his countrymen forever.

Through a long life in which much was achieved as well as left unfinished, he has become a permanent feature of the Irish historical landscape. He created the party with the largest popular support in Ireland, and it still dominates the present political scene. He is the figure against whom all others are judged.

De Valera first came to prominence during the Easter Rising against British rule in Ireland in 1916, a rebellion organized by Irish republicans hoping to liberate their country from what they saw as eight hundred years of foreign rule. Because of his American birth, de Valera was the only male rebel commander to be spared. He was tried and imprisoned, but he gained great prestige from being a survivor of this great patriotic act. This prestige carried an otherwise obscure young man on to half a century of intense political activity.

De Valera was born in New York, where his Irish immigrant mother had married a Spaniard who died soon after his birth. Brought back to Ireland in 1885, he was reared among his mother's people in East Limerick. Though never a farmer himself, he claimed to cherish these early experiences as a permanent model of Irish social life. He also looked to America and to the Irish-American community as a source of support in the long struggle for Irish freedom.

An intelligent child, he was sent to one of the country's leading schools, where he excelled in math. He lived quietly, working as a teacher. He and his wife were little known among the vigorous and often colorful cultural circles in the Dublin of WILLIAM BUTLER YEATS [8].

But politics soon took hold of him. In 1912 the British government offered Ireland home rule, the option to run their own affairs, except defense and foreign affairs, but this was not acceptable to a Protestant minority in Northern Ireland, who wished to remain a full part of the United Kingdom. A great political crisis ensued, which almost led to a mutiny of British army officers in Ireland. Though the Home Rule Act became law, it was suspended for the duration of the First World War, which broke out in August 1914.

De Valera joined the Irish Volunteers, a group which was organized to defend Ireland's rights to independence, and this led to his part in the Easter Rising, his work as "President of the Irish Republic" in America, the controversies surrounding the Treaty with Great Britain, and to the civil war in Ireland, which ended with him being imprisoned again, this time by the new Irish government.

In 1924 he was released. The antitreaty republicans who had fought in the civil war were a disparate group, ranging from revolutionary radicals to deeply conservative Catholics. In 1926 de Valera split from the Irish Republican Army (IRA) to form a new republican party, Fianna Fail, which quickly built up a following on the middle ground of Irish politics. The party entered the Dail (Ireland's national assembly) in 1927.

In 1932 de Valera came to power and quickly consolidated his sway over the country. On the world scene he began to play a useful but ultimately frustrating role in the League of Nations.

At home he began to pick at the treaty solution, and in 1937 he introduced a new constitution which provided for a president as head of state within a social framework based on the social teachings of the Catholic church. The idea of a written constitution came from America. Though amended from time to time, the constitution is de Valera's most lasting monument, and it still provides the basic law of Ireland.

Adroitly, he managed to keep Ireland out of the Second World War. Ireland prospered during the war, but there were social difficulties afterward which resulted in de Valera losing power in 1948. In 1951 he returned to power, but was again ousted in 1954. Reelected in 1957, he was faced with worsening economic conditions.

A solution to Ireland's economic malaise was begun by the first Program for Economic Expansion of 1958, the basis of the country's development since. But this was a scheme of his deputy SEAN LEMASS [14], a young man impatient for power. De Valera left politics and was elected to two terms as president. In 1973 he retired to private life, and died in 1975.

In a famous speech at the end of the Second World War, de Valera spoke of his vision of an ideal Irish society based on traditional rural and spiritual values. But by the time of his death, Ireland, with the advent of prosperity based on industry and electronics, and dominated by television and the wider interests of the day, had abandoned that vision.

De Valera remains a controversial figure. The details of his career are still debated. To a generation of Irish people whom he saved from the scourge of a world war, he was seen as a giant among modern statesmen, a visionary with an unblemished record of probity.

As always in public life, his political opponents differed. He was often seen, even by his friends, as aloof and cold. His years as a teacher of math and languages had left him with the pedantic attitudes of a calculating grammarian, delighting in the small points of a matter at hand, while others were impatient to settle larger issues.

Yet he retained the lifelong devotion of men of great capacity and integrity, and his certainty of mind gave confidence to many others. He once said that if he wished to know what the Irish people thought, he had only to look into his own heart. This outlook lies at the heart of the separation of Northern Ireland, one of the great issues he never resolved (having done so much to create it). He could not understand the unionist people of Belfast by looking into *his* heart. These contradictions are all a part of the de Valera legend, an aspect of the hold which he retains over the minds and imaginations of the Irish people.

A final judgment can be left to the historian Prof. J. J. Lee of Cork University, who writes of de Valera in his history of modern Ireland: "He was, in a sense, greater than the sum of his parts. Behind the ceaseless political calculation and the labyrinthine deviousness, there reposed a character of rare nobility. "

3

Michael Collins

1890–1922

Though he died fighting in the Irish Civil War at the age of thirty-one, Michael Collins remains for many Irish people the very epitome of the Irish rebel—bold, handsome, and romantic. He was the man who masterminded the guerilla war against the British army in Ireland between 1919 and 1921, but also lived just long enough to firmly lay the foundations of a democratic state in Ireland. Though divided from his former comrades by the civil war (1922 to 1923), he saw the Treaty with Great Britain as a stepping-stone to fully securing what many Irish people had longed for, a united thirty-two-county Irish republic. But he had to place responsibilities before dreams and accept what was offered, even though it meant the partition of the island. It had been effectively partitioned since 1880, and it has taken Irish nationalists another century to come to terms with the outlook of many Ulstermen.

Michael Collins was born on October 16, 1890, in Woodfield, Clonakilty, in County Cork. Like so many Irish leaders, he was the son of a small farmer. After being educated in the local national school, he went to London at the age of sixteen, where he joined the civil service as a clerk in the post office. Later he worked as a clerk for a stockbroker, which gave him some grasp of finance.

In London he joined the Irish Republican Brotherhood (IRB), the main group plotting for an Irish revolution—they derived from the original Fenians, who had attempted an invasion of Canada and an insurrection in Ireland back in the 1860s, a generation before Collins's birth. He returned to Dublin to take part in the Easter Rising in 1916, which the brotherhood instigated. He fought in the General Post Office in Dublin where the rebels had their headquarters, with PATRICK PEARSE [7], and was detained when the rebels surrendered. On his release from prison, he quickly came to the fore as a leading figure in the political party Sinn Fein, as well as in the Irish Volunteers, the military wing of the movement that became known, from its Fenian roots, as the IRA. Against the wishes of EAMON DE VALERA [2] and others, in 1917 he organized for a Sinn Fein candidate to run in a local election, and to win the seat. Many felt that Irish republicans should have nothing to do with British institutions of any kind.

In 1919, with the establishment of the first Dail—the assembly of Irish representatives who had been elected to the imperial parliament in London but chose instead to sit in Dublin—and the declaration of Irish independence, he became the minister of home affairs and later the minister of finance in the underground Sinn Fein government of Ireland. But it was not for these public roles that he became well known. He was also director of intelligence for the Irish Volunteers. While he was raising the National Loan to finance the activities of the new movement, with help from Irish Americans, he was also setting up an espionage system which infiltrated the British system in Ireland.

A forceful personality of great energy, he was also famous for his personal courage and contempt for danger. His coup in organizing the murder of fourteen British intelligence officers on a Sunday morning, November 21, 1920, led that afternoon to twelve fatalities at Croke Park when British soldiers opened fire on a crowd attending a Gaelic football match.

The British prime minister Lloyd George, an astute Welshman, realized that the excesses of the war fought the length and breadth of Ireland during late 1920 and early 1921 could no longer be sustained. A truce came into effect in July 1921, and a second Dail was assembled in August. Collins was one of those who went to London to negotiate the treaty signed in December 1921.

What might have been the end of Ireland's troubles and the beginning of a new era became instead the object of fierce objections from some republicans. Collins became chairman of the Provisional Government of the Irish Free State, and after the civil war broke out became commander in chief of the national army. On a tour of west Cork his party was ambushed at Béal na Bláth on August 22, 1922, and during the firefight which followed he was struck in the head by a ricocheting bullet and died almost at once.

He had been in his own country, the countryside of his childhood. As Cork writer Frank O'Connor later expressed it, "The countryside he had seen in dreams, the people he had loved, the tradition which had been his inspiration—they had risen in the falling light and struck him dead." His funeral, so soon after the sudden death of his colleague Arthur Griffith, was an occasion for an outpouring of national grief. But there were other men to succeed them, and despite the turmoil and terror of the civil war (far worse than anything that had been seen in the short war against the British) the Irish state remained stable.

This was, perhaps, Collins's greatest gift to his people, but his other qualities of bravery and leadership have given him almost mythical stature in modern Ireland. That Ireland is today a mature and thriving democracy owes much to the life and struggle of Michael Collins.

4

John Fitzgerald Kennedy

1917–1963

The election of John F. Kennedy as thirty-fifth president of the United States in November 1960 marked for Irish people everywhere a peak of achievement and national pride. He was the first Irishman and the first Catholic to be elected to that high office. Until then the prejudices which were deeply ingrained in American life had prevented both the Irish and the Catholics from getting to the White House. Though John Fitzgerald Kennedy, the wealthy son of a millionaire, was far removed from long-prevailing images of the Irish, his wit, handsome demeanor, love of the written and spoken word, and delight in politics of all kinds identified him as Irish through and through.

Kennedy's eventual visit to Ireland (June 26–29, 1963) was a momentous occasion, and a significant one. He spoke to the Irish nation on behalf of millions of emigrants. At the spot from which Patrick Kennedy had set out three generations before, he said: "When my great-grandfather left here to become a cooper in East Boston, he carried nothing with him except two things: a strong religious faith and a strong desire for liberty. . . . If he hadn't left, I would be working at the Albatross Company across the road."

The existence of that factory was an important development. For those heady days in the 1960s marked a transition from the older rural Ireland his grandfather had emigrated from to a new modern, industrialized Ireland, a democracy very much in the American model. For many commentators and historians, the Kennedy visit, coming so closely on the arrival of television in Ireland and the Vatican Council, brought about a rapid series of social and religious changes that transformed Ireland.

To many young people, Kennedy seemed to suggest a new kind of model for public life. Though his reputation has since been the object of much reassessment, his historical importance in the immediate days of the 1960s cannot be lessened. To Irish people everywhere he became the leading example of what the Irish nation could achieve.

His great-grandparents had come to the United States from Ireland, part of that great wave of people whom he would write about as the makers of America in his brief book *A Nation of Immigrants*. His grandfathers had been successful in business and politics, John Francis Fitzgerald being mayor of Boston. His father, Joseph P. Kennedy, achieved even greater success in business. A supporter of Franklin Delano Roosevelt, he became the first head of the Securities and Exchange Commission and served as American ambassador to London.

Joe Kennedy was naturally ambitious for his children. After the death of his eldest son, his ambitions became centered on Jack. Though Jack's education had been indifferent, he was widely read. As an explanation of why the war had come, he wrote *Why England Slept* (1940) during his father's time in London. During the war he served with the U.S. Navy in the South Pacific, and when his PT boat was sunk his old back problem reasserted itself. Illness was a problem for the rest of his life. Though it was not obvious to many except his family and friends, half the days of his life were days of pain, as his brother Robert later pointed out.

In 1946 he was elected to Congress from the eleventh Massachusetts district. He proved to be liberal and farsighted. In 1952 he was elected to the Senate, and in 1953 he married. Though he was independent-minded on many issues, Kennedy did not resist the demagoguery of Sen. Joseph McCarthy (a family friend). Hospitalized by recurring trouble from the back problem which responded only partially to treatment, he was unable to be present for the vote on the motion of censure in the Senate against McCarthy. It was during this illness that he wrote *Profiles in Courage* (1956), which won a Pulitzer Prize.

In the book he defined his own outlook: "A man does what he must, in spite of obstacles and dangers and pressures—and that is the basis of all human morality."

He failed to gain the vice presidential nomination in 1956, but began a campaign to secure the Democratic nomination for president in 1960. He gained this, and went on to fight Richard Nixon. The race was marked by the innovation of television debates, which many felt Kennedy won. Though he barely won the popular vote, he carried the electoral college, 303 to 219. He was the youngest man ever elected president, as well as the first Catholic, and the first born in the twentieth century.

The events of his brief presidency were memorable, but the most critical may have been the Cuban missile crisis in 1962. The most serious crisis since the end of World War II evolved out of Russia's presence in Cuba, the obverse of American presence in Asia. It was perceived as part of the worldwide menace of communism that then dominated public concern. The standoff ended on October 26, 1962.

It was under Kennedy that the inexorable growth of U.S. involvement in the defense of South Vietnam against the efforts of the Viet Cong and the North Vietnamese communists to unify the divided country began, but Kennedy also began efforts to disengage from the problem. He also met the Russian leader Nikita Khrushchev for a summit in Vienna in 1961.

At home, too, Kennedy faced many problems, but on two fronts he made great strides. He was a young man, and to the impatient but idealistic generation of the 1960s he seemed to speak with a recognizable voice. From the black community, then in the throes of the civil rights movement, led by Martin Luther King, Jr., he won respect. Kennedy, too, came from a community which had suffered exile, discrimination, and intolerance. But his liberal ideas were not always shared by other Americans, or other Irish Americans. His admirers knew that John Kennedy had enemies, but they could not have guessed what final form that enmity would take.

The achievements of John Kennedy have been eclipsed by the circumstances of his death (by assassination in Dallas, Texas, on November 22, 1963). For many people of Irish descent, his real achievement was not what he did as president, but that he was elected to that office at all. He remains one of the greatest of those of Irish descent.

5

Charles Stewart Parnell

1846–1891

One of the great influences on Parnell, the uncrowned king of Ireland, the almost mythical leader through the Land War to the edge of Home Rule, was his American-born mother. She was the daughter of Adm. Stewart of the U.S. Navy. Many of his contemporaries thought, and recent historians have confirmed, that he derived his abiding dislike of the English and their ways from her. An Irish journalist writing Parnell's life asked his mother why her son had such a rooted antipathy to the English. "Why should he not?" she answered with American deliberation. "Have not his ancestors always opposed England? My grandfather Tudor fought against the English in the War of Independence. My father fought against the English in the War of 1812, and I suppose the Parnells have no great love of them."

His great-grandfather, Sir John Parnell, had been chancellor of the Irish Exchequer in the last decades of the eighteenth century, when Ireland had its own independent parliament under Grattan, a parliament swept away by the Act of Union, in 1800.

Parnell was the son of a Protestant landowner in Wicklow who retained nationalist sympathies. Parnell was, however, educated at Yeovil and Chipping Norton, places quintessentially English. He went to Magdalene College in Cambridge, but left the university without taking a degree.

Parnell was not an intellectual in any way. However, he took a great interest in practical matters, such as the mines on his Irish estates, and liked nothing better than chemical experiments as light entertainment. He was solitary and difficult to know, but he was a master of men in public life, and of their emotions.

Elected member of Parliament from Meath in 1875, he joined the Home Rule group of Irish MPs at Westminster, led by Isaac Butt. He was in his element in the House of Commons, and soon mastered its procedures, and the techniques of obstruction, which the Irish party had used since they were created by Joseph Biggar. If the Irish could not rule Ireland, they would attempt to make England ungovernable. What is called filibustering in America drove the British parliament to distraction.

After Butt died in 1879, Parnell was a dominant personality in the party, which had many colorful and energetic people in it. He was asked by Michael Davitt to become the first president of the Land League in 1879, and it was through the Land War that he emerged as the preeminent leader of Ireland.

The Land War involved a great deal of violence and intimidation, and the British government arrested Parnell and other leaders. A compromise, called the Kilmainham Treaty, was reached while they were in jail in Kilmainham. Parnell was released, but a few days later a terrorist group murdered the Irish secretary in the Phoenix Park in Dublin. Coercion returned.

The Land League, however, was converted into the National League, and the efforts of Parnell were now directed not toward land reform, which eventually came, but to Home Rule—restoring to Ireland not full independence at once, but full control of its internal affairs.

This was not fully acceptable to all advanced nationalists. The Home Rule Bill of 1886 failed, and it was followed by the sensational accusations a year later by the *Times* of London that Parnell had been connected with the Phoenix Park murders. But at a special inquiry the letters that they published were soon proved to be forgeries, and though the violence of the Land War could not be concealed, Parnell was triumphantly vindicated in the eyes of his followers by the suicide of Richard Pigott, the forger of the letters. (These events echo all through the work of JAMES JOYCE [25], especially in *Ulysses*.)

However, later in 1890 Parnell faced another challenge. For many years he had been living privately with Mrs. Katharine O'Shea, the wife of a fellow Irish member of parliament, by whom he had several children. In December 1889, Captain O'Shea sued her for divorce and named Parnell as the other man. The scandal that ensued ruined Parnell in the eyes of many Catholics in Ireland, and the Irish bishops called on the Irish party to reject him as its leader. In the course of the ensuing split between the two wings of the party, Parnell suddenly died.

A few years after Parnell's death, a journalist put it to the prime minister, William Gladstone himself, that the Irish leader must have suffered intense pain in that last year. "Poor fellow! Poor fellow! I suppose he did; dear, dear, what a tragedy! I cannot tell you how much I think about him, and what an interest I take in everything concerning him. A marvelous man, a terrible fall."

With him died any hope of Home Rule for the time being, as the Irish party remained split until 1900. However, no sooner had it revived itself than it faced a new challenge from the rise of Sinn Fein, demanding outright independence and not merely Home Rule. Home Rule was granted in 1914, but suspended for the duration of the war. The Easter Rising and the following Anglo-Irish war led to the creation of the Irish Free State. Though Parnell was not a republican, he retained the admiration of many of them. His great achievement was to push the land question toward a conclusion, and to provide the Irish people with a quality of leadership they had not had since DANIEL O'CONNELL [20].

He remains a man of mystery, for he all too often kept his views to himself. He ruined himself over his love for Katharine O'Shea, and that was also, in the eyes of many of his followers, an admirable thing.

A flawed and tragic figure, Parnell survives in the memory of the Irish as one of their greatest leaders.

6

Mary Robinson

1944–

Irishmen as a whole have often been seen as male chauvinists. Yet in the past there have been great and influential Irish women, such as Queen Maeve, St. Bridget, GRACE O'MALLEY [46] and the Daughters of Eireann during the Irish Revolution, such as MAUD GONNE [52] and the COUNTESS MARKIEVICZ [52]. But the rise of the modern women's movement has had its dramatic effects in Ireland, as elsewhere. One of the fruits of this has been the extraordinary career of Mary Robinson. In many ways her success has been more in the American style than anything seen in Ireland.

She was born Mary Bourke into a prominent Mayo family (the Bourkes traced their origins back to the Normans in the twelfth century). Her family was connected not only to Irish republican politics but also to the British establishment. Her father was a medical man, with a wife ambitious for their children. Mary was sent to a leading convent school, and having attended a finishing school in Paris, she went on to study law at Trinity College at a time when entry to this Protestant university was closed to most Catholics by their bishops. Her education was not unusual for girls of her class, but her legal ambitions were.

She also studied at Harvard, and her experiences in the United States during the turbulent days of the Vietnam War had an important effect on her outlook.

She became a brilliant student of law at Trinity College, where she eventually was appointed Reid professor of law. Trinity College had long been seen by many nationalists as one of the bastions of British rule in

Ireland, but throughout the 1960s had emerged as one of the sources of
Irish reform. She married a Dublin lawyer with artistic interests, who
also emerged as a person of influence himself in the heritage conserva-
tion field. She managed to rear her three children away from the spot-
light of controversy, which was also an achievement given the nature of
modern media scrutiny.

Her work as a practicing lawyer and legal academic quickly
brought Mary Robinson to the firing line. She thought that matters of
private conscience, such as homosexuality and contraception, should not
be a matter of law. Her legal practice concentrated largely on constitutional and civil rights matters, and through her success she was able to
make changes that legislators had found difficult. Though Ireland shares
a common-law system with the rest of Great Britain, it also has a written constitution, and constitutional cases have become a testing ground
for public opinion.

She became involved in politics on the left wing of the Irish
Labour party, but her relations with party politics were not always calm.
She was elected to the Irish Senate as a senator from Trinity College.
During her terms as senator she introduced many bills which
attempted to change the social situation in Ireland. One was for legal-
izing contraception, but this was dismissed in controversial circumstances, as many Catholics in the country objected to it. She had
promised on her election to use the Senate as a "forum for new and
possibly unpopular views."

What these might be were indicated by her support for and
involvement in the newly emerging women's movement in Ireland.
However, these issues were, in her view, part of a wider spectrum of
rights that had to be developed in Ireland. These views alienated her
from the more traditional and conservative elements of Irish life, which
was tied to the fears of the old agricultural life on the land, which had
often been insecure and impoverished. With changing economic conditions social attitudes changed, and Mary Robinson became a figurehead
for changes already under way. On contraception, for instance, though
the church authorities denied it to Catholics, many theologians had
already moved on, taking the mass of the faithful with them.

But Mary Robinson was also committed to the European ideal,
and this was one area in which most of her people agreed. At Trinity
College she ran, with her husband, the Irish Center for European Law.

Though she had left the party, she was nominated for the office of
president of Ireland by Labour party leader Dick Spring in 1990. In

Ireland the post of president is a nominal, titular post rather than an administrative one, so she had no powers but the force of her own personality. Previously, the post had been filled by a range of retired politicians, and a judge who had been content to relax in the post. But her presidential campaign proved to be a watershed in Irish life and politics, dividing one era from another. In the future, historians will certainly see it as a benchmark date.

Mary Robinson quickly saw that even though she could not involve herself in party political matters, other social, academic, and cultural areas were wide open to her. She emerged through the presidency as one of the new vitalizing influences on Ireland. Her theme of reconciliation was echoed widely, but she also worked with the marginalized and disadvantaged. She made many visits to Northern Ireland, meeting and shaking hands with GERRY ADAMS [100], for instance. All over Ireland she concerned herself with those whom society and politics had previously excluded and ignored. She also made a special point of remembering those who had been forced to emigrate and make up the Irish community worldwide. A candle was kept burning in a window of the presidential residence in Phoenix Park in their memory.

She served only one seven-year term as president before advancing to a post with the United Nations as high commissioner for human rights. This would turn out to be as important a post on a universal scale as the presidency was on a national scale. For all that it has done in the past, the United Nations has not always managed to achieve enough, caught as it so often has been between political rivalries it could not control.

Now, in a new era, Mary Robinson may be one of those who will give the United Nations new authority in a still badly divided world, and though she now wishes to further her career elsewhere, she has made her mark on the world stage. In Mary Robinson the younger generation of Irish women have an extraordinary role model, though their mothers had been content to live in a domestic scene, exerting a powerful influence over the formation of Irish life and opinion in that way. She took herself into a wider world and triumphed. After Mary Robinson, no public office in Ireland could be considered an all-male preserve.

7

Patrick Henry Pearse

1879–1916

The leading inspiration of the Easter Rising against British rule in Ireland, Patrick Henry Pearse might seem to have been named for the American patriot Patrick Henry, whose battle cry was "Give me liberty, or give me death." But Pearse was, in fact, named after an uncle. Nothing was quite what it seemed in the life and career of Patrick Pearse.

Surprisingly for an Irish patriot, his father was an Englishman, a monumental sculptor who worked widely on the many Catholic churches which were erected around Dublin in the second half of the nineteenth century. His work, once neglected, is now much admired by art historians. Pearse's mother was Irish, however, and her family connections were an important influence on the growing boy.

He was born in Dublin at 27 Great Brunswick Street (now Pearse Street)—the name of the street was itself a constant reminder of the British royal family to Dubliners. He was educated nearby at the Christian Brothers school in Westland Row and attended University College, then part of the Royal University of Ireland, and was called to the Irish bar as a barrister in 1901. But the law was not his main interest in life.

Beginning in 1895 he was an active member of the Gaelic League, an organization founded to revive the use of the old native language as the everyday tongue of the people of Ireland. Though supposedly non-political, it was distinctly nationalist in outlook and Pearse was the editor of its influential weekly paper. He taught Irish in classes organized by the league, and one of his pupils, for a very short time, was the writer

JAMES JOYCE [25]. Joyce thought Pearse's remarks on the infelicities of the English language were merely silly, so he gave up the course. But many others were to find the mesmeric Pearse an inspiring figure.

To further his educational ambitions for Ireland, in 1908 Pearse founded St. Enda's, a Gaelic-speaking school which later moved to much larger premises in a mansion at Rathfarnham, in 1910. The school was patronized by many advanced and liberal-minded parents, and included many distinguished people among its staff, such as the poet Thomas MacDonagh.

In 1913 Pearse joined the Irish Republican Brotherhood, the underground movement that aimed to establish a republic in Ireland. He was soon co-opted into the inner circle of the Supreme Council. The IRB, which traced its origins back to the Fenians of the 1860s, was widely supported by Irish Americans and was a secret organization. Pearse was also on the central committee of the Irish Volunteers, an open organization which had been organized by Professor Eoin MacNeill to counter the Ulster Volunteers, who had been set up to resist the Home Rule Bill then passing through the British Parliament in the years 1913 to 1914. The Ulster Volunteers imported some thirty thousand rifles from Germany. When the Irish Volunteers imported 1,500, the incident led to shootings on the streets in Dublin, at Bachelor's Walk, an incident which was later to be seen as the first bloodletting of the troubles.

Pearse was largely responsible for organizing the funeral of the old Fenian revolutionary O'Donovan Rossa in 1915, who had died in exile in America. Rossa had been responsible for an active bombing campaign against English cities in the 1880s, and was a great hero to many Irish republicans. Rossa's belief that only physical force could drive the British out of Ireland was not, however, shared widely by those who supported the Irish party. But this funeral was to be a symbolic occasion. In his oration at the grave, Pearse claimed that "Ireland unfree shall never be at peace." It was a warning of what was to come.

With the outbreak of the First World War, the Irish Volunteers split. The vast majority went to fight with the Irish and British regiments on the western front, though a small number were determined to seize the opportunity for another insurrection. Pearse and his IRB friends planned to have the rising on Easter week, making use of the general mobilization of the Irish Volunteers, which was supposed to be a mere exercise. When he heard of these plans, Prof. MacNeill, the actual leader of the Irish Volunteers, tried to prevent the mobilization. Only a tiny fraction of the original one hundred sixty thousand volunteers turned out in support of the rising.

During Easter week Pearse was commander in chief of the Irish Army, president of the republic, and one of those who signed the proclamation. But the uprising failed from lack of widespread support among the people and its own military ineptitude. The leaders were court-martialed and sentenced to death.

Pearse bravely faced execution. In death, his influence would be far more profound than it had been in life. He remains for Irish nationalists of all kinds a central figure of history. His ideas about the Irish language and the sources of Irish nationality are still those of many, but the growth of Ireland since 1922 has been away from his core beliefs. His ideas of heroic blood sacrifice have been much criticized by revisionist historians and theologians, who see them as both mad and heretical. But such comments have not shaken his many admirers. Even today, Pearse remains for Irish people a controversial figure, capable of arousing fierce emotional debate.

Pearse was also a poet and a teacher. These sides of his personality are attractive in ways that the belligerent comic-opera figure of the uprising is not. His ideas about the education of children, through sensitive teaching, remain very potent. Perhaps the real Pearse was not the militant, but the sensitive poet and dedicated teacher. To later generations, these aspects of his life may well seem to represent the real importance of Patrick Pearse.

8

William Butler Yeats

1865–1939

The first Irishman to win a Nobel Prize (in 1923), William Butler Yeats combined within himself contradictory elements of Irish life and culture, but it is from the tension of those contradictions that his greatness as a universally admired poet emerged. Such poems as "The Lake Isle of Innisfree" and "Down by the Salley Gardens" won immediate appreciation, but he remained to the end of his long life a poet of increasing power and passion.

His father, John Butler Yeats, was a painter, and Yeats was reared in a close family atmosphere where art and poetry were admired and encouraged. As a painter, his brother JACK [26] took after the father, but William's interests were literary.

His schooling was unsuccessful, and for many years he had to eke out a living as a literary journalist and editor of anthologies. He barely scraped by until he was in his forties, but very quickly, when he was still in his teens, his exceptional talents as a poet were recognized. The sources of his lyrical verses, which he began to publish in the late 1880s, lay in the newly discovered ancient mythology of Celtic Ireland and the landscapes of the west of Ireland.

To these elements which would have been widely shared by many Irish artists, writers, and leaders of the day, he added his esoteric interest in the magical tradition of Europe. His conjuring of spirits was not mere fancy, but part of an increasingly elaborate belief system. But such was his skill as a poet that his personal symbols do not form an immediate barrier to the reader.

Though he was born in Dublin (at Sandymount, on June 13, 1865), and lived there for long periods, and in London and Oxford, it is with the western landscapes, especially those of Sligo and Galway, that his poetry is most closely linked.

Yeats's own people came from Sligo, which was a place of special significance to himself and his brother Jack. He often stayed with his friend Lady Gregory at her home, Coole Park, in Galway, and tied to this sense of landscape was a sense of Ireland's mythical history. Yeats was among the first Irish poets to draw upon the ancient literary tradition of Celtic Ireland for new purposes. In the old Celtic myths and legends he found a depth and passion that other poets in Europe found in the mythology of ancient Greece.

By the end of the 1890s, Yeats had been recognized as the most significant poet of modern Ireland. For all his seemingly dreamy appearance, he was a man of wide interests and great energy. His interest in drama led to the creation of the Literary Theatre, and later the Abbey Theatre. Though his own austere and allusive plays, often in verse, were not to everyone's taste, those of his friend Lady Gregory, which were comedies of rural life as well as patriotic tragedies, were immensely popular and made the Abbey Theatre's name.

The Abbey also provided an outlet for the genius of J. M. Synge, whose comedy *The Playboy of the Western World* provoked a riot in the theater in 1907, and later for SEAN O'CASEY [55], whose plays of the Irish troubles, such as *Juno and the Paycock,* are classics of world theater. For this alone Yeats would be remembered. His own play, *Cathleen ni Houlihan,* in which his friend MAUD GONNE [52] appeared in 1902, is now seen as having had a powerful effect on the imaginations of many of those who were later to be involved in the national movement.

However, it is as a poet that Yeats marked the world. He began as a lyric poet of misty landscapes and lost love. His early passion for the elusive Maud Gonne was one of the great love stories of Irish literature. But she did not take "dear Willy" too seriously, and preferred a life devoted to the politics of revolutionary Ireland. With maturity, his poetry took on more vigorous and somber aspects. He was deeply affected by events such as the Easter Rising and the troubles that followed, but his later poetry combines that sense of history with a mythical dimension which transcended the merely national.

By the 1920s he had become one of the most important poets of the century in the English language. Abroad, Yeats was seen as a great poet, but in Ireland he was also a leading public figure. He served two terms as a senator, appointed in part to represent the interests and opinions of the Protestant Anglo-Irish minority. In this role he helped to design Ireland's new coinage, but he also spoke out against the introduction of censorship and legislation to remove the right to divorce, fearing that the new state would pursue a public policy dominated by Catholic social and moral precepts. His speeches won him few admirers at the time, but are now significant for what they reveal about the evolving nature of the new Ireland; by the 1980s, public policy had come around to agreeing with Yeats.

By the time of his death he had become, for many, one of the greatest poets of all time. Though it was his early verse that made the greatest impact on the general audience, his later poems, in all their allusive and symbolic complexity, have come to be of central importance to Irish readers of today. They are often passionate, yet cold, combining the elements of ice and fire in a mysterious and powerful manner.

After a long illness, Yeats died in the south of France on January 28, 1939. His body was later brought back for a state funeral in Drumcliffe churchyard in Sligo. After death, his influence continued. He had gathered together a group of fellow poets, and his ideas and ideals pervaded his generation. Though the poets of the younger generation of the 1930s would eventually resent this, he nevertheless became an ideal even with them, through his perseverance against poverty, hardship, and literary disdain. Yeats was an Olympian, a man out of time, a genius.

9

John Boyle O'Reilly

1844–1890

When many Americans think of Irish poetry it is not always Yeats or Seamus Heaney that comes to mind, but the Bostonian John Boyle O'Reilly. His poetry was quoted by JOHN F. KENNEDY [4] when he spoke in 1963 to the Irish national assembly because it had been the poetry which had made Ireland come alive for many of the president's family in the nineteenth century.

The Fenian poet and editor was born the child of William and Eliza (Boyle) O'Reilly at Dowth Castle, on the south bank of the Boyne, near Drogheda, on June 28, 1844. His father was the master of the national school which had been established there by Lord Netterville as part of the Netterville Institute.

A clever boy, at the age of eleven John Boyle O'Reilly was apprenticed as a printer to the *Drogheda Argus*. Local newspapers played an important part of the life of rural Ireland, and by this time many were becoming strongly nationalist in political tone.

He later moved to England, working on the *Guardian* in Preston. The north of England had drawn many Irish people to work in the thriving industries there when no work could be found at home. It was in Preston that he joined the Fenians, or Irish Republican Brotherhood. He was sent to Dublin in 1863 to enlist in the 10th Hussars as part of a Fenian scheme to subvert the empire by secretly recruiting Irishmen from the British army into the ranks of the republican movement. However, he was informed on in 1866, arrested, and sentenced to death for failing to give information on an intended mutiny and conspiring to levy war against the queen. His sentence was commuted to life imprisonment, and he passed a year in solitary confinement in the notorious Millbank Gaol in London, where hard labor meant walking the treadmill for long hours every day. He also passed a period of hard labor in the brickyards at Chatham. He was then sent to the remote prison on Dartmoor, from which he managed to escape. Recaptured, he was sentenced to twenty years in the penal colony in western Australia.

O'Reilly was one of sixty-three political prisoners deported in 1867 to Australia—the first to be sent there since 1848. As convict No. 9843, he landed at Fremantle on January 10, 1868, and was sent to a convict settlement nearby. With the help of Fr. Patrick McCabe, a local Catholic priest, he escaped on a New Bedford whaler to America. At sea he was transferred from the whaler to an American barque, and at Liverpool was transformed into the third mate of the *Bombay*, landing in Philadelphia in November 1869. The day he landed he applied for naturalization.

Though he knew nobody in Boston, his fame as a poet and patriot had gone before him. He settled down in Boston, where he joined the staff of the *Boston Pilot*, a long established Irish-American newspaper of Catholic interest, owned by Patrick Donahoe. He frankly reported on the the mismanagement of the Fenian invasion of Canada from St. Albans, and within a few months of joining the paper he was appointed editor. He married an Irish girl, Mary Murphy, in August 1872; they had four daughters.

He quickly made a name as a writer and lecturer. His *Songs, Legends and Ballads* went into eight large editions. In 1876, along with Archbishop John Joseph Williams of Boston, he became part owner of the *Pilot* (which had a circulation of over one hundred thousand), and he remained its editor until his death. For the next two decades the paper played an important role in the assimilation of Irish Catholics into American society, through O'Reilly's editorial advice. Slowly, his youthful revolutionary ideals matured into a more conservative outlook.

Influenced by such men as Patrick Donahoe and Patrick Collins, his was a conservative, constructive, but still anti-British program of Irish-American acculturation. The paper supported Democratic candidates, and his own comments on the developing industrial nature of the United States placed him among the leading social reformers. When members of the Catholic community faced financial ruin in Boston following the fire and panic of 1872 to 1873, he began with Archbishop Williams a scheme to help local businessmen.

His novel *Moondyne* (1879), about his Australian experiences, was also a success. His volume of poems, *Statues in the Block* (1881), was also popular. Under his charge the *Pilot* became famous for its noted contributors, which included WILLIAM BUTLER YEATS [8] and other writers and poets of the new generation in Ireland.

He was refused permission to enter Canada in 1885 by the government. Liberal in his views, John Boyle O'Reilly opposed the anti-Semitic and antiblack prejudices of so many Irish Americans all his life. He was also interested in sports, being an excellent athlete and an enthusiastic canoer. He even wrote about sports: *Ethics of Boxing and Manly Sports* appeared in 1888. He was also deeply involved in Catholic activities in Boston, in the Irish-Catholic Colonization Association, and in promoting Catholic education to the highest levels.

Overworked and suffering from insomnia, he died from an accidental overdose of his sleeping potion at his summer home in Hull, on Boston harbor, in August 1890. He is buried in Holyhood Cemetery in Brookline, Massachusetts. There is a memorial in Boston, which his many admirers paid for through subscription, as well as a bust in the city's public library. He left a popular legacy of verse among the Irish at home and in America.

He was a favorite poet for the special occasion, such as the O'Connell Centenary, or the dedication of the Crispus Attucks monument on Boston Common. He had not fully developed as a poet when he died. Like many of the Irish poets he admired, such as Thomas Davis and D'Arcy Magee, his best work is his ballads. Over the years many of these have perhaps faded from memory, and modern critics prefer the shorter poems reflecting his interest in things spiritual.

Though his name as a poet has declined in Ireland, when he was quoted by that other famous son of Boston, President John F. Kennedy, on his visit to Ireland in 1963, it led to a revival of interest in him in America, Ireland, and Australia, as the significant figures of the nineteenth century are reappraised.

As editor of the *Pilot* or patriotic poet, John Boyle O'Reilly was one of the most influential Irish Americans of his day, reflecting their policies and piety in the editorials and poems he wrote, but never confusing the two. He was an advocate of Ireland's right to home rule, and he provided leadership to the Irish-American community on the issue, but he also saw that they were making their lives in a new country and laid equal emphasis on the duties of the Irish as American citizens.

10

Patrick Ford

1835–1913

All his life Patrick Ford was dedicated to a country of which he can only have had the vaguest and most youthful memories. He was the archetype of those Irish Americans whose influence was to pervade the country that their parents had once called home. He was born in Galway on April 12, 1835, and his parents, Edward and Anne Ford, died when he was an infant. In 1842 he was taken to Boston by family friends. He was reared and educated in America, and never saw Ireland again.

He attended public schools in Boston, including Boston Latin School. As a youth he worked in the office of the *Liberator,* the leading antislavery paper, edited by William Lloyd Garrison. Ford began his working life as a journalist in 1855. During the years 1859 to 1860 he was the publisher and editor of the *Boston Sunday Times.*

During the Civil War he joined the 9th Massachusetts Regiment and fought at Fredericksburg. In March 1863 he married Odele McDonald, and from 1864 they lived for two years in Charleston, South Carolina.

Later he moved to New York, where he founded the *Irish World,* which quickly became the voice of the Irish-American community, or at least of a very vocal and revolutionary part of it. This was in 1870, when the Fenian movement was still active and powerful in America. The chief interest of the editor—and the paper—was to forward the national cause of Ireland in every way possible. As time went on his hatred of England became almost irrational.

In 1874 he was one of the founders of the American Independent

National party, popularly known as the Greenback party, which held its first national convention in that year. Under the influence of the party the term *hard money* came into use to designate silver coins, distinguishing it from the "greenback," paper money, the value of which they wanted to inflate. In the presidential election of 1876, the party's candidate received over eighty-one thousand votes, advocating the use of paper money to pay all government bonds that were not tied to payment in coin.

In 1878 the party changed its name, having merged with some labor parties to form the Greenback Labor party, which joined with other groups to put forward James Weaver for president in 1880. He failed, but they got fourteen congressmen elected. The election of 1884 proved to be a disaster, and the party dissolved soon after, though many of its followers joined the Populist party, formed in 1891.

Ford, however, had turned to supporting the Republicans, and his paper is said to have been responsible for bringing thousands of Democrats over to supporting James Blaine in 1884. Both major parties seemed too conservative for Ford, and he switched his support, and his readers, from one to the other, as policies changed.

The influence of the paper and its editor was immense. Patrick Ford supported the Fenians, and later the Irish Land League, helping to set up 2,500 branches of the organization among Irish Americans across the United States. MICHAEL DAVITT [24], the founder of the Land League, called him "the most powerful support on the American continent of the struggle in Ireland."

He was said to have collected over half a million dollars for causes in Ireland, and he was identified by the British as a prime mover of American opinion against their Irish policies. He wrote two books, *The Criminal History of the British Empire* (1881) and *The Irish Question and American Statesmen* (1885). His journal was carefully perused by the secret police of the Special Criminal Branch in Dublin Castle, and inflammatory clippings from it were filed away for use as possible evidence. In *The Criminal History,* Ford himself quoted Gladstone's observation: "But for the work the *Irish World* is doing and the money it is sending across the ocean, there would be no agitation in Ireland." Gladstone preferred to blame Irish Americans for the political turmoil rather than British policies in Ireland.

Home rule, as advocated by CHARLES PARNELL [5] and William Gladstone, seemed to Ford a miserable compromise. Nothing but the complete independence of Ireland was good enough, and he saw Gladstone as an opportunist using Irish affairs to his own advantage.

The full title of Ford's newspaper was the *Irish World and American Industrial Liberator and Gaelic American.* Its editorial interests stretched beyond the questions that bothered Gladstone to American domestic issues. Ford was a champion of many social reforms: income tax, the government regulation of railroads and monopolies, and aid to farmers. He was a friend of Henry George, the advocate of a single tax and land nationalization. Ford's interests also extended to supporting the progressive-minded among the Catholic clergy in America.

The American social philosopher Fr. John A. Ryan, born in 1869, who grew up in an Irish family on a farm in Minnesota, recalled the effect of the paper: "One could not read the *Irish World* week after week without acquiring an interest in and a love of economic justice as well as political justice."

In time Patrick Ford mellowed, becoming a supporter of home rule and the constitutional Irish party. This was especially so after 1900, when it seemed that revolutionary politics was a completely spent force in Ireland and America, and that the niceties of constitutionalism might yet carry the day.

He died at home in Brooklyn, New York, on September 23, 1913—a crucial month in the history of modern Ireland, when Dublin was in turmoil over the great Lockout, which saw large crowds battle with the police in the city streets. (This arose from action by JAMES LARKIN [37] to improve the pay of carriers and other workers, which led to union members being locked out by the employers. For some historians these events were the beginning of the troubles in Ireland.) He did not live to see the fruits of his life's work in the Easter Rising and the creation of the Irish Free State.

Patrick Ford is an example of the crusading editor. He was ahead of his time, and that does not always pay. There was no money in his kind of journalism; it was carried on as a form of politics. Unlike JOHN BOYLE O'REILLY [9], he was not anxious to support an emerging Irish establishment in the United States, nor was he interested, as were so many other newspaper owners of the day, in creating a personal fortune. His battle was to free the enslaved, black and white, and to promote social justice.

The central idea that motivated him was Irish freedom. By giving expression to the emotions and aspirations of many millions who could not express them so well, he exerted a profound effect, perhaps difficult to measure. Today he is a figure largely known only to historians, but in his own day there was no doubt of his influence.

11

Wolfe Tone

1763–1798

It is to Wolfe Tone, and to his enthusiasm for the French Revolution, that modern Irish republicanism in its various forms traces its origins. Every year several political parties of different outlooks make their individual pious pilgrimages to his burial place in Bodenstown, County Kildare, to pay homage to his memory and rededicate themselves to eliminating the divisions in Ireland that they see as having been fostered by a foreign invader. But Tone's lasting influence over Irish life and politics is not as straightforward as they would hope to suggest.

Theobald Wolfe Tone was born in Dublin on June 20, 1763, the son of a prosperous coach maker with family connections with Kildare. A Protestant, he was educated at Trinity College, in Dublin. While a student he eloped with a girl of sixteen, and the marriage, though affected by his politics, was happy. Later Tone studied at the Middle Temple, the lawyer's college in London. He was called to the Irish bar in 1789, but like many impatient revolutionaries, he never had much taste for the law.

Like other lawyers of the day, he turned instead to politics, agitation, and writing. In 1791 he published what has proved to be a most influential pamphlet, *An Argument on Behalf of the Catholics of Ireland*. Along with Thomas Russell and Napper Tandy, he founded the Society of United Irishmen. Their aims were "to break the connection with England, the never-failing source of all our political evils . . . and to substitute the common name of Irishman in place of the denominations of Protestant, Catholic, and Dissenter . . ."

He was active in the Catholic Committee, and called the Catholic Convention in Dublin in 1792. The Catholic Relief Act of 1793 (one of a series that would end with full Catholic Emancipation in 1829) gave partial concessions to the aspirations of the native Irish, but not enough for Tone and his friends, who were deeply influenced by the French Revolution, just as the Irish Volunteers had been influenced by the American Revolution.

It should be remembered that at this time Ireland had its own parliament and could legislate for itself. Though dominated by Protestant landowners, this parliament could have evolved along the lines suggested by the American Revolution. But it was not to America that Wolfe Tone looked for either inspiration or help.

In 1794 Ireland was visited by a clergyman named William Jackson, an emissary of the French revolutionary government. Wolfe Tone prepared a note for him, claiming that Ireland was ripe for revolution. Jackson was arrested, but the authorities agreed that Tone would not give evidence against him, and that he could leave for America.

This he did, taking his young family with him. In Philadelphia he got letters of introduction to the French Directory, and was soon in France plotting an invasion of Ireland. For the French, of course, there was a great advantage in a sideshow in Ireland, which would distract the British from events elsewhere.

An expedition sailed in 1796, but was driven off by the weather. A second expedition, planned with Gen. Lazare Hoche, came to nothing with the general's death. When the uprising in Ireland broke out in the spring of 1798, Wolfe Tone renewed his efforts with the French, and other forces sailed later in the year—while Napoleon was invading Egypt, directly threatening British interests in the East.

One expedition landed in Mayo in support of the rebels there. Tone himself reached Lough Swilly on board a French ship in October, but was captured. He was quickly court-martialed, treated as a traitor rather than a French officer. Though he pleaded to be shot like a soldier, the authorities wished to hang him like a criminal. On the morning of the day appointed for his execution, in November 1798, he used a penknife to open a vein in his neck. Inevitably, Irish nationalists, rather than accept that Wolfe Tone, a deist, had committed suicide, claimed he had been murdered by the British government.

Though Tone's influence was immense, his ambition to bring the French to Ireland was unlikely to have brought either independence or peace to Ireland. The rebellion in 1798, which he had fostered, proved to be an appalling bloodbath in which Catholic insurgents murdered Protestants and local Protestant yeomanry exacted appalling revenge in their turn. This led to the Act of Union, which Irish Protestants saw as the only way in which their interests could be protected. Rather than break the connection with England, Tone's activities strengthened it. As is so often the case, the revolutionaries brought about a result quite the opposite of what they intended.

Though Tone's words are still quoted today, the experience of the French Revolution, whose support he had sought, cast a shadow over all of Irish nationalism that has still not been thrown off. Nominally democratic, the French Revolution quickly became arbitrary. In the cause of one kind of freedom, its deistic leaders attacked the church. Despite Tone's rhetoric, none of this could have had wide appeal to the Irish people, for subservience to Napoleon would have been an even worse fate than union with England.

Although he was high-minded and idealistic, the results of his life brought destruction and ruin to many. Yet in the end they also brought about the independence of a large part of Ireland. His autobiography, edited by his son in America, became one of the sacred texts of Irish republicanism.

Yet it was to the parliamentary tradition which he rejected that the Irish people as a whole clung and which forms the basis of the modern advanced democracy which Ireland enjoys today. Tone may be honored, but his revolutionary ideals have not found a place in the public life of modern Ireland.

12

Mike Quill

1905–1966

Once notorious, Mike Quill represents those Irishmen whose effect on the lives of millions is important, but who are themselves not seen as great figures.

Michael J. Quill was born in the west of Ireland of a family deeply involved in the national movement. He fought in both the Irish war of independence and with the irregulars in the civil war. In 1926 he was forced by the peculiar political circumstances of the Irish Free State to emigrate to the United States. There he joined Clan na Gael, the long-established American branch of the Irish Republican Brotherhood. After a series of short-term jobs he began working in the New York City subway system. There was an easy introduction to this position, as most of the workers on the system were foreign-born Irishmen.

A decade later he was one of the subway workers who came under the influence of James Gralton, the socialist organizer who was expelled from the Irish Free State in 1936. Quill was involved in organizing the Irish Workers Clubs in New York, through which Gralton's ideas, derived from JAMES CONNOLLY [16], were propagated. Connolly had, of course, lived in New York, and his study of the 1907 Yonkers (New York) trolley men's strike was used as an object lesson in setting up the tiny Transport Workers Union.

A group of Clan na Gael members had been trying to organize the subway workers into this union since 1934. The Communist party of the United States (CPUSA) was also at work in this area, and when Quill and his friends were refused support by the more conservative Irish-

American organization, the CPUSA came forward with money, organizers, lawyers, and both the editor and means to start a trade union paper.

Quill was well known in Irish circles, but many Irish Americans preferred to support revolution only in Ireland, not in the United States. Many Irish-American nationalists were indifferent to what Quill saw as class exploitation, and the poverty that was as common in their new country as it had been in Ireland, though with less excuse.

The working conditions on the subways—with twelve- to fourteen-hour split shifts in a seven-day work week—provided fertile ground for organizers. Quill brought to trade union organization some of the discipline for which the IRA had been famous back in Ireland. The union was infiltrated by informers (as the IRA had been), but Quill worsted them. It was thought that every fifth worker was in the pay of the employers (for an extra dollar a week) to spy on union meetings.

But advances were made. By 1938 the Transit Workers Union had won a union-recognition ballot, which gave them the status of the recognized union for railway workers, and was affiliated with the Congress of Industrial Organizations (CIO). Now known as Red Mike, Quill became a celebrity in New York City. As a representative of the Bronx, he was elected to the city council in 1937, 1943, and 1945. His way with words made him a joy for newsmen after a handy quote on local or union events. He broadcast regularly over the city-owned radio station WNYC.

The Communist links of the union's leadership made for difficult times in the period after the war, when the influence of CPUSA was under investigation. It is not clear if Quill himself was a party member, but in 1948 he opposed the party over two issues. Following the lead of the CIO, he supported Harry Truman rather than Henry Wallace for the presidential ticket that year. He also supported a raise in fares on the subway, which the party opposed. The extra money, he argued, was going in part to increase the transit workers' wages.

The union leadership split over the issue, and the Communists attacked Quill. He retaliated by throwing them out. In tune with the times, he spent some years pursuing Communists, but then readmitted some of those who had helped to found the union in the 1930s.

For years, Quill indulged in heady arguments over union contract negotiations with the mayors and city authorities. Though he always settled before it actually came to an all-out strike, in 1966, perhaps because of the more radical atmosphere of the day, a strike was called and Mike

Quill became a center of controversy. A mere fifteen minutes into Mayor John Lindsay's first term, the men ceased work, stayed out for twelve days, and ended with a 15 percent pay increase. Without transit workers, New York City, with all its multifarious activities—so important to the life and economy of the United States and the world—simply could not work.

During the strike, Quill was detained and jailed. Already in ill health, he collapsed in his cell and had to be admitted to a hospital. Three weeks later he died. During the strike he had told the press: "May the judge drop dead in his black robes." However, it was Mike Quill who passed away first.

For a generation, Mike Quill had been at the heart of life and politics in the largest city in the world. He brought to his public role the passion of an Irishman trained in the war against an ancient and unjust enemy. Through Mike Quill something of the radicalism that informed many members of the old IRA was transferred to the United States. He transformed the lives not only of those in his union, but the lives of all New Yorkers. He helped to make New York what it is, for better or worse, an extraordinary achievement for a poor boy from the west of Ireland.

13

George Boole

1815–1864

Science has never seemed a very strong part of the Irish tradition, yet Irish people and others whose life's work was spent in Ireland have made important scientific advances. George Boole, whose name is still honored in Irish scientific circles, was one of these. But scientists work in an international, not a national, mode. Boole is important not only because, as Bertrand Russell observed, he discovered pure mathematics, but because his work lies behind the modern computer revolution.

He was born in Lincoln, in the east of England, on November 2, 1815—the year of Waterloo. His father was a poor tradesman, which did not give young George much of a start in life. Indeed, if he had been poorer, initially things might have gone better for him. But he was clever, and at sixteen was appointed an assistant master in a small school in Doncaster. This was the beginning of a distinguished teaching career, and at the age of nineteen he opened his own school back in Lincoln. This was more civilized than the others he had attended or taught in, and it was here, while trying to teach mathematics to his own pupils, that his own deepening interest in the subject was aroused.

He worked alone. At first his main interest was invariants, without which Einstein's theory of relativity would have been impossible. He was almost the only mathematician in the British Isles to write about logic. His first thoughts were contained in a small booklet he published in 1847 called *The Mathematical Analysis of Logic,* but he later came to think of this as quite inadequate. It required more work, but what his contemporary, Prof. Augustus de Morgan, called the "splendid invention" of symbolic, or mathematical, logic was a major advance. It brought him the friendship of de Morgan and other workers, who urged him to go to Cambridge University as a student and begin an academic career. But Boole was happy enough to persist with his schoolwork.

Boole was not unambitious, however, and in 1849 was appointed professor of mathematics at the Queen's College in Cork (now University College Cork, a constituent college of the National University of Ireland). Here at last was an opening in which he could develop his thoughts almost free from monetary pressures and concern for the care of his elderly parents, who depended on him. In 1855 he married a relative of the explorer Sir George Everest, for whom Mount Everest is named, and "with whom he lived in perfect domestic happiness," as Mrs. Boole later told one of her husband's biographers. They had five daughters.

By this time his reputation as an advanced mathematician was already known. In 1841 he had published a paper entitled "Theory of Analytical Transformation," in the *Cambridge Mathematical Journal*. This led to a long friendship with the editor D. F. Gregory. He wrote what were then considered two important textbooks, *Differential Equations* (1859) and *Finite Differences* (1860).

But his most important and far-reaching work was *The Laws of Thought* (1854), in which symbolic language and notation were employed to express purely logical processes. "The design of the following treatise," he wrote, "is to investigate the fundamental laws of those operations of the mind by which reasoning is performed; to give expression to them in the language of a Calculus, and upon this foundation to establish the science of Logic and construct its method; and to make that method itself the basis of a general method for the application of the mathematical doctrine of probabilities; and, finally, to collect from the various elements of truth brought to view in the course of these inquiries some probable intimation concerning the nature and constitution of the human mind."

This ambitious work was widely influential, being followed up by works in Britain, Europe, and America, and it lies at the very root of the dependence of the modern world on computers, for it reduced the theoretical basis of logic to a choice between 0 and 1, the key to all modern computing science.

As professor E. T. Bell, the historian of mathematical thought, wrote, "The intricacy and delicacy of the difficulties explored by the *symbolic* reasoning methods would, it is safe to say, defy human reason if only the old, pre-Boole methods of *verbal* logical arguments were at our disposal. The daring originality of Boole's whole project needs no signpost. It is a landmark in itself."

After writing his masterpiece, Boole did not live much longer. His health had not always been good, and he worked long hours. He was also involved in the difficult academic politics of the college, which were often very overheated and outspoken. Going into college in the winter of 1864 he contracted a cough, which was followed by pneumonia, from which he died on December 8, 1864.

Nineteenth-century mathematics laid the foundation for twentieth-century physics. Early in this century, Boole's work was brought to a wider audience by Alfred North Whitehead and Bertrand Russell, and it has been further developed by many others since. Boole's creative work in *The Laws of Thought* laid the foundations for the computer revolution, a fact which only became clear as modern machines began to develop from the primitive machines of the 1940s. The modern information revolution which is transforming the whole nature of life itself owes an immense debt to the work and influence of George Boole and his study at Cork a century and a half ago. Every computer that is turned on in the world today is a child of George Boole's genius.

14

Seán Lemass

1899–1971

Now seen as the architect of modern industrialized Ireland, Seán Lemass had for much of his life been the follower of EAMON DE VALERA [2], whose vision of Ireland was based on the rural nation he had grown up in. But Lemass was a city man, and realized that in large part the future of Ireland would lie in its cities. Even by 1959 the contrast between the two cultures of Ireland had become an extreme one.

A Dubliner, Seán Francis Lemass was born on July 15, 1899. He was educated by the Christian Brothers at the O'Connell Schools, where a special brand of Catholic nationalism was imparted to all the boys. He was a clever student, winning the Junior Grade scholarship in the state exams. For a whole year after he left school he attended a practical business college.

In January 1915, at age fifteen, he joined the Irish Volunteers, serving at first in de Valera's own company. He and his elder brother Noel took part in the Easter Rising in 1916, but because Seán was so young he was not deported. A Dublin policeman who knew the family recognized him and drew the attention of a British officer to "the nipper." "But he's old enough to handle a rifle," said the officer. He was released nevertheless. To his annoyance, his parents sent him back to his studies.

Lemass began his working life in the family hat shop and drapery business in Capel Street in the heart of the city, but he also continued his activities with the reorganized volunteers (by then a republican movement), and was soon a full-time officer. He was arrested in

December 1920, and this time was sent to Ballykinlar internment camp to join other leading figures in the movement.

In the summer, after the truce came into force, he was released, but was among those who rejected the treaty settlement, again following the lead of de Valera. During the civil war he fought with the republicans in the Four Courts, an important city center building, which had been occupied by Rory O'Connor, in imitation of the Easter Rising of 1916. When the garrison fell he was arrested, but managed to escape and rejoin the republicans in the field. But he was captured again in December 1922, and this time was interned in the Curragh in Kildare until the end of 1923. His brother Noel was captured and murdered by free-state agents, and his body was dumped in the Dublin Mountains—one of the grimmest events of that war of comrades.

Lemass was released in December 1923, but by then he had read every book on economics and history he could find on the camp bookshelves. He was elected to the Dail (the Irish assembly) in 1924, and sat for the same constituency until he retired from politics in 1968. He was, by then, a leading figure in the new party, Fianna Fail, which de Valera formed to escape from the dead end of the civil war.

In 1932, at the early age of thirty-two, he became the minister of industry and commerce in de Valera's first government. He began to improve the sorry state of Irish industry through a protectionist policy. The war years, with materials of all kinds in very short supply, were a major challenge to the country, which he largely dealt with. He founded Irish Shipping to create an independent Irish merchant fleet. He also set up the Tourist Board, which created a major new industry in Ireland. Lemass held the same office until he was elected Taoiseach (prime minister) in June 1959. He had been de Valera's deputy since 1945.

With remarkable energy, he developed Ireland's industry behind a secure tariff wall, then changed this policy, indeed, reversed it, establishing free trade with the United Kingdom in 1965, which was seen as a first step toward entering the common market (now the European Community).

He earned a cover story in *Time* magazine, which featured a traditional leprechaun drawing aside a green curtain to reveal a spanking new factory. This coverage was typical of a change in the international media's interest in Ireland, From the mid-1960s onward a new economic and social situation emerged, leaving the old, traditional Ireland behind. In this new scheme of things he was ably assisted by a new professional class, among whom T. K. WHITAKER [98] was outstanding.

From now on the dark shadow of emigration and a falling population, coupled with high unemployment, began to pass from Ireland. Indeed, in 1965 it had reverse migration—more people entered than left—and the country at last began to retain many of its young people, especially those with higher educations. Everyone knew that Ireland had a past; now it seemed that it might also have a future.

In January 1965 he also began a serious rapprochement with Ulster when he visited the new prime minister, Captain Terence O'Neill, in Belfast—a visit brought about by earlier discussions between O'Neill and T. K. Whitaker at the United Nations in New York. Lemass hoped to promote a federal solution to the problem of the island's partition, though this did not appeal to Belfast. The visit had important results, but may also have generated a rising tide of expectation that in 1969 exploded into a quarter of a century of bloody warfare. The new policy represented another break with the past policy of his party and of other Irish governments.

Lemass resigned as prime minister in November 1966, just after the celebrations of the fiftieth anniversary of the Easter Rising. In retirement he left his successors to run the country without having to look over their shoulder all the time. This, too, was a sign of a new maturity in the country. He died in Dublin on May 11, 1971.

In time, the shy schoolboy who had taken part in the uprising grew into an accomplished, if reserved and enigmatic, man of affairs. By far and away, Seán Lemass was the key man in the making of Ireland as it is today. He had presided over what came to be called the managerial revolution. The generation which has followed since he left public life owes him a debt which it has not fully realized.

15

James Craig, Lord Craigavon

1871–1940

A central figure in the creation of Northern Ireland, and a staunch unionist in the face of a rising tide of Irish nationalism, James Craig, the son of James Craig of Craigavon, a wealthy Belfast distiller, was born on January 8, 1871.

By this time Belfast was beginning to emerge as the major industrial center on the island of Ireland, imitating Glasgow in its growth and outstripping Dublin, Cork, and Limerick. Indeed, it rivaled some of its Scottish counterparts. It was this new industrial growth, and the prosperity that it generated largely for Ulster Protestants, that Ulster unionists were anxious to protect by retaining what they saw as their essential link to the United Kingdom.

Craig's childhood was dominated by the emergence of the Orange Order from being a quasi-secret society. It had once been banned, and was accused of plotting to put the Duke of Cumberland on the throne in place of Queen Victoria. It now established itself as a powerful element in Ulster life and Irish politics. Though feared by the Catholic majority, the Orange Order had important links of religion and friendship with influential persons in high places in British society and government.

Craig was privately educated in Ulster, and then at Merchiston Castle School, in Edinburgh. He became a stockbroker by profession, and fought with the Royal Irish Rifles in the Boer War, that great imperial adventure in which some Irish nationalists supported the Boers.

He was elected a unionist member of Parliament from East Down, a strongly Protestant area of Ulster, in 1906. With Edward Carson, a Dublin-born barrister, he became a leading figure in the party, which was allied with the British Conservative party. They were determined to resist the intention of the Liberal government to grant Home Rule to Ireland. Carson, with a busy London legal practice, was active in government at Westminster, while Craig was the organizer of the Ulster Volunteers at home in Belfast. They armed in defense of the union in 1914, importing weapons from Germany to do so. It was their actions, together with a series of rebellions by women suffragettes, trade unionists, and Irish Nationalists which doomed the Liberal party.

Craig was the Ulster representative at the Buckingham Palace Conference on the Third Home Rule Bill, when the king hoped to hold all the parties together. Home rule was passed by Parliament and given royal assent, but it was suspended for the duration of First World War. Craig fought on the western front from 1914 to 1916. He was quartermaster general of the 36th (Ulster) Division, which consisted mostly of Ulster volunteers. He was knighted in 1918, and served as a parliamentary secretary in the government from 1919 to 1921.

By now home rule was a dead issue. But if the rest of Ireland was to have some greater or lesser measure of self-government, Ulster unionists were determined that they would have home rule for themselves. This they received under the Government of Ireland Act of 1920. Its measures were not enough for the south, but they gave Craig and his followers a parliament in Belfast, which the king opened for them the following year.

Elected from North Down in 1921, in June of that year Craig became the first prime minister of Northern Ireland. The rest of Ireland came to different terms with the British, and in 1922 the Irish Free State under MICHAEL COLLINS [3] and Arthur Griffith came into existence. With Collins, Craig agreed on the protection of northern Catholics, who had been the victims of pogroms in 1920, in return for a settlement of the border. Though a commission investigated the border and reached a settlement, hopes that Northern Ireland would be unviable were not to come true. Craig maintained himself and his statelet. He was elevated to the peerage as Lord Craigavon of Stormont in 1927.

In 1929 he abolished proportional representation, which had been intended to secure the rights of the Catholic minority in the six counties of the north, saying the people did not understand the dangers of it.

The nationalists had adopted a policy of not attending the Belfast parliament (for a time EAMON DE VALERA [2] was an Ulster MP!). In 1934 Craig could tell the Ulster assembly, "We are a Protestant parliament for a Protestant people." It was a definition that excluded the Catholics from the civic life of the country they lived in. Whatever he did of practical value for the status and economy of Northern Ireland was balanced by policies of discrimination and prejudice. It was the same racial intolerance that in other forms stalked other parts of Europe. The Ulster unionists may have felt that they were defending an outpost of Christian civilization against barbarians, but the Catholics of the country felt they were being treated like blacks in the southern United States.

A friend spoke of his "sagacity, honesty of purpose, and courage," and said he possessed qualities of a high order, that he was "a man of undoubted courage, high character, sound judgment, and devotion to duty, and his powers of leadership were conspicuous." To his political opponents among the liberals and nationalists, he had every appearance of being bigoted, outdated, and vindictive.

Craigavon died on November 24, 1940, soon after the Second World War began, leaving Northern Ireland with an entrenched unionism which would take another two generations to resolve into a state that had room for all. Yet in politics, the spirit of "that old bull Craigavon," as the poet Louis MacNiece called him, roams at large whenever the Orange Order parades through Catholic streets or defies the will of the British government. Among all the elements that affect the future of Northern Ireland, the heritage of Lord Craigavon looms large.

16

James Connolly

1868–1916

Though his career was brutally cut short, James Connolly remains the most influential personality in Irish left-wing politics, and his many writings have remained widely read and influential to this day, even in an Ireland that heartily embraces the market economy. All cultures need such a critic.

He was born of Irish parents living in Scotland, in the Cowgate district of Edinburgh, then a slum, on June 5, 1868. Like so many working-class children, he was sent to work at the early age of eleven. At fourteen, however, he joined the British army, then, as now, a resort for those with ambitions to escape a background of poverty. For a time he was stationed in Ireland. He was determined, however, to marry a Wicklow girl he had met in Scotland. To support his family he left the army to work as a carter.

At this time he began to take an interest in socialist and trade union matters. In 1896 he was sent to Ireland as a paid organizer for the Dublin Socialist Club, one of the first organizations of its kind in Ireland. He founded the *Workers' Republic,* the very first Irish socialist paper.

From these first tentative beginnings grew the Irish Socialist Republican party, whose main aim was to secure "the national and economic freedom of the Irish people." These activities soon brought him to the attention of the British authorities, and the secret police in Dublin began to make regular reports on his activities.

Life was hard for his family. Having made a tour of Britain and the United States in 1902, he eventually returned to America with his family in 1903. He stayed in the United States for seven years, working under the auspices of the Socialist Labor party. He established the Irish Socialist Federation in New York and published a monthly journal of Irish interest called the *Harp*. He was one of those who helped to found the Industrial Workers of the World (the Wobblies), whose aim was the creation of "one big union" which all working men could join to defend their interests in the era of the great trusts.

But as an almost unknown figure from Ireland, Connolly was an outsider in the Irish-American communities with their Catholic, conservative leadership. His espousal of trade unionism and women's rights, when added to a raising of Irish consciousness, was not popular among the established nationalist groups. Though admired by many, he could not break through the parochial and racial prejudices of the Irish Americans, to many of whom socialism, in any shape or form, was anathema.

Even among American socialists he had difficulties. His Irish nationalism, religious and spiritual ideas, and Catholic-inspired opposition to divorce were intolerable to many other socialists, largely of European, and especially German, background. He received little support among American socialists for the *Harp*, which soon failed.

He then turned to the Industrial Workers of the World, and in 1910 became editor of the *Newcastle Free Press*, a Wobbly-supported paper published for workers in the heartlands of the industrial district dominated by the steel trust.

Convinced that his American venture had been a regrettable mistake, he went back to Ireland in 1910 and worked as the Ulster organizer of the Transport and General Workers Union. It was at this time he wrote his most extended work, *Labour in Irish History*. This was an attempt to discover, or perhaps create, a legitimate role for the left in the course of Irish history—to justify his claim on the future by calling on the country's past struggles against oppression.

Among employers there was widespread resistance to accepting trade unions, and this led to the great lockout in Dublin in 1913, in which the workers were led by JAMES LARKIN [37]. When Larkin was eventually jailed, Connolly took over the union leadership.

The families of the Dublin workers suffered greatly at this time, as did the protesting workers themselves when they were attacked by the police in the city center. Along with Capt. Jack White, Connolly set about organizing the Irish Citizen Army, based in the union's headquarters in Liberty Hall.

Afterwards Larkin went to America. Connolly, on the outbreak of the First World War, opposed it. He saw capitalism, whether in Britain, America, or Germany, as the real enemy of peace and social justice. Working people were being led away from their true interests by the siren call of nationalism.

But Irish nationalism would be Connolly's own nemesis. In 1916 he took part in the Easter Rising with PATRICK PEARSE [7] and Thomas MacDonagh, even though the aims of his organization were very different from those of the Irish Republican Brotherhood, which they led. He was appointed military commander of the Dublin district, and the members of the Irish Citizen Army that could be mobilized fought alongside the Irish Volunteers in the city garrisons. While in command at the General Post Office he was badly wounded in the leg, but still gave orders from a mattress laid out on the floor of the building.

After the rebels surrendered he was detained in Dublin Castle, but after a court-martial he was executed by shooting, sitting in a chair in Kilmainham Gaol, on May 12, 1916.

Like the other leaders of the uprising, Connolly took on even greater significance in death. His ideas remained influential not only among members of the general trade union movement in Ireland, but also among more radical republicans, in both Northern Ireland and the south. His son and daughter carried on his work in radical politics into the middle decades of the century.

To the Irish left, Connolly remains a hero. To Irish people in general, many of whom would not share all his views, his life is a constant reminder that social justice, rather than the pursuit of wealth, must remain the ultimate aim of all social organization. In recognition of his role in Irish history, a statue of him now stands in Beresford Place in Dublin, facing the new Liberty Hall, one of Dublin's first high-rise buildings, erected in the 1960s. Times change, and even trade unions change with them.

17

Brian Boru

c. 941–1014

One of the most important figures in ancient Irish history, Brian Boru was always thought of in the popular imagination as having broken the power of the Viking invaders, or Danes as they were once called in Ireland. But the actual situation was more complicated than that.

When he was born in north Munster in about 941, the Vikings were well established in strongholds around the Irish coast, and the Irish annalists made much of their raids into the Irish interior. Incidentally, at this time the Irish themselves had colonies in Scotland and Wales, and had made past excursions into Europe itself. The Vikings are now seen more in the light of colonists and settlers rather than raiders, and their role in Irish culture a more positive one.

The problem that faced Ireland was its own political structure. Though the island of Ireland shared a common culture, it was divided into many petty kingdoms. To achieve unity among them was a hard task. (The analogy is with the American colonies, which would have collapsed if they had not managed to unite in 1776.)

In 976 Brian succeeded his brother as king of Dál Cais, in Thomond, an area now covered by County Clare in the southwest of Ireland. At once he laid claim to the kingship of the province of Munster. He became king of Munster in 978, and then began to grapple with the high king of Ireland, based at Tara. Brian himself raided with his armies far into the northern half of the island. Máel Sechnaill, the high king of Ireland, was eventually forced to concede power to Brian, and in 997 at a meeting at Clonfert they partitioned the country between them.

However, in 999 the Leinstermen revolted and allied themselves with the Norse in Dublin. Brian counterattacked, defeated them, and seized and plundered Dublin. But this was not the end of the Norse; rather, it was the beginning of an alliance with them. Brian married Gormlaith, the mother of King Sitric of Dublin, and married his own daughter to the king—a double marriage, cementing the alliance.

Brian now felt secure enough to make claim to the northern part of the island. Máel Sechnaill failed to obtain the support of the northern O'Neills, and yielded to Brian, who became high king of Ireland at the age of sixty-one. In 1002, with a great army, he marched north to Armagh, the city of St. Patrick in which the church in Ireland was centered, where he made a gift of gold and confirmed the city's bishop as the primate of Ireland. Into a page of the *Book of Armagh* his secretary wrote an inscription in Latin referring to Brian as *imperator scotorum,* "the Emperor of the Irish." The next year he made a circuit of the north, subduing the O'Neills by taking hostages. This was how he got his traditional Irish name—Brian Boru means "Brian of the Tributes."

In 1012 the O'Neills and the Leinstermen rebelled against his authority. Brian, now an old man of seventy-two, laid siege to Dublin in 1013 but failed to take the city and returned home for Christmas to his own stronghold of Kincora on the shores of Lough Ree on the Shannon above Killaloe.

Before spring, the Norse had summoned help from abroad, and allies came from the Orkneys and Man. The armies met on the field of Clontarf, a little to the north of Dublin, on Good Friday, April 23, 1014. The Norse and the Leinstermen were defeated, though Brian himself was slain by a fleeing Norse warrior while praying in his tent. Brian's son and grandson also died in the battle.

This battle, far from being an attempt to drive out the Norse, was part of an internal Irish struggle. From recent investigations, the Vikings have now emerged in a more positive light as the bearers into Ireland of new cultural norms, such as coinage, towns, ships, and international trade. They are no longer seen as some earlier version of the English, ravishing the idyllic Celtic nation of Ireland.

The death of Brian marked the last chance Ireland had to create a centralized state under a principal king, as was emerging all over Europe. Brian was called the Emperor of the Irish in imitation of the achievements of Charlemagne (who had died in 814), the protagonist of European unity and Christian culture. Though he had been styled Emperor of the Irish, his empire was short-lived. Again the Irish petty kings fell to local quarrels, and the Irish people failed to create the unitary state which alone would have preserved the integrity of the island from invasion and usurpation.

As it was, despite the achievements of Brian Boru, the country and its ill-led people lay open for a more determined invasion by the Normans, which followed in due course. Brian ultimately failed in what he had hoped for, but it was a noble failure of the kind that the Irish admire, and which her poets and annalists have lamented ever since.

18

Alfred Harmsworth, Lord Northcliffe

1865–1922

The power of the modern press, for both good and evil, was created by men like Irish-born Alfred Harmsworth. His chief titles remain to this day, and the influence he had hoped to exert through them continues. We live today in an era of immediate mass media largely because of his activities a century ago. His notions transformed the nature of the modern world.

Alfred Harmsworth was born in 1865 in the little village of Chapelizod, just outside Dublin, the setting for JAMES JOYCE's [25] book *Finnegans Wake*. But that epic of noncommunication had little in common with Harmsworth's driving ambition to be a great communicator. Two years after Alfred's birth his father moved to London to work as a barrister. His health broke down when Alfred was still in his late teens, so Alfred was largely self-educated. He was also the virtual head of a family.

After leaving school, Alfred Harmsworth began in a small way as the editor of *Bicycling News* in Coventry, where many of the bicycles which were then the latest craze were made. They were a new means of mass transport, and changed the lives, and courting habits, of a generation. The mobility provided by the bicycle was a symptom of the age.

It was an era of mass demand, and Harmsworth conceived the idea of a new kind of newspaper which would cater to the new class of readers which had been produced in England by the Education Act of 1870.

By making elementary education compulsory for all throughout the United Kingdom, the act had given new importance to the printed word.

The Reform Act of 1867 had extended the franchise to city workers, and that of 1884 to laborers in the countryside. The working class, of which the working-class Irish were an important element, was now of political importance. They were becoming the new masters, and newspaper proprietors were keen to gain their support. Harmsworth was one of the first to sense the new drift of things. After some years as an active freelancer he decided to go into publishing himself. His entry into publishing in 1888 marks a distinct new phase in the history of the free press.

His paper was called *Answers to Correspondents,* and was exactly what it said it was, a kind of *Notes and Queries* for the working classes—or ill-educated upstarts, as his critics said. (*Notes and Queries* was a well-known magazine of the academic classes.) The title was soon shortened to *Answers,* but it was the first outpost of an empire. He was joined by his brother Harold (later Lord Rothermere), and within five years the paper was selling over a million copies a week. Other papers and magazines followed, which became the Amalgamated Press, then the largest publishing group in the world.

In 1894 Harmsworth bought the *London Evening News* and returned it to profit, an achievement in itself. Then, in 1896, along with Kennedy Jones, he launched the *Daily Mail,* intended to be a new kind of newspaper. His staff was instructed to "explain, simplify, clarify": it was a paper for the busy person in a modern democracy. Its circulation rapidly rose from a daily average of 202,000 in its first year to 543,000 at the end of its third. Yet many grandees saw it as a vulgarization of government and public life.

The essential feature of the new journalism was not to inform its readers or to support reforming causes, but simply to make money. Its sensationalism was in the cause of pure commercialism, and circulation figures were all that mattered. The large circulations naturally attracted the even richer reward of large-scale advertising, and the smaller papers quaked in the advent of these new giants.

A weekend paper followed called the *Sunday Dispatch.* Seeing that "the new woman" was another force to be reckoned with, Harmsworth began an illustrated paper, the *Daily Mirror,* in 1903. Though originally aimed at the female market, the *Daily Mirror* quickly established itself as a cheap picture paper. Finally, in 1908, he acquired the *Times* of London, perhaps the most august paper in the British Empire, whose reputation as "the Thunderer" was supposed to make the great of the world quake. This brought Harmsworth to the heart of the establishment that ruled the United Kingdom and the expanding British Empire beyond.

Harmsworth (like newspaper proprietors in the United States) conceived that his keen touch for what the public wanted gave him the duty to mold their minds. The backing of the *Times* was an important influence in bringing about the settlement of the Irish situation, in 1921. Though his influence on politicians was slight, his later years were marked by a megalomania that resulted in his breakdown and death on August 14, 1922.

Yet Harmsworth's real influence over history was in the creation of the advertising practice which is so well developed today. Special circumstances brought about the expansion of the press in the 1890s: paper, now made of wood pulp, was cheaper, and machinery was better and faster. Readers, especially businessmen, wanted a digest of the previous day's news rather than long opinion articles. All these factors came together for Alfred Harmsworth.

The daily life of the twentieth century in America or Europe is inconceivable without the daily paper and its range of wonderful advertisements for a consumer lifestyle. Whether or not this is a good thing has become for many social critics a pressing question of the day, for consumerism affects everything from the health of individuals to the survival of the planet itself.

Harmsworth was not self-consciously Irish, but he was representative of those countless millions from his native land who made their way in Britain, America, and Australia through their pertinacity for commerce. They are not always counted among the cultural heroes of Ireland, but in their own spheres they have helped to make the modern world what it is.

Though his influence over day-to-day politics was not as great as he would have hoped, Harmsworth created a whole new market for periodicals. This made his fortune, but it also opened the way for many others. He remains among the giants of press history.

19

Edmund Rice

1762–1844

In 1993, Pope John Paul II declared Edmund Rice, the founder of the Christian Brothers and Presentation Brothers, to be a man of heroic virtue—the first step on the road to his canonization as a saint. Among all the Irishmen of his day and since, Edmund Rice has affected more people than can be imagined through the foundation of these two Irish teaching orders as a force in education worldwide. "Educate that you may be free" was a maxim of the Irish patriot THOMAS DAVIS [23]. Edmund Rice helped make this a reality.

He was born at Westcourt near Callan, in County Kilkenny, and into a well-connected family on June 1, 1762. His father was a prosperous farmer, so he did not lack either material comfort or an education. He received his early education at a "hedge school," an informal school often in the open or in a cottage, for the children of Catholics living in the Callan area. Having gone on to a commercial academy in 1777 at Kilkenny as a preparation for a business career, he went to work in Waterford in 1778 with his uncle, who died and left him the business. He married Mary Elliott, the daughter of a Waterford merchant, in 1785. His great wealth did little to cushion the shock of his wife's death in 1789, when she fell from her horse while out hunting. The child she was expecting was born prematurely and disabled.

Her death was the turning point of Rice's life. Having made ample provision for his daughter Mary, he now decided to retire from business and devote himself to charitable work. At first he thought he might go to Europe and join an enclosed order. One day he called on his friend, Fr. John Power. While they were talking they heard the shouts of young boys fighting in the street outside. Power's sister remarked, "Well, Mr. Rice, you are thinking of burying yourself in a monastery on the Continent. Will you leave these poor boys uncared for? Can't *you* do something for them?" He realized then that a truer vocation lay at home, helping his own people.

In 1796 Rice sought permission from Rome to create a religious society which would provide the poor with free education, and he helped establish a Presentation convent for girls in Waterford in 1798. With the approval of the church authorities in Rome and Ireland, he opened a school for poor boys in Waterford in 1802. Rice was joined by two companions, and they began to live as a community in rooms over the school, which was in a converted stable. Then, in 1803, they moved into a specially built school and monastery called Mount Sion. The town itself was a prosperous seaport with glass and other industries, with a thriving trade to Newfoundland, the United States, and the West Indies. Nevertheless, it the midst of plenty, it also had its poor.

This first venture was a success; other schools followed, but the arrangements for their control were unsatisfactory. Yet, from the success of the schools sprang a congregation of men (approved by the pope in 1820) called the Institute of the Brothers of Christian Schools of Ireland. These men were not priests like the Jesuits or other teaching orders, but unordained brothers who nevertheless took vows of poverty, chastity, and obedience. As Rice saw it, they were there to serve a pressing need. However, they faced opposition from Bishop John Murphy of Cork, which led eventually to the creation of another congregation, the Presentation Brothers.

In 1829 came Catholic emancipation, which would open up many new opportunities for young Catholics to advance their careers. But it had the rather absurd consequence of bringing with it a new penal law to provide for "the gradual suppression and final prohibition" of male religious orders. Rice and his colleagues found they were in an illegal situation, and though there were some difficulties, in the end the regulation proved a dead letter.

The introduction of the national school system in 1831 provided another problem for the brothers. Though some of their schools at first joined the state system, it proved unappealing and controversial, and eventually Rice withdrew. Rather than depend on state funds, the schools survived through the good will of benefactors.

Rice himself retired in 1838; there were then twenty-two houses of the Christian Brothers in the British Isles. Among them was the O'Connell Schools in north Dublin, founded in 1828, a place of great influence in the city. His last years were clouded by further controversy and dissension within the order, as his successor found it hard to live so close to the founder. In 1840 he made a farewell tour of the schools. Soon afterward his health and mental faculties began to give way.

Edmund Rice died at Mount Sion in Waterford on August 29, 1844, but since then the system he inaugurated has spread with the Irish people throughout the world. The Christian Brothers combined practical teaching for boys with deep religious influence and a patriotic fervor which has marked the lives of countless people since. Their discipline was harsh to present-day eyes, but they gave to generations of Irish people with few advantages in the world the greatest boon of all— a decent education.

They also gave nearly all of them a sense of national identity, fostered through their own specially prepared schoolbooks, which is seen as one of the most important elements in the creation of modern Ireland. For everyone in public life who had attended a fashionable Jesuit school there were scores who had gone to the Christian Brothers. They all left a mark somewhere.

20

Daniel O'Connell

1775–1847

It may seem strange to place Daniel O'Connell only in twentieth place in this list, long after other patriots and public figures. Gladstone called O'Connell "the greatest popular leader the world has ever seen." His influence was certainly great, but it was also marred. If he had managed to achieve all he wished or his people wanted, he would have been further up the scale. But he did not, and that was his tragedy and Ireland's.

The creator of the modern Irish democracy sprang from the old Irish rural world of Kerry. O'Connell's people were not peasants, however, but Catholic landlords in their own right, whose wealth derived partly from a vigorous smuggling business.

He was born near Cahirciveen in August 1775, and was adopted by his uncle Maurice (Hunting Cap) O'Connell, the head of the family. Daniel spoke Gaelic and was reared in contact with the realities of rural Irish life. He knew country people thoroughly, a knowledge that served him well in later life, both as a lawyer and a political leader.

As there were then no schools in Ireland for landed Catholics, he was sent to college abroad at St. Omer and Douai in France. There he was exposed to the bloodier sights of revolutionary France, which gave him a lifelong loathing of political violence. The school was expelled from France by order of the government, the boys being jeered by the crowds and forced to wear the tricolor of the revolution. O'Connell's last gesture as the boat sailed out of Calais was to tear the cockade from his hat and throw it into the sea. His contemporary WOLFE TONE [11] saw such violence as the nation's salvation. O'Connell was wiser.

He studied law in London at Lincoln's Inn and read widely in European literature. His reading led him to the position of Catholic liberalism and laissez faire economics, which would remain his political view to the end of his life. He was called to the Irish bar in 1798, the year of rebellion in Ireland, in which Tone took part. The appalling scenes throughout the island in the wake of that aborted uprising confirmed his prejudice against revolution.

In 1802, he married his cousin, Mary O'Connell, raising with her a large and energetic family. He got up at four o'clock every morning and worked on his papers till ten. With hard work he became a figure of substance on the southern legal circuit. Surprisingly for a Catholic, he was also an active Freemason, involved in lodges in Tralee, Cork, and Dublin.

Dublin, of which he was later to be lord mayor and over whose main thoroughfare a huge statue of him now looms, was resolutely controlled by Protestant interests. In 1815 he bitterly attacked the corporation, and the exchange of personalities led to him being challenged to a duel by alderman John D'Esterre. O'Connell did not have the reputation as a duelist that D'Esterre did, but in the duel it was D'Esterre who was fatally wounded. The memory of the duel haunted O'Connell for the rest of his life. He wrote at once to Mrs. D'Esterre, who accepted a pension from O'Connell for her daughter, which was paid for thirty years, until his death. He never went to communion again without wearing a white glove on his right hand, and in passing the D'Esterre house he would raise his hat and pray for the repose of D'Esterre's soul.

After 1798, the Act of Union had promised Catholic emancipation, but this was resisted. In 1823 O'Connell began the Catholic Association, which introduced a new notion. Hitherto politics had been the preserve of the few, and was financed by them. O'Connell now proposed a "Catholic rent"; "a penny a month, a shilling a year" was to be the basic contribution. Backed by the clergy, it yielded £1,000 a week. O'Connell did not become rich out of this, for it was for party purposes. But in an age of democracy it introduced the technique by which political parties of all kinds would fund themselves.

O'Connell's great work was toward the achievement of the Catholic Relief Bill of 1829. In Ireland this is often seen as a measure only for Ireland, but of course it affected Catholics in the public life of the United Kingdom as a whole. Through the Catholic Association he created the first countrywide political organization, the forerunner of the modern parliamentary parties. He was elected from Clare in 1828, and emancipation was conceded the next year.

Leaving the bar and relying on an annual collection to maintain his family, he turned to the frustration of repealing, if he could, the Act of Union. But though he was not a separatist in the way Wolfe Tone and other republicans had been, an independent Ireland (such as had flourished briefly under Henry Grattan in the last two decades of the eighteenth century) was not appealing to British leaders. Through the difficult 1830s he persisted, but it was only when the Whigs fell from power in 1841 that the repeal movement began to take on energy. O'Connell was elected lord mayor of Dublin, and began to hold enormous meetings around the country, one at Tara collecting three-quarters of a million people. Another was to be held at Clontarf, and people were already gathering when the government banned it. O'Connell, fearful of exposing his unarmed followers to army guns, called it off. This loss of nerve, as it seemed to young men round the nation, was a turning point. O'Connell was arrested and jailed but soon released. Old, tired, and ill, he had no resources left; there were rifts in the associations and potato crop failures in the country. He left Ireland, and after a last speech in the House of Commons set out for Rome, but he died in Genoa in May 1847.

Balzac said that O'Connell "incarnated a whole people," and his European reputation among liberals was immense. He remains a controversial figure, but there is no doubting the extraordinary effect he had (for all his faults) on the Irish people. That Ireland remains a democracy, which has been unswayed by the further assaults of revolutionary violence upon its civic institutions, can be seen as his greatest legacy. In the distracted decades since his death it is no small one.

21

Arthur Guinness

1725–1803

Ireland was once seen as a purely agricultural country. Lacking natural resources other than its green fields, industry seemed a hopeless dream. The figure who above all helped Ireland begin the transition from field to factory was the first Arthur Guinness, the founder of the now world famous Guinness brewery in Dublin. It is one of only a handful of businesses that have survived in Ireland from the eighteenth century, and as such it has a historic and influential place in Irish life.

Arthur Guinness was a Protestant born in Leixlip, though both his ancestry and his paternity are mysterious. Though the family later claimed to be descended from an ancient Ulster clan called Magennis, this was not so. More likely, they were the descendants of a Cromwellian soldier from Cornwall called Gennys. It has also been suggested that Arthur Guinness was the natural son of Dr. Arthur Price, Anglican bishop of Cashel, who lived in Celbridge, employed his father, and left Arthur a legacy of £100, with which he was able to start his first small brewery.

In September 1756 he leased a brewery at Leixlip, and this was the first stage of his career. When he was thirty-four he moved into Dublin to continue his business there. Such were the regulations against Irish exports at the time that at first he thought he might move to Wales to work, but in the end he settled in Dublin.

In 1759 he bought a brewery at St. James's Gate from another businessman. At first he brewed beer and ale, but in 1778 he began to make porter, a dark beer made with roasted barley, which was named after the porters in the London markets who had begun to bring the dark brew into favor. For a long time, until the middle of the twentieth century, porter was the mainstay of the business. But stout, a heavier, even darker roasted beer, came to replace it.

By 1799 the dark beers were the sole product of the firm. At this time he began to develop an export trade to England and elsewhere. Guinness was a leading figure among Dublin brewers, and was their member on the city council. A religious man, he founded the first Protestant Sunday school in Ireland in 1786. When the Orange Order was founded in Dublin, the toast was drunk with Arthur Guinness's Protestant beer.

In 1803 Arthur died. The business passed to his son Arthur, and when he died it passed to Benjamin Lee Guinness (who was made a baronet in 1867). When he died he was followed by Sir Arthur Guinness, later Lord Ardilaun. His brother Edward Guinness, later earl of Iveagh, broke the immediate connection with Dublin, as he lived largely in London after 1900.

His son, the second Lord Iveagh, presided not only over the growth of the business in Ireland and Britain, but also in the establishment of breweries in Nigeria and Malaysia. His son, Viscount Elveden, was killed in the Second World War, and the business passed to his son. It was in this generation that Guinness became a public company and control passed from the family.

Arthur Guinness and his descendants are among the most remarkable Irish families of the last three centuries. The extent of their success in business surpassed all others at home. They were also generous to Dublin, to Ireland, and to charities elsewhere. Their history was a mixed one, however, heavily marked with personal tragedies, so much so that many thought some kind of curse hung over the more recent generations, with deaths by suicide, drugs, and driving accidents. Indeed, the social life of the Guinnesses and the scandals attached to them have kept countless journalists and several authors busy over the years. (A book by the novelist Frederic Mullally gives details not only of the main branches of the family, but also the multifarious side shoots, which are as full of human interest as the main ones. They include respectable bankers, reckless jockeys, and dedicated missionaries.)

Yet, in their overall impact on the Irish economy, they have been, until recently, one of Ireland's most successful companies. Naturally, this meant personal wealth for the family, but it also meant prosperity for Dublin.

The economic value of the firm was and is immense. The materials were supplied by Irish farmers; the product employed thousands of Dubliners to make it, and even more thousands of people to sell and drink it. Though now drunk and made around the world, Guinness stout is so closely associated with the image of Ireland as to be safely called its national drink. It has become de rigeur for visiting dignitaries, whether American presidents or British prime ministers, to be photographed drinking the stuff—whether they like it or not.

22

Sybil Connolly

1921–1998

For nearly her whole life, Sybil Connolly was synonymous with Irish high fashion, a genre she could be said to have invented. Irish people of fashion had been accustomed to follow the lead of Paris and London. A la mode meant designs and fabrics conceived and created abroad.

Connolly was brought up in Wales with two sisters. As a young girl, she was taken by her mother to see Balenciaga, and this made a great impression on her. Educated at the Convent of Mercy at Waterford, she joined Bradleys in London as an apprentice at the age of eighteen, where she studied design. Almost forgotten now, the firm was one of the big names between the wars in London, and employed some fifty apprentices. The ninety-eight fitting rooms were always busy with fashionable customers, and once or twice she was even sent to Buckingham Palace to assist in royal fittings for the strong-minded Queen Mary.

Soon after the outbreak of the war, in 1940, she was persuaded by her family to return to live in Dublin. There she brought her London experience to Richard Alan, a leading Dublin shop then owned by Jack Clarke, of which she became a director in 1943. The firm specialized in tweedy country wear, stylish but far from high fashion. The owner of the firm gave her the opportunity to design her own dress line in 1952. One dress, called Bal Masque, created a stir. She then established her own firm in 1953.

Success on an international scale followed. Three dresses from the first show went to New York to be shown in an international show which included the likes of Dior, Jacques Fath, and Hardy Amies. She held a fashion show at Dunsany Castle (the ancient home of the Plunketts) for American buyers and fashion writers. Sheila, Lady Dunsany, was among her first clients, and when she visited the United States with her husband Lord Dunsany, she wore clothes designed by Sybil Connolly. This collection crossed the Atlantic and was shown in "The World of Fashion" exhibition in Boston along with gowns from other great European couturiers such as Schiaparelli, Patou, and Fath. She was on the cover of *Life* magazine, with five pages featuring her inside.

Gabrielle Williams, longtime fashion correspondent of the *Irish Times,* records that her first shows received immediate and wild enthusiasm. "She had done the unthinkable: transforming the clothings of the Irish peasant into haute couture, using traditional Irish fabrics throughout. It had never been done before."

Orders soon followed from the United States, which she often visited. There she met her great friend, the doyenne of the American fashion world, Eleanor Lambert. She also made many visits to Australia. Miss Connolly was trained to cater for these tastes in a Dublin fashion house, but in the late 1940s she began to make her own mark. It was not merely her flair for line and color, but her desire to use Irish fabrics, light tweeds, linens, and lace woolen fabrics of other kinds that made her work distinctive.

She was, it must be admitted, lucky in her connections, for she managed to establish herself with Bergdorfs in New York, and it was her clientele in the United States that made her famous worldwide, with features on her work in *Harper's Bazaar, Vogue, Time,* and other magazines. She made dresses for Jacqueline Kennedy and other society hostesses in New York, Boston, and San Francisco. Mrs. Kennedy was painted wearing a Sybil Connolly dress for her White House portrait.

Miss Connolly diversified her range of designs, moving in fabrics and interiors, becoming in due course a designer for Tiffanys in New York of china, pottery, and crystal, all made by Irish craftspeople. Watercolors of floral subjects were converted into chintzes for Brunschwig and Fils, and bed linens for Martex. She became a popular lecturer in North America, and wrote two books, *In an Irish Garden* (of which she was coauthor) and *In an Irish House.* From time to time she served on various committees involved with the arts, yet at home she lived quietly enough, as her imagination and energy was concentrated on the American market rather than the Irish social scene.

However, she remained clearly identified with Ireland. Her own magnificent home in Dublin's famous Georgian area, Merrion Square, made an elegant showroom for her creations, and for several decades this was her base, where her clients could view her creations, come for advice, and also buy antiques or other items of Irish design.

Her most influential years were the critical ones of the late 1950s and 1960s. Today, when fashion has broken out of its old rigid molds, Sybil Connolly can be seen as a figure who united the best of both approaches. Her clothes were lovely in an elegant, classical way, but they were also bold and often daring in the choice of materials and the colors. She brought Ireland as a fashion center into the consciousness of the world, and so opened the way for two generations of other Irish designers who have followed her, such as Irene Gilbert, Paul Costelloe, and John Rocha.

There was a deep irony here, in that she based her most successful designs on the clothes and fabrics of the rural Irish, whom poverty had driven out to America. Yet in her hands they became romantic, charming, and beautiful.

23

Thomas Davis

1814–1845

For a man with so short a career, Thomas Osborne Davis has exerted an influence over generations of Irishmen of all kinds which is surprising. Arthur Griffith, the president of the Irish Free State in 1922, said Davis was "the prophet I followed throughout my life, the man whose words and teachings I tried to translate into practice in politics." It is to Thomas Davis, a Protestant, that Catholic Ireland owed much of its political maturity.

He was born in Mallow, a town in Cork, on October 14, 1814, the posthumous son of a British army doctor who had died in September. His mother was a Cork woman. With her child she moved to Dublin, taking a house at 67 Lower Baggot Street, which was Davis's home for the rest of his life.

He was an indifferent scholar, and a worse athlete at school. In 1831 he entered Trinity College, in Dublin, and enjoyed himself there, graduating in 1836. He then set off on a tour of Britain and Europe. On his return he was called to the Irish bar in 1838. On renewing his studies for the law at Trinity he became auditor of the college historical society. He joined the Repeal Association in 1841, which DANIEL O'CONNELL [20] had created to campaign to repeal the Act of Union, passed in 1800, which bound Ireland to Great Britain.

He found much of the inspiration for his own ideas in the Irish past, then only being opened up by native scholars, and in a famous speech at Trinity College, then seen as a bastion of British rule, he pleaded for Irish historical studies. His great watchword was "Educate that you may be free." (The annual lectures by Irish scholars and writers which are broadcast by the Irish State service are named for him.)

He was one of the group of young men, impatient as young men often are with their elders, who banded together to found the *Nation* newspaper in Dublin in 1842. The paper was the brainchild of Davis and his friend John Blake Dillon, another barrister. While walking in the Phoenix Park they discussed the matter with another friend, CHARLES GAVAN DUFFY [82], who agreed to put up the money.

The first issued appeared on October 15, 1842. An augury of things to come, it contained a poem by James Clarence Mangan. It was in its pages that Davis published his own poetry and ballads. Such songs as "A Nation Once Again" and "The West's Asleep" are still sung today. Among the other contributors was Jane Elgee, later the mother of OSCAR WILDE [97].

The paper proved to be a great success, and soon the *Nation* had a nationwide readership. Rather than the gleanings of a foreign newspaper, shipping news, and parliamentary reports, which is what most papers of the day contained, the *Nation* set about a program of practical education and liberal enlightenment. The songs and ballads were published as *The Spirit of the Nation* in July 1843 and became an instant bestseller. This was the first of a series of inexpensive publications on history and politics called *The Library of Ireland.*

Thomas Davis was one of the founders of Young Ireland, a political movement which would instigate a rebellion in the summer of 1848. But Davis contracted scarlet fever and failed to throw it off. He died at the age of thirty in his mother's house in Dublin in September 1845, but his ideas became the shaping inspiration of generations of Irish people.

The national ideal as espoused by Davis and his friends might have claimed to be an ancient notion, but was in fact a new and lately fashionable mystique. All across Europe the provinces of the empires and large states were discovering their "nationalities," so Young Ireland had parallels in many other countries. Though it was an idea hailed with enthusiasm in the nineteenth century, it was the cause of two world wars in the twentieth.

The problem was not in the idea of nationality itself—the sense of a shared heritage and culture. It lay in the idea that a nation had exclusive claim to one piece of land and was therefore entitled to drive out anyone who did not share that culture, or to make them second-class citizens.

Of course, Davis and his friends were high-minded idealists, but their ideas were responsible not only for much bloodshed, but eventually for the partition of Ireland, for their nationalism could leave no room for other aspirations. It has taken Ireland and other countries of Europe many decades to undo the damage and to find new grounds for allegiance in the European Union.

Yet Davis was the Protestant son of an Englishman. Many of his ideas have proved influential, especially that of reviving the Irish language and the knowledge of ancient Irish history and culture. So, too, were his ideas about education in Ireland, and the need for the widespread use of the Queen's Colleges. He was also right about the industrial development of Ireland, expounding the need to use turf and water as sources of power. An early death cut off the full development of his ideas, though what he did manage to say and publish was wonderfully effective.

24

Michael Davitt

1846–1906

The title of one of Davitt's six books, *The Fall of Feudalism in Ireland,* encapsulates the work of his life and his influence in Irish history. He dedicated himself to making the Irish the owners of Ireland. His career covers the whole spectrum of Irish politics, from revolutionary action to parliamentary debate.

Davitt was the son of a small Mayo farmer, born in the famine years, who saw his family evicted from their small holding at Straide in 1851 and forced to emigrate to industrial Lancashire in England. He went to work at a very early age. At the age of eleven, in 1857, he lost his right arm while working in a cotton mill. However, he never let this disability restrain him in anything he wanted to do. He might have lost his arm, but he was far from incapacitated.

He joined the Irish Republican Brotherhood in 1865—they were strong among the Irish workers of the north of England—and became an organizing secretary of the IRB by 1868. The year before, in February 1867, he was one of the party of Fenians who attempted to seize Chester Castle, the preliminary to the Fenian uprising in March.

In May 1870 he was sentenced to fifteen years in jail with penal servitude for arms trafficking—which meant breaking stones in Portland. Through the agitation of Isaac Butt and CHARLES PARNELL [5] he was eventually released on ticket of leave (a form of release conditioned on not re-offending) in 1877. He invited Parnell to join the IRB (on the train from London to St. Helen's in Lancashire, of all places), but Parnell wisely declined.

Davitt then left for America, and there, with other former Fenians like JOHN DEVOY [43], he worked out the so-called New Departure policy, which aimed at gaining for Ireland the twin achievements of self-government and land reform. It would also give a new direction to many Fenians, taking them from furtive rebellion to constitutional activity.

Davitt returned to Ireland in 1878, but he found the IRB still dedicated to revolutionary action and Parnell equally reluctant to take up the challenge of land reform. But he brought Parnell to speak in Westport, and this was the beginning of the Land League, with Parnell as president, and of the Land War. This meant political and social turmoil in Ireland during 1879 and the following year, at a time when agriculture was passing through a difficult period in Ireland, with crop failures and near famine.

This ended with the Land Act of 1881, which gave Irish tenants fair rents, fixity of tenure, and free sale. The league, however, also wanted tenant ownership, and this was resisted. The leaders were jailed. Davitt was arrested and returned to penal servitude in 1881, having broken his ticket-of-leave pledge. Released again in May 1882, just after the Kilmainham Treaty, he was arrested yet again for a seditious speech in 1883.

Davitt's followers saw his political slogan, "Land for the People," as a small-farmer proprietorship, while what Davitt meant was the actual nationalization of the land. Davitt was influenced by the American theorist Henry George, but his notion was not popular. Davitt thus lost his leading role in politics, but he continued in public life. He was elected MP from Meath in 1882, from North Meath in 1892, from Northeast Cork in 1893, and from South Mayo in 1895.

He and Parnell saw the Land War as a step on the road to securing home rule, and ultimately independence. But the fall and death of Parnell left the Irish party divided and impotent. Davitt was never again to be quite at the forefront of Irish politics. His role became that of a sort of freelance nationalist and democratic reformer working for Irish independence and social justice through constitutional means. He was widely known as an MP throughout Ireland and Britain and all over the world. The last twenty-four years of his life were striking and active.

He withdrew from parliament in 1899 and went on a visit to Australia, writing *Life and Progress in Australasia* (1898). He was delighted with what he saw there, and with the country's progressive political developments, so different from the state of affairs at home. During the Boer War, like many other Irish people, he identified with the Boer stand, visiting South Africa and publishing *The Boer Fight for Freedom* (1902). He was disappointed that the Irish Americans had not made more of this situation when they might have aided the Boers, some of Britain's most resolute opponents. He also made further visits to the United States in 1901 and 1902.

Unlike many Irish patriots, Davitt was a man of international interests. In *Within the Pale* (1903) he exposed the contemporary massacres of the Jewish population of the capital of Bessarabia, northeast of Odessa. He visited the city on behalf of the Hearst papers in America. The sufferings of the Jews aroused his every sympathy, and the book, one of the best he wrote, is a passionate plea for Zionism.

"When in Palestine, nearly twenty years before," his first biographer Frank Sheehy-Skeffington noted, "he had been greatly impressed by that country, and imbued with the idea that something should be done to preserve its unique character . . . But when he saw the evils endured by the Russian Jews, he came to the conclusion that the root of their sufferings was the fact that they possessed no national home . . .; and the suggestion that they should be allowed to settle in Palestine, the original home of their race, appealed to him irresistibly." His experiences there made him not only "a convinced believer in the remedy of Zionism," but an effective opponent of anti-Semitism in Ireland, Britain, Russia, and elsewhere.

His most famous work, however, is none of the above, but *Leaves From a Prison Diary* (1885), a chilling account of his life as a prisoner of the queen, which has achieved the status of an Irish classic.

He died in Dublin on May 31, 1906. Though he had requested no ceremonies, huge crowds visited the church in Dublin where his body rested before it was taken to Mayo for burial at Straide. As a model of what an Irish patriot should be, Davitt comes high on the list, both as a man of courage and a man of conviction.

25

James Joyce

1882–1941

Along with W. B. YEATS [8], James Joyce has exerted an immense influence on the development of modern literature both in Europe and America. Though in his own day *Ulysses* was seen as a scandalous work, it quickly achieved the status of a modern classic. There can be few writers since who in some way or another have not been aware of the literary and moral example of James Joyce.

He was born in Dublin on February 2, 1882, the eldest surviving child of a Corkman, John Stanislaus Joyce, and his wife, formerly May Murray, whose people came from Longford. At the age of six-and-a-half he was sent to the Jesuit college at Clongowes Wood. He eventually transferred to Belvedere College, another school in Dublin, from where he went on to University College, but these, too, were run by the Jesuits. Joyce revolted against his religious training, but to the end his mind remained imbued with the tenets and traditions of the Catholic church, working with and reacting to the Thomistic philosophy of his teachers.

He was a brilliant, indeed precocious, child. From an early age he was interested in the use of words and the study of language. At college he studied modern languages, and later taught English as a foreign language. Through his studies he became widely read not only in older literatures, but in such contemporary writers such as Henrik Ibsen.

He had abandoned a medical career to go and live in Paris when he was summoned home to the harrowing scenes of his mother's death from cancer in 1903. After an idle, drifting year, he left Ireland accompanied by Nora Barnacle, a Galway girl who was to be the mother of his two children. Though he revisited Ireland briefly in 1909 and 1912, he spent the rest of his life in Europe, first at Trieste (then the port city of the Austrian Empire), in Switzerland for much of the First World War, and finally in Paris until he was forced to flee after the German invasion. He and some of his family escaped to Switzerland and settled in Zurich, where he died unexpectedly on January 13, 1941.

Ireland was a largely rural country in the nineteenth century, and the art of Yeats and other writers of the Irish literary revival looked to the ancient traditions and language of the countryside for their inspiration. Not so James Joyce. He was a distinctly urban genius: The city and its people were the perennial source of his inspiration. But the culture and history of the city, as he showed in later work, was as rich in linguistic and mythological overtones and undertones as the west of Ireland, beloved of Yeats and John Synge.

He began his career in an unexceptional way as a poet of some very slight lyrical poems, but these and some later ones are very minor works indeed, and largely of autobiographical interest. But with *Dubliners* (1914), a collection of sharply observed short stories, he instantly established his place as a distinctive voice in modern Irish literature. The impression which these stories had made was reinforced by the publication of the deeply autobiographical novel *A Portrait of the Artist as a Young Man* (1916), which provided an account of an Irish-Catholic upbringing which was often unsparing in its painful detail, but executed with cool precision. The character based most closely on Joyce himself, Stephen Dedalus, closes the novel with a passage in his diary as he is about to leave Ireland: "I go to forge in the smithy of my soul the uncreated conscience of my race."

He wrote a play, *Exiles* (1918), which was largely considered a failure and even a minor work until it was given a triumphant production by Harold Pinter in London in 1971, which at last restored its tortured intimacies to their proper place in the Joyce canon.

If his short stories had been objective, and his novel subjective, these two modes were combined in his next work. He moved on to explore his personal urban world, which he developed in *Ulysses* (1922) and *Finnegans Wake* (1939), which represent, respectively, the hectic day and the dreaming night of a great modern city. Leopold Bloom, the central figure of *Ulysses*, represents the moral conscience of the city through his encounters with its diverse citizens, while *Finnegans Wake*, through the dreaming hotel keeper H. C. Earwicker, contains the backward and forward history of the universe. Neither work is capable of simple explication. They have to be read and experienced for themselves.

But just as important in *Ulysses* is the figure of Molly Bloom, the wayward wife of the wandering Leopold. Joyce's women are of two kinds, the icy virgin and the voluptuous mother goddess. Molly Bloom's rambling thoughts on the verge of sleep fill out the end of the novel, and are among the most remarkable impressions of the female psyche achieved by a male writer. They close with her passing into sleep, the sleep where Mr. Earwicker and his family are discovered at the opening of *Finnegans Wake,* reminding us that Joyce's books are not separate items, but parts of one long and continuous creative work.

These books, especially *Ulysses,* broke new ground in that they dealt with human actions in words which many thought broke down the proper amenities of literature. However, for writers of the early part of the century, Joyce's linguistic and technical experiments were of profound consequence.

In Ireland he was the inspiration of two generations of writers who found their material in the life of the city, and his influence can be traced in such diverse figures as Flann O'Brien and J. P. Donleavy.

In America, where *Ulysses* was banned, Joyce was seen as the leader of the vanguard of modern literature. This was not a comfortable place to be. It obscured many of the classical features of his writings and the profound debt which they owed to the medieval thought of the Catholic church. Though it might seem that Joyce had renounced, indeed denounced, the God of his fathers, his own mind and imagination was deeply grained by the history, culture, and mental attitudes of the Irish people.

26

Jack B. Yeats

1871–1957

Jack Yeats was the brother of the poet WILLIAM BUTLER YEATS [8], and the son of the painter John Butler Yeats. Without doubt, he is the greatest Irish painter of the twentieth century, in a class which includes whatever great masters one would like to mention. Some would even say he is the greatest Irish painter of all time. These may seem to be extravagant claims, but his work has these important distinctions.

Jack Butler Yeats was born in London on August 29, 1871, while his father was living there in hopes of making a name for himself as an artist. But though he was delighted with many aspects of city life, it was rural Ireland that awakened the boy's imagination when he was sent home at the age of eight to stay with his grandparents in Sligo, on the western coast of Ireland. To the end of his life his drawing and paintings were filled with images and scenes drawn directly from the world that he then began to explore.

Though his education was skimpy, he began studying in art colleges in his teens, and contributed black-and-white drawings to various papers and magazines in London. He even did work for the *Boy's Own Paper*. For thirty years, beginning in 1890, he worked as a professional illustrator at a time when journalism depended on the facile pens of many artists in a way which is no longer the case. He also worked in watercolors, of which he had several exhibitions.

He married Mary Cottenham ("Cottie") White in 1894, but he and his wife had no children. In 1897 they moved away from London to live in rural Devon. At this time he was a close friend of the poet John

Masefield, who shared his delight in ships, pirates, and the sea. In 1910 he returned to live in Ireland—he had never felt fully at home in England. At first he and his wife lived in Wicklow, but later moved back into Dublin, where Yeats had a studio on fashionable Fitzwilliam Square, high up in an old Georgian mansion.

He had traveled in the west of Ireland with John Synge, illustrating the playwright's articles for the *Manchester Guardian* with drawings of life in the west of Ireland. He returned to these scenes in his book of 1912, actually called *Life in the West of Ireland.* He began painting in oils, at first as a continuation of the close observational style of his earlier work, but over the years moved into a looser, more mythopoetic style. This growth as an artist was much like that of his brother the poet, who moved from the lyrical to the great poems of his old age. Jack Yeats was among the significant artists who exhibited at the influential show of international modern art held in 1913 at the New York Armory.

His imagination was much engaged by the Troubles, and he was far more radical in his politics than his brother. Jack painted several scenes of incidents in the troubles, such as *Bachelor's Walk—In Memory* and *Communicating With the Prisoners,* which have become icons of Irish history. Though his poet brother supported the Free State and accepted an office as a senator, Jack Yeats's sympathies were with the republicans, and images of heroic defeat which echo events in the civil war can be found in his later paintings.

Living quietly in Dublin, he exhibited from time to time. His painting, however, continued to mature and to become technically looser and more expressionist, with a vivid sense of color while beginning to employ personal symbolism drawn from the life he loved in the west.

He was also a writer, but his plays and novels are largely of interest for what they reveal about the painter rather than for themselves, though all share the beguiling tenderness for past scenes that makes his work so attractive to many. His inspiration, he once said, for both his paintings and writings was "affection, wide, devious, and sometimes, handsome."

He was brought to the attention of the wider world by the critical writings of Sir Kenneth Clarke, then the director of the National Gallery in London. "Color is Yeats's element in which he dives and splashes with the shameless abandon of a porpoise." In 1945 a major exhibition of his works was held at the National Gallery, and another in Dublin. From then he held regular, almost annual exhibitions in both cities.

Jack Yeats's friend, the Irish poet Thomas MacGreevy, thought that the painter was the equal of Titian and Rembrandt: "If universality of outlook and the last refinements of artistic technique were attainable for a religious painter in the little Republic of Venice, and for a bourgeois painter in the little republic of Holland in the seventeenth century, why should they not be attainable for an artist of the life of the people in the little almost-republic of Ireland in the twentieth? Universality of outlook and technical mastery of art are both a question of the capacity to understand, the capacity that is the second gift of the Holy Ghost, that was the one gift Solomon asked of the Lord. I am of the opinion that the Lord bestowed the capacity to understand on Jack Yeats."

His work has often been compared with the poetry of his brother, but as an expression of the Irish imagination he had far more in common with JAMES JOYCE [25]. Both share an early realism, a mature and humane middle style based on city life, and a final late stage in which the words of *Finnegans Wake,* so complex in their symbolic allusiveness, parallel late paintings such as *Men of Destiny.* Joyce even owned a Jack Yeats picture of the River Liffey. Yet, oddly, his paintings remained at a price which enabled many to buy them from his exhibitions.

Yeats died in Dublin in 1957, but since his death his reputation has grown continually, and his paintings now achieve astronomical prices which would have come as a great shock to such an essentially shy and retiring man. His paintings have an intense literary quality, unusual for a twentieth-century artist, which makes them accessible to a wide audience. They are a pageant of the spiritual odyssey of the Irish people over the last two centuries, the full depths of which are now coming to be appreciated. In time he will, indeed, be ranked with Titian and Rembrandt.

27

Archbishop
Thomas Croke

1824–1902

Every year the finals of the All Ireland Gaelic Games of hurling and football are held in Croke Park in Dublin. It is the most important date in the sports calendar of Ireland, and draws crowds not only from Ireland but from abroad, especially from the United States.

The stadium, now one of the most up-to-date in the country, belongs to the Gaelic Athletic Association, and is named after Archbishop Thomas Croke, the great nineteenth-century archbishop of Cashel, who promoted Gaelic games as a patriotic movement, and so helped to create in a large way the popular national identity of modern Ireland.

Thomas William Croke was born in Ballyclough, in County Cork, in January 1824. His father William was a Catholic, but his mother, formerly Isabelle Plummer, was a Protestant, though she converted to her husband's religion four years before she died. Such mixed marriages were by no means uncommon in nineteenth-century Ireland, especially in the southern counties, where intolerance was less than in Ulster. But most Protestants in the south were Anglicans, and hence closer to their Catholic neighbors than the Calvinistic Presbyterians of the north in many aspects of their beliefs.

Croke studied for the priesthood at the Irish College in Paris between 1840 and 1844. He spent a final year, 1847, in Rome before being ordained. He taught for a time at the diocesan college in Carlow, and then again in Paris until 1849. Being abroad, he was away from the devastation caused by the famine, especially in parts of Cork. Yet no one of any sensitivity could be unaware of its effect on the Irish character. During the postfamine years of 1849 to 1858 he did missionary work in the Diocese of Cloyne, in the south of Cork. He was made the first president of St. Colman's College in Fermoy, where one of his pupils for a brief time was the father-to-be of JAMES JOYCE [25]. He was then parish priest of Doneraile in County Cork from 1865 to 1870.

Croke attended the Vatican Council as theologian to Bishop William Keane of Cloyne. This was one of the defining events for Catholics in the nineteenth century, leading as it did to the definition of papal infallibility. But for Croke it had a surprising outcome. From there he was sent, as so many priests of the day were, from Ireland to New Zealand. The Irish community in New Zealand was an active one, but not as significant as that in Australia. His stay lasted only five years, as on a visit to Ireland in 1875 he was elevated to the archdiocese of Cashel and Emly, one of the most important in the country, covering as it did not only the fertile areas of Munster, but also the impoverished hill country in the Galtee Mountains.

Croke, conscious of these contrasts in Irish life, was a keen advocate of education, and everywhere he went he promoted the building of churches and schools. Like most Irish clergy he supported the temperance movement, which had begun in Cork in the 1830s, but he was also an enthusiast for the Gaelic League and the revival of the Irish language.

These activities as a pastor were as nothing compared to his national work. In his younger days he had been a follower of DANIEL O'CONNELL [20] in his campaign for the repeal of the Act of Union. After O'Connell's death he supported the Young Ireland movement, which had ended in the abortive uprising of 1848, which took place in Munster. That unhappy failure did not prevent him from being a supporter of the Irish Tenant League in the 1850s at a time when there was no real Irish party, merely a group of Irish MPs with nationalist interests.

However, when Croke became archbishop in 1875, a distinctive political movement was emerging under Isaac Butt, and he also became an advocate of home rule. Butt was followed by the more aggressive CHARLES STEWART PARNELL [5] and the Land League. Though these were looked upon with dismay by more conservative figures like PAUL CARDINAL CULLEN [44], Croke happily embraced them.

Croke was a nationalist to the core. This inevitably got him into trouble with the government. The British, through influential English Catholics, attempted to poison Rome's opinion of him. In 1887 he wrote an unwise letter to the main Nationalist paper, the *Freeman's Journal*, criticizing the government's use of Irish taxes to fund the repression by the police of those who paid them. This seemed to have overstepped the mark, and to be encouraging Catholics to not pay legal taxes, so he was denounced in Rome. However, his friends Archbishop William Walsh of Dublin (himself a nationalist), and Cardinal Henry Edward Manning of Westminster, smoothed the troubled waters.

Croke was as dismayed as many other followers of the Irish party were by the shocking revelations of the private life of Parnell and Mrs. O'Shea, during the divorce action naming Parnell, brought against her by her husband, Captain O'Shea, in 1889–1890. The Irish party split when the Irish bishops announced that they could no longer support such a public sinner. Disillusioned by party politics, he slowly withdrew from that arena.

But his enthusiasm for the Gaelic Athletic Association (GAA) remained. Started in the early 1880s by Michael Cusack and some other enthusiasts at a time when both rugby and soccer were being organized on a more professional basis, the aim was to bring the benefits of healthy sport and competition to the parishes of Ireland. Rugby and soccer were denounced as "foreign" games, played only, it was claimed, by the garrison and Castle Catholics. Gaelic football and hurling, which had been played since time immemorial, were provided with new rules and a league. The GAA was organized everywhere, and soon had a large following.

Many of its members shared Croke's disillusionment with the Irish party and the older politics. In time, of course, it formed a parish-by-parish ready-made organization for Irish republicans to infiltrate in order to promote a new wave of revolution in the early twentieth century. Croke remained a great heroic figure to the movement, which now has worldwide links. The promotion of sport has been one of the great social movements of modern Ireland; its influence has been for the most part wonderfully beneficial, and is indissolubly linked with the name of Archbishop Croke.

However, Croke died at Thurles on July 22, 1902, and did not live to see the emergence of the new nation exactly a century after he was born.

28

Cyrus Hall McCormick

1809–1884

History (in the schoolbook sense of history) seems to be dominated by political figures who create their own self-importance. It is often forgotten what profounder social changes are brought about in the human condition by those who push forward not political, but technical, change. Their influence is what really creates and changes the world.

Americans in the nineteenth century felt themselves less bound by conventional ideas than Europeans did, and this was especially true of inventors. The McCormick dynasty, Ulstermen by origin, are among these. Robert McCormick (1780–1846) was a farmer dependent on labor, which was often in short supply, so he contrived many labor-saving devices for work on the farm and fields. In 1809 he invented a reaping machine, which he improved by degrees over the years, incorporating into it a horizontal reel and vibrating sickle. Though he was a pioneer of mechanized farming and popularized harvesting machines through the United States, he was not the first.

The first application of steam to the plow was patented by the Irish landlord Richard Lovell Edgeworth (the father of the novelist MARIA EDGEWORTH [91]), but this was not developed until 1852. A reaping machine had been invented by the Rev. Mr. Bell of Carmylie, Forfarshire. But invention was one thing, development for widespread use another. In the opening up of the American continent, the nation was faced with what seemed to be limitless acres of arable land on the western prairies. As the founder of the McCormick Harvesting Machine Corporation, which was influential in the introduction of the harvesting machine throughout the United States, Robert McCormick was the true pioneer of industrialized agriculture.

His son was Cyrus Hall McCormick, who inherited his father's interests. He was born in Walnut Grove, Rockbridge County, Virginia—a name redolent of the older forms of agriculture. In 1831, at the age of twenty-two, he took up the challenge that had defeated his father, to construct a really workable grain-cutting machine. His reaper, a development of his father's earlier and cruder machine, was first used in the late harvest of 1831 and patented in 1834. It transformed the nature of agriculture and the provision of food to the great urban centers, which were emerging in American and Europe in the nineteenth century.

It should be remembered that in 1820 the population of the United States was 12,866,020, centered in what is now Moorefield, West Virginia. By 1880 the population, now demographically centered in Ohio, had grown to 50,155,783. The state of New York alone had a population of five million; by the turn of the century the U.S. population had grown to nearly seventy-six million. It was to feed these teeming masses that mass-produced food was needed.

The Irish writer JONATHAN SWIFT [34] had remarked that whoever could make two ears of corn grow where only one grew before deserved better of mankind and did a more essential service to his country "than the whole race of politicians put together." Growing ears of corn was one thing; harvesting them for the market, as the McCormicks did, was just as important a service to humanity.

Further years perfected the harvesting machine. By 1843 McCormick was able to sell the rights, and with the capital set up a factory in Chicago in 1847. One of his new machines was exhibited at the Great Exhibition in London in 1851—perhaps the most important showcase of new ideas ever held. The *Times* of London, the leading British paper of the day, said that if McCormick's machine fulfilled its promise, it alone was worth the cost of the whole exhibition.

Like most inventors and manufacturers, McCormick was beset by legal problems: Inventors are notoriously litigious. There were other inventors in the field as well, such as Obed Hussey, who announced his invention of a reaping machine in 1834. Yet the factory flourished. During the Civil War, McCormick's machines helped to make the Union victory possible by ensuring a food supply to the armies in the field.

The firm expanded in the years after the Civil War, when the western regions of both the United States and Canada began to develop. New markets were found in Europe and elsewhere. In 1871 the family, having lived in Washington, New York, and Europe, settled permanently in Chicago. Cyrus was awarded many prizes and distinctions. In 1879 the Academy of Sciences in France elected him a corresponding member for having done more for agriculture than any other living man.

Cyrus Sr. died in Chicago on May 13, 1884, and was in turn succeeded by his son, Cyrus Hall McCormick II (1859–1936), then only twenty-four. A serious-minded young man, he was already well versed in the details of both the machines and the buisiness. He settled all the outstanding legal problems with fellow inventors, and began a new stage in the development of the firm.

In 1902 the firm became the International Harvester Company, one of the largest corporations in the world. Inevitably, the size and near monopoly of the firm attracted the attention of federal trust-busters, but the company eventually came out of this situation intact. Cyrus II ceased the day-to-day direction of the firm in 1918, and died in June 1936.

As befitted their Ulster origins, the McCormicks were Presbyterians and gave freely to many church and philanthropic causes, especially the Young Men's Christian Association (YMCA). Yet their inventions more profoundly shaped western life than any charity. They literally helped put bread on the tables of the industrial masses for a century or more, and their enterprise lies behind the extraordinary agribusinesses of today. While such people as Cyrus Hall McCormick may not always appear in history books, the influence they have exerted over the shape and structure of modern life is profound. But mere inventors do not often receive their just honors.

29

John L. Sullivan

1858–1918

Born in Boston of Irish parents, John L. Sullivan found that the way to the top could be achieved through sport. Sports of all kinds now dominate the lives of so many people, either as participants or spectators, that it is often forgotten how recent the development of the professional sportsman is.

The great boxer was one of the first, and made it possible for many another poor boy, black or white, to crawl his way out of some urban slum or rural backwater to gain fame and fortune. But he also showed that this was not an easy road, or one that always ended happily.

John Lawrence Sullivan was born in Boston. His father, Michael Sullivan of Tralee, a fiery little Kerryman, provided his temper. His mother, a lady weighing 180 pounds and built on a generous scale, provided his physique. As a boy he demonstrated his great strength, and he was fond of sports and got many offers to play baseball.

Sullivan left school at sixteen and worked as a plumber's mate, enjoying nothing more than a rowdy drunken Saturday filled with drink and fist fights. One evening at the Dudley Street Opera House in Boston there was a boxing display, and he was asked into the ring. He knocked his opponent clear into the orchestra pit. He announced that he could "lick any son of a bitch in the house." The legend of J. L. Sullivan was already in the making.

As a sport, boxing had been around since 1719, but it had passed through ups-and-downs of popularity since then. The first, though unofficial, heavyweight championship of the world was fought in London in

1819 between an American black, a freed slave, and the English champion. In mid-century, gamblers tainted the sport. Bare-knuckle fighting, in any case, was a brutal business with almost no rules and was illegal in many countries. The Marquis of Queensberry rules of 1867 began to bring improvements, and by 1890 boxing had recovered the popularity it maintains to this day. This was largely due to J. L. Sullivan.

Sullivan spent a year giving boxing exhibitions in a variety show run by another Irishman named William Muldoon. He began his career as a professional pugilist in 1880, when the American champion was another Irish boxer, Paddy Ryan. Sullivan, in the way of the boxing world, had to fight his way up to a challenge with the champion. In Mississippi City, Mississippi, on February 7, 1882, the match came off. It was fought with the customary bare knuckles on grass, and Sullivan knocked Ryan out in the ninth round. He was the idol of the crowd, and he received a tremendous reception on his journey back to Boston. He toured the country giving exhibition fights, offering $500 to anyone who could last four rounds. These efforts gave boxing a new respectability and wider popularity.

For a long time "the Boston Strongboy" carried all before him. He stood five feet, ten-and-a-half inches high, and in fighting condition weighed 180 pounds—just like his mother. He was quick tempered and fiery, with blazing hazel eyes and extraordinary self-confidence. Though he drank a great deal, even when not in condition he could "knock a horse down." His manager, Jimmy Wakley, welcomed all challenges, except one from the black fighter Peter Jackson. Like many Irishmen, Sullivan was a fierce American patriot and slightly racist in his views. He scorned foreign and black fighters. For instance, he slaughtered the New Zealand boxer Henry Slade (known as the Maori) at Madison Square Garden in August 1882.

But in May 1883 he had real difficulty with the English boxer Charlie Mitchell, who actually managed to knock Sullivan down—an unheard of feat. Such was Sullivan's anger that the police had to stop the fight in the third round to spare the Cockney's life.

His size, weight, strength, and "hurricane" style of attack generally meant that he could overcome his opponents in two or three rounds. On August 8, 1887, at the Boston Theater he was presented with a $10,000 diamond-studded belt by his admirers. Later that year he went to Europe on a wave of sporting enthusiasm. He visited Ireland and England, and met the Prince of Wales, himself a great sportsman. A fight with Charlie Mitchell at Chantilly on the estate of the Baron

Rothschild lasted some three hours and ended, to Sullivan's annoyance, in a draw. Both of the boxers were arrested; Sullivan posted bail and fled the country.

But the end was in sight. The next year his condition was bad, but Muldoon brought him up to scratch. In a fight with Jake Kilrain in Richburg, Mississippi, in July 1889 after seventy-five rounds in the open heat of the sun he took the match—just. This was the last bare-knuckle fight. After this match, boxing with gloves under the Marquis of Queensberry rules became the norm.

Sullivan now claimed to be world champion, as Kilrain had beaten Jem Smith, the English champion, to a draw. Three years later, on September 7, 1892, "Gentleman" Jim Corbett, after a fight lasting twenty-one rounds, brought the Boston Strongboy's career to an end by knocking him out. The match, held in New Orleans, is often seen as the first heavyweight title fight under Queensberry rules, with gloves and three-minute rounds.

Sullivan was now in a bad way. In his riotous lifestyle he had lost everything, even the diamond belt. He managed to pick himself up, however, and toured in plays and in vaudeville, opened a bar in New York, and took a share in one in Boston. The Irish talked of putting him into Congress.

He had married a chorus girl in 1883 named Annie Bates, but she left him soon after. In 1905, having taken the pledge of temperance, he became a reformed character. He divorced Annie and married Kate Harkins from Roxbury, in Boston, whom he had known since his youth. In 1912 they bought a farm in rural Massachusetts. Kate died in 1917. Sullivan lingered on, spending his time on the farm with an old sparring partner until he, too, passed away on February 2, 1918.

John L. Sullivan, who retained the regard and affection of many beyond the circles of boxing fans, had made boxing a respectable sport, yet in the end he died obscurely and in poverty, his passing largely eclipsed by the news of the First World War.

30

Richard Croker

1841–1922

On July 1, 1907, the city council of Dublin elected and admitted Richard Wellsted Croker as the twenty-first honorary burgess of the city. To a list that included Gen. Ulysses S. Grant and CHARLES PARNELL [5], Richard Croker, the former head of Tammany Hall and a by-word for civic corruption, made a curious addition. If the life of the Irish Americans was city centered, men like Richard "Boss" Croker were at the heart of it as the architects of Irish-American urban politics.

Croker was born just before the famine in Clonakilty in west Cork in the south of Ireland on November 23, 1841. Though in later years he allowed his followers the impression that he came from an impoverished peasant background, this was not true. Impoverished his father, Eyre Coote Croker, may have been, but he came from landed gentry of largely English extraction. The family, in which there were nine children, emigrated to New York City when Richard was three. He was educated there in public schools, beginning his working life at the age of thirteen.

His first job was as a machinist, but he was big and strong, and in his late teens was a fighter with a reputation on the Upper East Side as leader of the Fourth Avenue Tunnel Gang. All his life he retained the outlook and morality of the street gang.

He soon entered local politics, disguising his past. He even became a Catholic to forward his political ambitions. He joined Tammany Hall, then led by the notorious "Boss" William M. Tweed, and soon had the ambition to lead it himself. Croker became an alderman in

1868, putting his foot on the first rung of city promotion. He was later appointed coroner of New York City at a salary of $25,000 a year.

He succeeded "Honest John" Kelly, a leading Democrat, as Tammany leader in 1886 and held power for seventeen years. He added to his positions the equally lucrative ones of fire commissioner and city chamberlain. Croker had opposed Tweed, and claimed that his only ambition was to save a great city from that crook's clutches. However, the investigations into the corruption of local politics made life more difficult for him in New York. He was already tainted by a rumor that he had murdered a man. Certainly, on election day in 1874 an opponent of Croker's was shot and killed. Though Croker later claimed that one of his henchmen had done the deed, some thought that "Boss" Croker himself was responsible.

Through a system of local patronage, he creamed off the spoils from a great city, allowing, however, his henchmen their share. The investigations of the Lexow Committee marked the beginning of a move against Tammany. In 1894, to put some distance between himself and the law, he retired to England, though he later moved to Glencairn, a large mansion outside Dublin.

There he was the greatest of the "returned Yanks," as people in Ireland called their countrymen who returned laden with money from the New World. His income had always been something of a mystery. The British tax authorities, a more rigid organization than he was used to dealing with in New York, estimated his income in 1900 at $100,000, and fixed his tax at $5,000. He adopted the style and manners of the country squires from whom he sprang, breeding a famous Derby winner, Orby, in 1907—the first Irish horse to win that classic race. From the chief herald of Ireland he gained a grant of a coat of arms; given his true family background this posed little problem. The New York crook had become the complete Irish gentleman.

When his first wife, from whom he had long been estranged, died in 1914, he married Beula Benton Edmondson, a princess of the Cherokee Nation from Oklahoma, who was many years younger. This alliance led to disagreements with his children, which continued after his death in 1922, resulting in a spectacular law case heard in Dublin at which it was alleged that the beautiful Beula, far from being an Indian princess, was actually the wife of an Italian plumber. The citizens of Dublin queued around the block for weeks to hear the evidence.

For Irish people, Boss Croker was an extraordinary personality, though silent and reserved. His funeral at the end of April 1922, when his remains were buried in the grounds of Glencairn, was attended by leading members of the new Irish government with an honor guard of Irish Free State soldiers.

Undoubtedly Boss Croker was corrupt to the core, but from the point of view of his Irish constituents, he was the man who made the system, so long controlled by American Protestants, serve the needs of the new Catholic Irish. The whole basis of the Democratic party in the great cities of the northeast rested on this arrangement. In that he served the interests of his own community well, Richard Wellstad Croker's influence was immense. What was unforgivable in the eyes of many others was the corruption of the civic institutions of a great city which accompanied it.

31

Joseph R. McCarthy

1908–1957

The senator who led the campaign to root out Reds from the public service and other areas of American life was in his day seen as a dangerous threat to American civil liberties. This remains true, but there were other dimensions to the senator from Wisconsin. He remains perhaps the most controversial Irish-American politician of this century, having given his name to a particular brand of free-wheeling political activity.

Joe McCarthy was born in Grand Chute, Wisconsin, on November 14, 1908. His family were Catholics of mixed Irish and German origins. His early education was in the public school system, at Underhill County School rather than the parish system. Having worked on a farm, he started his own chicken farm. Then, at nineteen, he moved to Manawa, enrolled in Little Wolf High School, paying his way by working in a grocery store and ushering in a theater. Ambitious, he was also bright, for he completed the four-year-school in one.

In 1930 he entered Marquette University to study engineering, but changed to the law school, graduating in 1935. He was then in private practice as a lawyer until he was elected circuit court judge of the tenth district in 1939, and he remained a judge until his election to the U.S. Senate in 1945. Between 1942 and 1945 he fought with the U.S. Marines in the South Pacific.

The war had been won by a grand alliance of the western democracies and the Soviet Union. After the war and the occupation of

Eastern Europe, and the establishment of Communist regimes in the countries under the control of the Soviets, this alliance changed into a cold war. An iron curtain, in Winston Churchill's famous phrase, divided Europe.

In 1946 McCarthy was elected to the Senate, and served there until his death. In his first year as senator, McCarthy took up what he saw as the challenge of the penetration of members of the Communist party into the government and other areas of American life. In this he had the support of a section of the Republican party, led by Robert A. Taft. In 1950, in a speech in Wheeling, West Virginia, he leveled the charge that Communist agents in the State Department were influencing American foreign policy. This was followed up by a hearing of the Tydings Committee.

In the House, the Un-American Activities Committee gave rise to alarming charges, though President Harry Truman dismissed these as red herrings. Yet some two million federal employees were investigated, 526 of whom resigned and 98 were dismissed. In 1948 twelve Communists were tried for attempting to overthrow the government.

Under Truman, McCarthy attacked George C. Marshall, then secretary of state and creator of the Marshall Plan to aid the recovery of postwar Europe—a plan deeply resented by many conservative Americans.

Others such as Asian adviser Owen Lattimore, who had been involved in policy in the Far East, were also suspect. A narrow test of loyalty was espoused that focused on resistance to the alliance with the Soviets during the Second World War.

In 1950, with the beginning of the Korean War and the conviction of Alger Hiss, the country was alive to the Communist menace. Alger Hiss, a former State department official, was accused by Whittaker Chambers of passing documents to Communist spies or agents, which he denied. Hiss was convicted, not of espionage, but of perjury; and the matter remains deeply controversial to this day. J. Edgar Hoover announced that there were fifty-five thousand party members in the United States and some five hundred thousand sympathizers and fellow-travellers, that is, those non-Communists whose radical sympathies for the poor and oppressed in America were traded upon by Communists for the advantage of the party.

The election of President Dwight D. Eisenhower (who took office in 1953) led to more effective political resistance against McCarthy and his methods. On January 2 a report by a Senate privileges committee on the activities of the senator found that some had been "motivated by self-interest." McCarthy's investigation of the army, conducted in hearings from April 23 to June 17, 1954, came at a time when he was already losing influence in Washington and the Eisenhower administration was following a line more or less like that of Truman. These hearings were televised, and the counsel for the army, John G. Adams, dramatically defeated McCarthy's charges.

These hearings led the army to level charges that McCarthy and his counsel Roy Cohn had attempted to obtain special privileges of leave for an army private (with whom, it seems, Cohn was sexually involved). This was controversial and unpleasant material, though not fully aired at the time.

Eventually the Republican party distanced itself from McCarthy, and he was censured by the Senate. A censure resolution was passed on July 30, 1954, and in a vote of a special session of the Senate on December 2, he was condemned for his conduct in chairing the Senate committee.

His early death in Washington, D.C., on May 2, 1957—he was only forty-eight—did not, however, end the right-wing attack on either American liberal policies or Communists in places of influence. McCarthy had achieved a large following among conservatives of all religions and had a large Irish-Catholic following. His influence was immense and remained so.

With the fall of the Soviet Union and further investigations by historians, the actual extent of Communist influence has become clear. Paranoid though McCarthy was, the American Communist party had nevertheless infiltrated many areas of American life as a matter of policy.

McCarthy's extravagant style reflected the intense patriotism of an Irish American deeply anxious to prove his loyalty and that of his part of the community by focusing on the disloyalty of another one. A generation before, much of what he said about Communist America had been said about the Irish themselves as agents of papal power attempting to subvert American democracy. That had not been true, and for many Senator McCarthy's charge also belongs to what has been characterized as "the paranoid style" of American politics.

Yet even today, when communism has disappeared as a force in international politics, and so long after his death, Joseph Raymond McCarthy remains a model of a particular kind of American patriot for a significant number of Americans. As the journalist Nicholas von Hoffman points out, he introduced into public life a notion that all men were suspect, and therefore engendered a culture of total security at all levels of public and private life that has become the great obsession of the late twentieth century. These show, adds von Hoffman, that "the view championed by Joe [McCarthy], that the world is a perilous place penetrated by treachery and poised to attack, has gained wide acceptance."

32

Robert Boyle

1627–1691

Ireland is not always thought of as the cradle of scientists, perhaps because science at its purest has little in the way of national character. However, Robert Boyle is a figure which any country would be proud of. "Boyle's Law," as we are taught at school, is a key scientific fact. He was interesting as both a philosopher and a physicist and chemist. His contemporaries were aware of his curious position, as a friendly Irish epitaph described him as the "Father of Chemistry and the Uncle of the Earl of Cork."

He was born in January 25, 1627, at Lismore Castle in County Waterford, in the south of Ireland, the seventh son of the famous first earl of Cork, an important figure in the plantation of Munster. He was a serious child with a taste for study which impressed his father. He was sent to Eton College at the age of eight, and there (according to a fragment of autobiography that he left unpublished) a chance reading of Quintus Curtius "conjured up in me that unsatisfied appetite for knowledge that is yet as greedy as when it was first raised."

After four years study at Eton he returned home to be taught by tutors, and was then was sent around Europe with his French tutor, becoming fluent in French and Italian, then the languages of culture. In Florence in the winter of 1641 to 1642 he came into contact with the new ideas of Galileo. These travels were made difficult because the money sent by his father was stolen, and the party had to return to England slowly by a roundabout route. In 1644 he retired to Dorset, in the south of England, on an estate he had inherited from his father.

However, he found that rural life kept him far from the center of things in the capital.

Boyle was one of what was called "the invisible college" of scientists and philosophers, which was to become the Royal Society, and though he was still in his late teens he acquired an impulse toward investigation that lasted his lifetime. He visited Ireland in 1652 to deal with his estates, but found it "a barbarous country, where chemical spirits were so misunderstood, and chemical instruments unprocurable, that it was hard to have any Hermetic thoughts in it." Instead he turned to anatomy, Ireland having a ready supply of dead bodies in those days. On returning to England in 1654 he settled in Oxford, where he lived until moving finally to London in 1668.

He erected a laboratory where he and his assistants worked, and created a small scientific society around him. In 1659 he invented, with the help of Robert Hooke, the "machina Boyleana," the first air pump, which he used in experiments that led up to the propounding of Boyle's law.

His first experiments with the properties of air were published in 1660. In 1662 he published what came to be seen as his magnum opus, *The Skeptical Chymist . . . Touching the Experiments Whereby Vulgar Spagirists Are Wont to Endeavour to Evince Their Salt, Sulphur, and Mercury to Be the True Principles of Things.* In this work he overthrew the Aristotelian concept of the four elements of earth, fire, water, and air. In proposing the modern idea of an element as a substance which cannot be decomposed into simpler ones, he had grasped the idea on which all modern chemistry was later founded.

His interests covered many areas, including the possibility of transmuting base metals into gold. But he is remembered for proving that air is a material substance, having weight, its volume being inversely proportional to its pressure. This relationship is Boyle's Law, which he expressed and was later proved by Edme Mariotte. This is still among the first basic facts of science that all students learn at school.

He also made observations on the effect of a change in atmospheric pressure on the boiling point of water, collected many new facts in relation to magnetism and electricity, and explained the action of heat as a "brisk" agitation of particles.

But it was as a chemist that Boyle excelled. He was not a theorist, but an experimenter, and as such, the first modern chemist. He distinguished elements, mixtures, and compounds, prepared phosphorous (though he did not discover it), collected hydrogen in a vessel over water (though he called it "air generated *de novo*"), and inquired into the forms of crystals as a indicator of their chemical structures. He introduced the vegetable color tests of acidity and alkalinity, the construction of hermetically sealed thermometers, and the use of freezing mixtures.

He was also a devout Christian, and learned Hebrew, Syriac, and Greek, the better to understand the scriptures. He used a large part of his personal fortune in the propagation of the faith, and in his will left a sum of money to support the annual Boyle Lectures, eight sermons a year by a minister "for proving the Christian religion against Atheists, Theists, Pagans, Jews, and Mohammedans, not descending to any controversies among Christians themselves."

As a philosopher he thought that God had made the world in the beginning and that His "general concourse" was continually needed to maintain its being and motion. This was a return in part to earlier Hindu and Islamic ideas of continuous creation and re-creation, but was also the physical aspect of the Christian doctrine of immanence.

Boyle died in London on December 31, 1691. He was thought by all to be a man of fine character, and was very popular among his colleagues. His reputation was an international one, and he was always at the service of visitors to the Royal Society. But his fame will rest on his invention of "the experimental method" by which all scientific research now proceeds.

33

Hugh O'Neill

1540–1616

The departure in 1607 of Hugh O'Neill and other leaders from Ireland—what later came to be called the Flight of the Earls, was seen by many as the end of the old Gaelic order and any chance of its restoration. If a date is needed for the start of modern Irish history, with its saga of war, famine, and exile, this might be it.

O'Neill's career was a hectic one, in which all the vacillations of Ireland under the Tudors were displayed. With his departure and eventual death in Rome, an epoch had been reached. If he had succeeded in what he had hoped, he might have made himself a king of a united Ireland (fulfilling that old dream of BRIAN BORU [17]), and with Spanish aid to drive the English out of Ireland. But this was not to be.

Hugh O'Neill was the son of Matthew O'Neill, himself the illegitimate son of Conn, the first earl of Tyrone. In Irish eyes the earl was "the O'Neill," an old Gaelic title. The new English title had been bestowed on him by the queen on the surrender and regranting of his (or rather his people's) land. In 1559 he was taken by Sir Henry Sidney, the viceroy, to his castle at Ludlow, converted to Anglicanism, and taught English manners. In 1562 Hugh succeeded his murdered brother Brian as baron of Dungannon.

The English historian William Camden described O'Neill at this time as a man "whose industry was great, his mind large and fit for the weightiest businesses . . . he had much knowledge in military affairs and a profound, dissembling heart, so as many deemed him born either for the great good or ill of his country."

O'Neill returned to Ireland in 1568. Having been educated in both Ireland and England, he approximated more the English idea of a nobleman than an Irish chieftain. Unlike his relative Shane O'Neill, who was cast more in the old Gaelic mold, Hugh tried to avoid direct conflict with the powerful English. Indeed, he helped them in their campaign against the rebel Gerald Fitzgerald between 1574 and 1587. He was rewarded for his supposed loyalty by Queen Elizabeth, who made him earl of Tyrone in his own right in 1585.

But all was not well. In 1588 he aided the survivors of the Spanish Armada that were cast up in Donegal. In 1593 he revived for himself the ancient Irish title of "the O'Neill," the use of which had been banned under English law. He was thought to be in league with Hugh Roe O'Donnell and Hugh Maguire when they rebelled in 1594. Accused of treason, he finally joined their revolt in 1595.

He proved to be a great asset to the Irish forces through his skills as a diplomat and a soldier. He was cool, farsighted, and calculating. Allowed a certain number of men under arms, he changed them frequently, so that a large number of his clansmen were trained in modern arms. Claiming he needed the metal to roof his castles, he had bought large quantities of lead and saved it for bullets. His careful planning and cautious strategy provided the Irish with the natural leader they had long lacked. He also sought the help of both Scotland and Spain against the common English enemy.

The true campaign began in 1596, and O'Neill led the Irish to a great victory at the Yellow Ford (on August 15, 1598). But the English began to strike back. Anxious for Spanish aid, O'Neill made an interim peace with Essex. But Lord Mountjoy deployed his army, and O'Neill and his allies were cornered at Kinsale, where he was defeated after rashly choosing to attack.

The war went on until O'Neill was pardoned and his land holdings were confirmed by James I. But it was obvious which way the tide was turning. English interference continued. Soon O'Neill had had enough of it all. On September 13, 1607, O'Neill, together with Rory O'Donnell, left Ireland, sailing from Rathmullen on the shores of Lough Swilly with an entourage of more than ninety of the Ulster nobility. Landing in Le Havre, they made their way to Flanders, and from there to Rome. O'Neill was outlawed by the Irish parliament, and the last of his estates were now confiscated and planted.

The Flight of the Earls left the way open for a final solution, so to speak, of the Irish problem. The lands of O'Neill and O'Donnell to the west of Lough Neagh were confiscated and planted with Protestant settlers from England and Scotland. Derry became Londonderry, having been granted to companies in the City of London. This plantation might have worked if it had been wholesale, but the policy was not consistently applied, and so there remained enough of the old stock of the Irish to foment further troubles in later centuries. W. B. YEATS [8] spoke of the Flight of the Earls as one of "Four bells—four deep, tragic notes in Irish history." Though the Gaelic ways lingered on here and there, they had been badly damaged by Mountjoy's campaign. The Gaelic Chieftans never again came as close to achieving the success as they had under O'Neill at the battle of the Yellow Ford.

O'Neill heard little of this. The last years of his life were passed in melancholy and idleness in Rome as a pensioner of the pope and the king of Spain. He died there on July 20, 1616.

34

Jonathan Swift

1667–1745

Though the author of *Gulliver's Travels* is often spoken of as an English writer, he was a Dubliner by birth and death. Though he enjoys universal fame as a writer, Jonathan Swift also has a more local reputation as an Irish patriot of an unusual kind.

The posthumous child of an English father, he was born on November 30, 1667, in a little square in the shadow of the Dublin Castle. He was educated at Kilkenny College and at Trinity College in Dublin, where his training was strictly Anglican. Though he enjoyed literature at the university, he did not care for either philosophy or the formalities of rhetoric. But he was no student, and his degree was specially granted to him. In 1689, having sought his mother's advice, he was appointed secretary to Sir William Temple (whom some have suggested was his real father) at Moor Park near London. There he stayed between 1689 and 1694.

Having been ordained in the Church of Ireland in 1695, he was given a living in a small Ulster prebend at Kilroot, outside Belfast. He did not find this agreeable, as the parishes were rundown and the local people mostly dour Presbyterians. He went home to Moor Park, where, among other duties, he had to tutor Esther Johnson (or Stella, as he calls her in his writings), the daughter of a companion of Temple's sister. It has been supposed (again, by a few) that Stella was also Temple's child by another mother.

At this time he wrote his earliest poems anonymously, as well as *The Battle of the Books,* which deals with the superiority of the classics

104

over the modern writers, and *A Tale of a Tub,* a satirical account of the consequences of the Reformation and Christian divisions. In January 1699 Sir William Temple died, so Swift had to seek another place. In 1700 he was given another livelihood in Ireland, at Laracor in Meath. He took a doctoral degree at Trinity College in 1701. For a while he divided his time between Dublin, where he was a social success, and London, where he gained a reputation as a political writer. A natural conservative, he took the Tory side in politics, satirizing the dominant Whigs (who had been in power since the fall of James II). His life in the heat of English politics is described in his *Journal to Stella.* She and Swift had gone to live in Dublin after their patron died.

When the Tories came to power Swift had hoped for a bishopric, but the queen's advisers influenced her to refuse him. However, he was given the deanery of St. Patrick's in Dublin. The return of his political foes, the Whigs, ensured there would be no further advancement in the Anglican church for him. Initially he saw himself as exiled in Dublin from the real life in London, and with no hope of an English bishopric.

When he returned to Dublin, Swift was followed there by Hester Vanhomrigh—the Vanessa of his later writings—whose family had been prominent in the life of the city. She was infatuated with him, and he was unable to untangle himself from her. Swift's relationships with Stella and Vanessa remain shadowy and mysterious, though the notion that Swift and Stella were half siblings might go a long way in explaining odd aspects of his behavior. It may be that he was married to Stella secretly in 1716, and that he had sexual relations with Vanessa, but none of this is certain.

To many of his contemporaries he appeared as what one writer called a "scabrous, mad misanthrope, faithless priest, and heartless lover." The modern judgment would be different. Now we are more aware of the literary and rhetorical devices by which he masked his own personality with that of others, from Isaac Bickerstaff to Capt. Lemuel Gulliver.

It was in Ireland that Swift wrote *Gulliver's Travels,* published anonymously in 1726. Though this became, in part, a children's favorite, the book itself has a very adult theme, for it is filled with Swift's loathing of mankind.

In Dublin and his own journeys around the countryside, Swift became conscious of the condition of Ireland itself. The English politician grew into the Irish patriot. The Ireland he was defending was, of course, largely that of English settlement, but Ireland was changing at the time, and the defense of Ireland's interests was to the benefit of all.

His satirical writings, such as his essay "A Modest Proposal" (1729), in which an "economist" (of the kind we still have with us!) argues that the surplus babies of Ireland should be fattened for eating, concerned the abuses of English rule in Ireland. In the *Drapier Letters* (1724–25) he defended the economic interests of Ireland against the exploitation of English adventurers, in particular William Wood of Wolverhampton, who had been granted coinage rights.

Swift remained in touch with his friends in England, but his mind slowly gave way. He was not insane, but it is now thought he suffered from Ménières disease, which began to affect him about 1736. In 1742 he retreated into depression, was declared legally insane, and was confined to his home, where he died on October 19, 1745.

Swift left all he owned to found St. Patrick's Hospital for the mentally ill, an institution which survives to this day. At midnight he was buried in his cathedral, beside Stella. His epitaph, in his own words, is on a plaque above the spot, inscribed in Latin, which translates as:

> Here lies Johnathan Swift, Doctor of Divinity, Dean of this
>   Cathedral . . .
> Where savage indignation can lacerate his heart no more.
> Go traveler and imitate if you can
>   his brave struggle for human liberty.

That, at least, is the record of the patriotic dean who was admired by the Dubliners he lived among. Swift was among those who began the process of creating the identity of modern Ireland as a country with mixed cultures.

For the world at large, *Gulliver's Travels* remains one of the great books of all time. Swift's satiric anger has been a major influence on writers since. In clear and limpid language, he lashed out not only at the passing abuses of the day, but also those perennial failings of human nature which he scorned.

35

George Berkeley

1685–1753

Geor012e Berkeley was one of the most important and interesting philosophers that Ireland has produced, though his career ranged from England to America. He was born at Dysart Castle near Kilkenny on March 12, 1685, and educated at Trinity College. He became a fellow in 1701, and taught at the university as a fellow and tutor until 1713.

His main studies were of Descartes and Newton at a time when Locke's *Essay on Human Understanding* (published in 1690) was already influencing philosophical investigations. From 1705 to 1706, he kept his *Commonplace Book* (published in 1871) which reveals the general trend of his thinking. In this he first outlined his new principle of philosophy that matter, substance, and cause have no meaning apart from the conscious spirit of man.

His first books were *Arithmetica* and *Miscellanea Mathematica* (both in 1707), and in 1709 he took holy orders. He made a wide impression in 1709 with the publication of *An Essay Towards a New Theory of Vision*. The idealistic ideas in this were developed further in *A Treatise Concerning the Principles of Human Knowledge* (1710). In 1711 he published *A Discourse on Passive Obedience*.

JONATHAN SWIFT [34], then at the heights of his London years, introduced Berkeley to the court and into the intellectual circles of the city. *Dialogues Between Hylas and Philonus* (1713) was a popular outline of his ideas. He told Dr. Johnson, "I had no inclination to trouble the world with large volumes. What I have [written] was rather with a view to giving hints to thinking men who have leisure and curiosity to go to the bottom of things and pursue them in their own minds."

Though worked out before he was thirty, his chief ideas were expressed in these publications. As a philosopher, Berkeley attempted to solve problems Locke left unresolved. It was Locke's work that suggested to Berkeley the central principle that nothing existed apart from perception (*esse est percipi*, "to be is to be perceived"). He said that this principle was intuitively obvious and manifest common sense. Dr. Samuel Johnson, a bluff, down-to-earth personality, thought that kicking a stone—what in the world could be a more densely material object?—was proof enough that Berkeley's extreme idealism was absurd, and other contemporary people of common sense would have agreed with him.

Hume claimed that Berkeley was attempting to show the nonexistence of matter, and that everything in the universe was merely idea.

Berkeley argued that everything that is seen, felt, or heard, or in any way observed is a real being, that it actually exists, while a thing not perceived cannot be known, and without being known (that is, perceived by a mind) cannot exist. The only intelligible cause of all phenomena is mind. Pain and pleasure cannot exist apart from their being felt.

Between 1713 and 1721 Berkeley traveled in Europe as the chaplain to Lord Peterborough, and then as the tutor to Bishop Ashe's son, but his mind was as much on the countries he had left behind, as shown by the publication of a further essay on the state of the nation, which he blamed on the decline of religion and public spirit. The collapse of the South Sea Bubble, a huge investment scheme that swept the country like a mania and proved a disaster for investors of all kinds, had just taken place (with an effect rather like the stock market crash in New York in 1929).

Berkeley was appointed dean of Dromore in 1722, and dean of Derry in 1724. He then became involved in a scheme to create a college in Bermuda. This was intended to be an intellectual base from which the American continents could be Christianized and brought within the pale of civilization. Through Robert Walpole, the prime minister, he received a promise of a government grant of £20,000 for this, and in 1728 left for the Americas.

However, he never reached Bermuda, but spent three years (1728–1731) in the colony of Rhode Island. There he made a contribution to the growth of American academic life and philosophy. One of his innovations was the introduction of the seminar as a teaching device. At last he realized that his grant (as is so often the way with government promises) would not be forthcoming.

His *Alciphron, or the Minute Philosopher,* a defense of religion against deists and others, was written in Rhode Island and published in

London in 1733. A supplement, *Visual Language,* showing the immediate present providence of a deity, appeared the next year.

Berkeley returned to Ireland, where he was appointed bishop of Cloyne, in Cork, in 1734, through the favoritism of Queen Caroline. This found him on the verge of a controversy concerning mysteries, that is the spiritual, transcendent elements in religion, which rationalists denied. This arose from a passage in *Alciphron.* Some free-thinking mathematicians (influenced perhaps by JOHN TOLAND [38] and the ancestors of many of today's scientists) held that mysteries were fatal to the moral authority of religion. *The Analyst* (1734) was Berkeley's answer, and *The Querist,* which dealt with matters of social economic policy, followed from 1735 to 1737.

He turned his mind to other inventions, math, the social problems of Ireland, and questions of religious toleration. In 1739 the diocese of Cloyne was greatly affected by famine and the associated cholera fever. From his experiences in America, Berkeley had been much taken with the medicinal properties of tar water. (Tar water was a preparation of pine resin, which was steeped in water for several weeks, strained, and then taken with milk three times a day as a remedy for all kinds of illnesses.) His experiences set off a train of thought. In his mind the properties of tar water became associated with the studies of Plato, the neoplatonists, and other mystics which he had been following for years. Tar water, as a universal healer, a panacea in the literal sense, suggested to him the final interpretation of the universe.

Siris, published in 1744, was ostensibly about the benefits of tar water, but its pages contain some of Berkeley's most profound metaphysical speculations. Though it was to be George Berkeley's last word on philosophy, it was also a most curious book on metaphysics. But his high flights of speculation were obscured by the controversy that followed on just whether or not tar water was a panacea.

He resigned in 1752 due to ill health, and left Ireland to live in the calmer academic atmosphere of Oxford, where he died in January 1753. He is buried in Christ Church, Oxford.

Berkeley's idealism was very influential on both Hume and Kant, but it was not perhaps until the middle of the nineteenth century that his ideas began to receive more sympathetic treatment. Since then they have had a critical influence on the development of philosophy in both Europe and America. Among his other Irish admirers was W. B. YEATS [8], who saw Berkeley as an exemplar of that Anglo-Irish tradition which he elevated to one of the great cultures of the world.

36

U2

Late Twentieth Century

Though Ireland had long been famous for its poetry and music, these had nearly always taken traditional forms. With the advent of the rock group U2—a sly allusion to the famous American high-flying spy plane—the country of W. B. YEATS [8] and JAMES JOYCE [25] produced a new phenomenon, a world-famous rock band. Completely breaking with what had been thought of as traditional Irish music, they achieved worldwide fame, and their style of music and approach to life has proved immensely influential. Their tours, especially of North America, have brought a new meaning to the words *Irish culture*.

The band consists of four Dublin musicians: Bono, or Paul Hewson, born May 10, 1960; the Edge, or David Evans, born August 8, 1961, at Barking in Essex; Adam Clayton, born March 13, 1960 at Chinnor in Oxfordshire, England; and Larry Mullen, born in Dublin, October 1, 1960. They were the band's vocals, guitar, bass, and drums, respectively.

They met at school on the north side of Dublin, in one of the rapidly expanding suburbs that represented the new Ireland of today, often rough, raw, and Americanized. In 1976 Larry Mullen pinned a note to the notice board of Mount Temple School, a formerly Protestant school that had been turned into a coeducational comprehensive. He was looking for others to form a rock band, and out of the responses chose three. Initially they played versions of the Rolling Stones and Beach Boys as a group called Feedback; then they called themselves Hype. Their final name, U2, came in 1978.

Hewson was supposed to play guitar. "I was such a lousy guitar player," he told a local magazine in 1982, "that one day they broke it to me that maybe I should sing instead. I had tried before but found I had no voice at all. I remember the day I found I could sing. I said: 'Oh, that's how you do it.'"

For the boys, rock would be "about sweat, about the real world." In 1978 they won a competition in Limerick and were taken up by manager Paul McGuinness. A signing with CBS records followed. A song from their first album, *Out of Control*, in 1979 rose rapidly to number one on the Irish charts. This was followed the next year by another number one, *Another Day*. Oddly, CBS did not want to take them on in the United Kingdom, so they signed with the more innovative Island Records. However, the first singles for their new company made little impact. Early in 1980 readers of the Irish music magazine *Hot Press* voted U2 the number one band in five categories. They had arrived.

The first Island album, *Boy*, released in October 1980, was produced by Steve Lillywhite. It drew on all of the feeling of adolescence in a new style which listeners found both moving and inspired. But U2 was not studio-bound. They went on tour to support the album, and the effects of Bono's singing, and the tight playing of the others showed them to be an important new arrival.

In November 1980 the band toured the east coast of America—always important these days in building a universal reputation. Their second album, *October*, released in October 1981, had an impassioned religious feeling powerfully evangelical in its effect. A song inspired by the Polish Solidarity movement, which had begun to crack open the Communist colossus, was called "New Year's Day." The critical welcome of U2 continued with *War* (February 1983), on which the song "Sunday Bloody Sunday" reflected the same theme of religion and politics. *Under a Blood Red Sky* reached number two on the U.K. album chart.

The band was now on its way to joining the all-time great of rock music. Playing with Bob Dylan at Slane Castle, an Irish venue, united the old guard with the Young Turks of rock. As Ireland at this time seemed to be bubbling with talent, the band set up its own company to bring some of it on.

The growth of their own talent was seen on *Unforgettable Fire* (1984) which won a place on the U.S. charts. The ideals of the band were supported by their appearance at Live Aid and at Self-Aid, a similar charity event in Ireland. They were also involved with Amnesty

International. In these concerns they carried many of their young followers with them, as posters of U2 and Amnesty International crowded bedroom walls and school dormitories. A world tour brought them further audiences outside of their core areas. *The Joshua Tree,* released in March 1987, elevated U2 to one of the most important bands in the world. The album rose to the top of the charts in the United Kingdom and the United States. Two more albums brought the decade to a close.

Inevitably in a competitive world, other bands now began to make their appearance. Though U2 continued to grow and mature, its music had to be seen in this wider musical context. The band commanded immense attention from Irish commentators and writers. Whatever the further development of its music may be, it had an authentic voice that had come out of the contemporary culture of Ireland. Its concerns of spiritual quest, social commitment, and awareness of the real dangers lurking in the modern world were those of its admirers. Where in the past an important Irish poet, at the age of forty-five, might have accumulated a few thousand constant readers, the lyrics of a rock band such as U2 reach countless millions. They moved those millions with the same power which Irish poetry has always had, but in a new context which transcended the narrow borders of national identity into the realm of universal humanity.

There is little doubt of the stature which the band achieved on the Irish scene. This had great benefit not only for raising the mood of the young population as a whole, but in demonstrating to other ambitious bands that no heights were barred to Irish people of talent. They could challenge the world and triumph. But to triumph with material as deeply felt, and as resonant of centuries of spirituality, was another great achievement. Though now an international supergroup deeply committed to selected causes, for U2 rock is still "about sweat, about the real world."

ST. PATRICK
(Hays Collection)

EAMON DE VALERA
(Hays Collection)

MICHAEL COLLINS
(Hays Collection)

JOHN FITZGERALD KENNEDY
(CORBIS/BETTMANN-UPI)

CHARLES STEWART PARNELL
(New York Public Library)

MARY ROBINSON
(Associated Press/Donald Stampfli)

PATRICK HENRY PEARSE
(Hays Collection)

WILLIAM BUTLER YEATS
(Hays Collection)

PATRICK FORD
(Brown Brothers)

WOLFE TONE
(Hays Collection)

BRIAN BORU
(Hays Collection)

DANIEL O'CONNELL
(New York Public Library)

ARCHBISHOP THOMAS CROKE
(Hays Collection)

CYRUS HALL MCCORMICK
(Hays Collection)

John L. Sullivan
(Culver Pictures)

JONATHAN SWIFT
(Hays Collection)

GEORGE BERKELEY
(New York Public Library)

EUGENE O'NEILL
(Hays Collection)

ST. COLUMBAN
(Hays Collection)

GEORGE BERNARD SHAW
(Hays Collection)

MAUD GONNE MACBRIDE
(Hays Collection)

CONSTANCE GORE-BOOTH,
the Countess Markievicz *(Hays Collection)*

37

James Larkin

1876–1947

Along with JAMES CONNOLLY [16], James Larkin was one of the leading figures in the development of both the trade union movement and democratic socialism in Ireland. But where Connolly was more of a thinker, Larkin was a man of action, a street rebel.

One of his biographers, the historian Emmet Larkin, wrote: "His accomplishment was unique and representative—unique partly because it was representative. His rich and complex personality allowed him to harmonize the three most dissonant themes of his day. For he claimed to be at one and the same time a Socialist, a Nationalist, and a Roman Catholic." His career was representative because it "mirrored to a larger extent than did that of his equally colorful comrades [Eugene Debs, Tom Mann, and James Connolly] those attributes that were the hallmark of this generation of working-class labor leaders."

He was born in the slums of Liverpool, the great English seaport, in 1876 to poor Irish parents. As a child he witnessed not only the grim poverty of the families around him, but also had to watch the death of his father from tuberculosis. He had hardly any schooling, but was sent home to spend at least a part of his childhood with his grandparents in Ulster. He returned to Liverpool at the age of nine, and began his own working life at the age of eleven.

He spent some time at sea—he stowed away in search of adventure and then became a laborer on the Liverpool docks. When not yet seventeen he joined the Liverpool branch of the Independent Labour Party. He rose from docker to foreman, becoming the youngest worker at the docks. He lost his job for attempting to organize his men and joined the National Union of Dockers in 1901. In 1905, after a bitter strike at his firm, he was appointed an organizer for the union.

In Belfast in 1907, Larkin began the blacking of goods—that is, the refusal to handle any goods which had not been made or transported by unionized labor. However, he fell out with the union and went to Dublin, where in 1909 he set up his own union, the Irish Transport and General Workers Union (TGWU). Perhaps no other city had such scenes of poverty as Dublin had then. He strove to improve not only working conditions, but workers' lives by widening their cultural horizons. His union grew rapidly, and the inevitable clash with employers came to a head in 1913. Though the workers were forced back, their rights had been established. Larkin had drawn a line in the sand.

The epic days of the long summer of 1913 have entered into the folklore of Dublin—the hardship caused by the employers' lockout, the riots and deaths on O'Connell Street, the clash with the clerical authorities over the sending of workers' children to England to be fed. For six months twenty thousand men and women, on whom another eighty thousand depended for their bread and shelter, were locked out because they would not sign the pledge of the Employers Organization not to join the TGWU. For trade unionists throughout Britain it became the battlefront of the day. Larkin won support in England and America, and even Lenin, then lurking in Zurich, had to admire Larkin's revolutionary zeal.

Larkin then went to America, where he lectured and wrote about the causes close to him. But socialism was already in decline. As in Europe, its failure to resist the First World War had shaken its whole edifice. And there were other problems for Larkin. He was out of the country during the crucial years of the troubles, when Ireland took new directions he could play no part in. In 1920 he was sentenced to ten years and jailed in Sing Sing for attempting to overthrow the U.S. government at a time when the United States was passing through its first "Red scare." He explained his point of view as best he could: "[A]t an early age, I took my mind to this question of the age—why are the many poor? It was true to me. I don't know whether the light of God or the light of humanity or the light of my own intelligence brought it to me, but it came to me like a flash. The thing is wrong because the basis of society is wrong."

He became the focus of an international campaign to free him from prison. In 1923 he was pardoned and released and returned to Ireland, but once again he fell out with his union, and left it to set up the Workers Union of Ireland. Elected to the Dail (the Irish national assembly) and the Dublin city council, he continued his struggle for workers' rights.

For Larkin and the labor movement these were often difficult years. He played an important part in the making of the new Ireland, where the needs of the economy were tempered with the equally important needs of the workers. When he died on January 30, 1947, his funeral was a huge one even by the standards of political Dublin.

"It is hard to believe this great man is dead," the playwright SEAN O'CASEY [55], himself the product of the Dublin slums, wrote on the day of Larkin's death, "for all thoughts and all activities surged in the soul of this labor leader, for he combined within himself the imagination of the artist, with the fire and determination of a leader of a downtrodden class."

Yet for all his admirers said, there was an element of the maverick in Larkin. His critics could admit that he was a powerful and charismatic figure, but he was also demagogic, abrasive, and all too often divisive. His support of the International and the Communist movement made him anathema to many, but to others closer to the streets of Dublin he was a giant among men, a prophet of a better life for all. He remains a complex but powerfully influential figure, a legend among Irish leaders.

38

John Toland

1670–1722

The Irish hold themselves to be a deeply religious people, but that religion can often take curious forms. None was more so than the career of the theologian John Toland, the man who gave the concept of "free thinker" to the world.

Born into a Catholic family at Inishowen near Derry on November 30, 1670, Janus Junius Toland, as he was christened, became a zealous Protestant in 1686 at the age of sixteen. He was educated at Glasgow University, where he received his master's degree in 1690. In 1692 Daniel Williams's Presbyterian congregation sent Toland to Leyden (where he studied with the famous scholar of the day, Friedrich Spanheim). He had plans to become a Non-conformist minister, but he lost his faith, and became simply a nonconformist.

By 1694 Toland was at Oxford. In 1696 he anonymously published *Christianity Not Mysterious, or, A Treatise Shewing That There Is Nothing in the Gospels Contrary to Reason, Nor Above It; and That No Christian Doctrine Can Be Properly Called a Mystery*, a book which aroused immense controversy. Toland wished to show that true religion (deism, in fact), and natural morality were practically synonymous. Any notions which transcended reason, such as the Trinity, the Incarnation, and Grace, ought to be discarded as mere superstitions. What he sought was a religion (or more properly an ethical position) "as old as creation" and not dependent on church views. Though these were scandalous notions in the seventeenth century, such ideas can be found today among advanced theologians of many Christian outlooks.

He acknowledged the book as his in its second edition the same year, and was prosecuted for irreligion by the grand jury of Middlesex, which covered part of London. He escaped to Dublin in 1697, but found further troubles in his native land. He was attacked by churchmen and others, and in September the Irish parliament ordered his book burned by the common hangman for being godless and subversive of morals. An order for his arrest was made. In a country rife with persecution, Toland was soon driven back to England.

The term *free thinker* was used for the first time in history by William Molyneaux of Dublin in a letter to John Locke in 1697, in which he calls Toland "a candid free thinker." (Molyneaux's own book, *The Case of Ireland Stated,* advocating Irish independence, was also burned by the hangman in Dublin.) Fifteen years later JONATHAN SWIFT [34] referred to "atheists, libertines, despisers of religion, that is to say, all those who usually pass under the name Free Thinker." It is an achievement of the first order to bring a new concept and term like this into use.

Toland later wrote *A Life of Milton,* which proved almost as controversial. In the manner of so many outspoken young men since, intent on shocking their elders, he referred to "the numerous supposititious pieces under the name of Christ and His apostles and other great persons." He was accused of doubting the authentic nature of the New Testament, and replied to these charges in a book entitled *Amyntor, or a Defence of Milton's Life,* which attempted to open up the whole question of the canon of scripture and how it had come down to us. This is a still vexing question in this day, but in Toland's time a critic of biblical texts put his life in danger.

Toland was in Hanover in 1701 as part of a government embassy, and was received by the Electress Sophia on account of his recent book *Vindicius Liberius* (1702), a defense of the Hanoverian succession which, of course, affected the throne of England. In this book he admitted that *Christianity Not Mysterious* had been "a youthful indiscretion." In 1703 he was again in Hanover and in Berlin, where he was received at court once more.

His travels to Hanover and Prussia brought him into contact with German philosophers and contributed in a small way to the emergence of the German enlightenment. In a book which resulted from these visits, *Letters to Serena,* he attacked Spinoza and anticipated some of the ideas of modern materialism. In 1707 he also published his *An Account of the Courts of Prussia and Hanover,* which remains an important source for the career of Frederick I, King of Prussia.

The rest of his life was lived in some obscurity. He seems to have been a spy for the British government from time to time. He continued to publish on politics and religion, and in 1709 was in the Hague, where he published *Adeisidaemon* and *Origines Judaicae.* Another theological work appeared in 1718 called *Nazarenus, or Jewish, Gentile, and Mahometan Christianity.* In this he claimed that the early Christians of the first century had been *Jewish* Christians following the old Mosaic law. They were the later Nazarenes (or Ebionites) and Elkesaites, condemned by the church as heretics. To Toland's mind it was nicely ironic that the organized church should persecute true Christians, so to speak.

His *Pantheisticon* (1720) introduced the term *pantheism,* that is, an identification of the deity with the universe, of God with Nature, and it outlined a society of pantheists. This caused as much offense to the pious as his first book. To his critics, it seemed that he had reduced God to the material universe and to have made Him little more than a mechanical law of nature.

Toland lived these years in great poverty, sinking to the position of a semipolitical hack writer, dependent on the patronage of Harley, Shaftesbury, and others. He died, pen in hand, in Putney outside London on March 11, 1722.

In 1726 a collection of his writings was published, which included his *History of the Druids,* a key work in the development of ideas about the ancient past of Ireland. He asserted that the Druids (about whom little is known) were, like him, pantheistic philosophers. This view is maintained to this day by the Druid orders. One of these, the British Circle of the Universal Bond, claims to descend (through the poet William Blake) from a group organized by Toland in 1717 at a meeting on Primrose Hill north of London. This curious claim may have arisen from a group related to the Socratic Society, which Toland wrote about and which he seems to have been organizing at the time of his death.

Toland was one of the most influential Irish philosophers; deism as a notion begins with him in 1696, largely a consequence of the application of the Cartesian method to religion. The eighteenth-century encyclopediaists in France, the German enlightenment, and the religious debate in England continued his ideas and developed them as an increasingly rationalist approach to religion.

Deism was never a mass movement, though its influence can be seen in the Unitarian church. Toland's ideas were effective elsewhere, for deism easily moves away from any kind of theism and into atheism. He certainly contributed to the beginning of the decline of religion as a social force.

His ideas about pantheism can be traced through some of the poets and writers of the romantic movement, and even among some, like Wordsworth, who were Christians. Again, like deism and free thought, John Toland had brought a new idea before the world. He can therefore be seen as an important source of many New Age notions which remain vital to this day.

39

Tony O'Reilly

1936–

Today, Tony O'Reilly is widely seen as one of the most remarkable Irishmen of his generation. His extraordinary career, not just as chief executive officer of H. J. Heinz in Pittsburgh, but as the owner of a host of companies around the world, makes him one of the most notable Irishmen of all time.

Born in Dublin during the difficult years of the Depression, he had to work hard for success from early on. He makes no secret of his illegitimate birth, but it seems to have given him a drive that many of his Irish contemporaries lacked. He never rested. He was educated by the Jesuits at Belvedere, JAMES JOYCE'S [25] old school. There he was a success, in the classroom and on the sports field. At college he played rugby for Ireland on the international level.

His first job was with the Irish Sugar Company, a state-owned and -directed firm which was organized along old-fashioned, semisocialist lines. The Irish economy was not very developed then, and the Irish Sugar Company was one of the country's larger employers. In an economy where agriculture was a core business, the Irish Sugar Company was important.

O'Reilly took over from a former military man who had run the business with an eye on the best interests of the small farmers who supplied the sugar beet to the factories. He promoted new management techniques and introduced new products. In these early days his greatest coup was the rebranding of Irish butter as Kerrygold for the British and European markets, and it remains one of the most successful operations of its kind.

Some of these ventures were done in association with Heinz, and in 1969, when O'Reilly was only thirty-three, he was head hunted for their London operations. Four years later he was made president of the company, and in 1979 he was named CEO of Heinz.

O'Reilly had undoubted business flair, but this was based not only on his great intelligence but also his immense charm. "He has a million stories and tells them well," according to Richard M. Cyert, a fellow director at Heinz. "When you sit down to lunch with him, it's like going to a movie theater for entertainment." O'Reilly's native Irish wit was only part of his character. He could also make hard decisions.

He proved to be a charismatic leader of the company, among the most important in the United States even then, and he quickly revived its fortunes through the 1980s. Investors on Wall Street were impressed. He cut expenses, improved Heinz's market share, and expanded sales worldwide. Profits rose rapidly. The total shareholder returns averaged 31 percent a year in the 1980s, which was twice the average stock index of 16.8 percent. He had his reward, for during the first six years of the 1990s he earned $182.9 million, placing him near the top of the world's highest paid executives. But this was by no means all there was to Tony O'Reilly.

Though he spent much of his time in the United States, he remained an Irishman. Through an Irish investment company called Fitzwilton he bought into such international household names as Wedgwood China. He bought up the *Irish Independent* newspapers, Ireland's largest newspaper chain with several national and provincial titles. Newspaper interests were also developed in Australia and South Africa. He owns the *Sowetan,* one of the most influential papers among black readers in the politically sensitive townships around Johannesburg. This makes him an important player in the public life of South Africa, struggling to overcome the disadvantages of decades of apartheid.

In Ireland he is also the major shareholder of Dromoland Castle, a country mansion hotel of world class, and through Arcon, an Irish oil-exploration company, he shares in the new fields being sought around the coasts of the British Isles.

By the middle of the 1990s his investments were valued at over $787 million, moving him up among the richest men in the world. In any year he may travel up to three hundred thousand miles around the world on business matters. Though always keen to improve and expand his interests, especially in the rapidly developing area of telecommunications, O'Reilly never lost sight of Ireland or her historical problems.

In the United States he became one of the driving forces behind the establishment of the Ireland Funds, now an international trust with associations among Irish people not only in the United States, but also in Canada, Australia, and elsewhere. The aim of the fund is to support the social and cultural infrastructure in Ireland, north and south, and in this way to promote peace and reconciliation, social development, and economic welfare. Since its inception, the Ireland Funds have had a major impact, providing seed money and support for countless projects, large and small. In many ways they transformed aspects of Ireland. In North America, businessmen of Irish descent saw a way of sharing their good fortune with a country which their ancestors had had to leave generations before, often in great poverty. In Ireland this aid was much appreciated.

Tony O'Reilly has emerged as a new kind of Irishman, deeply imbued with pride in his country and its achievements, keen that these should be improved upon and appreciated, but also a man whose influence reaches far beyond Ireland or the United States. At home in Ireland or in Pittsburgh, he and his family lead a hectic social life, which is all part of the life of modern businessmen of his stature. Yet in a small country like Ireland, where social life was once lived on a less lavish scale, he has brought about a change of style which is widely influential.

In financial circles in the United States and in Europe, he is a man widely respected for his achievements. Upon his retirement from Heinz he was able to devote more of his time and energy to his own business interests. These included not only those already in hand (like Waterford Crystal), but also new acquisitions, such as the London *Independent* in 1998.

O'Reilly is also the sort of man from whom great surprises can be expected in the future. He was even talked about as a possible president of Ireland. Though this is a nonpolitical office of honor, it would have been a final crown to his career, and some think a just tribute to his achievements. It is clear now that there are more of those to come, as his still expanding business interests suggest.

40

Terence Vincent
Powderly

1849–1924

In the 1880s Terence Vincent Powderly was a key figure in the Knights of Labor, one of the first trade union organizations. He helped it develop from an oath-bound semisecret society into an open labor organization, the forerunner of the American Federation of Labor, the sort of union which many Americans are proud to be members of today.

Born in Carbondale, Pennsylvania, on January 22, 1849, Terence Vincent Powderly was one of twelve children of Terence Powderly and his wife, Margery Walsh, both poor Irish immigrants. They had come from Meath in 1827, and after a few years farming in New York State had settled at Carbondale, where the father was a teamster at the coal mine.

Young Terence attended the local school from the age of seven. He was then sent to work on the railways at the age of thirteen, quite the usual thing in the 1850s. After four years as a switch tender and car repairer, he was accepted as a machinist's apprentice in Scranton, Pennsylvania, and he worked there for some eight years.

In November 1871 he joined the Machinists and Blacksmiths Union. After the Civil War, American industry was moving away from the older life, represented by the blacksmiths and the local machine shop, and toward the manufacturing activity represented by the machinists. America was on its way to eclipsing Germany and Britain as the world's leading industrialized nation, and Powderly soon rose to prominence in the union.

In 1874 Powderly served as an organizer for the short-lived Industrial Brotherhood. But that same year he joined the Knights of Labor in Philadelphia. In 1876 he returned to Scranton, where he was an active organizer of Local Assembly No. 222. Later he became the corresponding secretary for District Assembly No. 5.

In 1878, on a Greenback-Labor ticket, he was elected mayor of Scranton, an office he held until 1884. He had begun to study for a law degree, but gave this up for union work when he was elected grand worthy foreman in 1879, and a little later that year, grand master workman of the Knights of Labor.

The Catholic church, of which Powderly was a devoted member, was equally dismayed by the secretive nature of the older trade brotherhood, yet the newer trade unions were heavily influenced toward socialism by European immigrants. Powderly worked to remove the almost Masonic and secret rituals and oaths, which the church disapproved of. He provided JAMES CARDINAL GIBBONS [42] with the information and documents to present to the papal authorities in Rome in defense of the Knights of Labor. It was not an easy task. As he observed, "Between the men who love God and the men who don't believe in God I have a hard time of it."

The expansion of the Knights of Labor under Powderly's leadership was due in large part to the expansion of industry rather than to any special talent on his part. At heart he was an idealist rather than an aggressive union leader, such as was coming into vogue. He preferred to emphasize the fraternal aspect of labor movements rather than deal with local and national issues of working conditions and wages. He was an enthusiast for a system of producer cooperatives such as George Russell and HORACE PLUNKETT [54] espoused in Ireland. His real energies went into campaigns for temperance, in which the church always was involved, and land reform. He supported Henry George, who advocated land nationalization, and greatly influenced MICHAEL DAVITT [24], for mayor of New York.

Powderly returned to the law in 1893, when his leadership of the Knights of Labor ended. He described his labor years in his most important work, *Thirty Years of Labor*, published in 1889. He was admitted to the bar in 1894, and in 1897 was raised to public office when he was appointed U.S. commissioner general of immigration.

Here he was called upon to deal with the rising number of immigrants, now largely from eastern Europe rather than Ireland, which were transforming the United States from the Anglicized nation it had been into the "melting pot" it was to become in the twentieth century. A few years earlier the Immigration Restriction League had been organized, and for the next quarter of a century it would spearhead the drive among nativist Americans to restrict immigration, especially from southern and eastern Europe. But Powderly was as conscious as President JOHN F. KENNEDY [4] that the United States was nothing if not "a nation of immigrants." He was not reappointed by Theodore Roosevelt in 1902.

In 1906 Powderly was made special representative of the Department of Commerce and Labor to study immigration. (By this time concern was focused on Japanese immigration to the West Coast.) Later he was made chief of the Division of Information of the Bureau of Immigration. Here it could be said that he exerted an influence over the racial changes which would transform the United States. His political activity was chiefly on behalf of Republican candidates, but he retained his links with labor publications for which he wrote, and he often addressed labor conventions.

In his later life, Powderly fell away from the church, but during his time as a labor leader his work had transformed the workers' movement in the United States. By reconciling the Catholic church to the American-style organization he enabled the United States to avoid at least some of the unhappy experiences of the church and workers in Europe. That in itself was a great achievement.

He died in Washington, D.C., on June 24, 1924—the year that the National Origins Act was adopted, setting a ceiling on the number of immigrants and establishing discriminatory national-racial quotas. Though the Irish benefited under this, it was not what had made the nation great.

41

John Louis O'Sullivan

1813–1895

If there is one phrase that sums up the ambitions of many Americans in the nineteenth century for the future of their young republic, it is "manifest destiny." That highly influential idea was the original concept of John Louis O'Sullivan. He came from a long line of Irishmen involved in the struggle for Irish freedom, a lost cause in the eyes of many sensible men. O'Sullivan saw that the future lay in America, but he espoused it with all the enthusiasm of his ancestors for their native land.

His great-grandfather, John O'Sullivan, who had been born in Kerry, was an adjutant general in the army of Prince Charles that invaded England in 1745, and was lucky to escape from the field of Culloden when the Jacobite cause was finally defeated. His grandfather, T. H. O'Sullivan, had been a member of the Irish Brigade in the service of France, but during the American Revolution he had fought with the British in New York. His father had settled in America as merchant and sea captain, and served in Francisco de Miranda's expedition of 1806 to liberate Venezuela.

According to family tradition (not always a reliable source), John Louis was born on a British warship in the harbor of Gibraltar in November 1813. He was educated at a military school in France, then at Westminster School in London, and finally entered Columbia University. He received law degrees in 1831 and 1834 and practiced law in New York City until 1837.

In that year he began publishing the *United States Magazine and Democratic Review* in Washington, D.C., with S. D. Langtree. Later they moved the journal to New York City. O'Sullivan's aim, so he claimed, was "to strike the hitherto silent string of the democratic genius of the age and the country." America was in an expansionist and nationalist mood, and the westward course of empire excited him and his friends. They saw it as enclosing not only the whole North American continent (including Canada), but also Cuba. It was in an article he wrote in the summer of 1845 for the July-August issue of the magazine that O'Sullivan coined the phrase "manifest destiny." No words could better have exemplified the nationalist spirit of the day. Dealing with the annexation of Texas that year, which had basically been seized from Mexico by America, he wrote of "our manifest destiny to overspread the continent allotted by Providence for the free development of our yearly multiplying millions."

Soon the term gained wider currency in the dispute with Britain over the Oregon Territory and the border with Canada. It was also made use of by those interested in seizing Cuba from Spain. To many Europeans, the "freedom-loving" Americans were merely on a course of colonial occupation, leading to the creation of an American empire.

There was another side to the journal, for it had contributions from Nathaniel Hawthorne, Henry David Thoreau, Edgar Allan Poe, William Cullen Bryant, and many others. This was a splendid gallery of talent. Among his other interests was the *New York Morning News,* which he edited from 1844 to 1846. He was also a member of the New York state legislature, in which he advocated the abolition of capital punishment, a novel and progressive idea for that day and age.

He married a daughter of Dr. Kearny Rodgers in 1846, and from 1849 to 1851 supported Narciso Lopez on his expeditions against Cuba, then a Spanish colony. Twice he was charged with violation of the neutrality laws. Though he was not convicted, he later claimed that through these schemes he had "been ruined for Cuba."

However, in February 1854 he was made chargé d'affaires in Portugal and later resident minister. He stayed there until 1858, expounding the doctrines of American expansion and manifest destiny. In 1858 he resigned and lived first in Lisbon, then in London, and finally in Paris, until 1871.

O'Sullivan's last years were spent in obscurity in New York. Julian Hawthorne, the son of his old friend the novelist, knew him during these years. He described O'Sullivan as "handsome, charming, affectionate, and unlucky, but an optimist to the last." He died in New York City on February 24, 1895. By that time, the idea of manifest destiny had returned again to inspire the American imagination. The United States had already taken California and the southwestern states from Mexico, and a large part of Oregon from Britain. Alaska had been bought from the Russians. Part of Samoa was placed under American control in 1889. In 1898 the United States annexed Hawaii (American settlers having overthrown the native government of Queen Liliuokalani in 1893 with the assistance of three hundred U.S. marines). At the end of the Spanish-American war in 1898 the United States seized Puerto Rico, Guam, and the Philippines from Spain. Cuba was liberated under American domination, while Spain assumed its national debt.

Many Americans were appalled. The steel tycoon Andrew Carnegie even offered to buy the Philippines for $20 million and give the people their freedom. But other Americans invoked John Louis O'Sullivan's heady concept of manifest destiny. This was the beginning of imperial America as a world power, which would eventually see the decline of the other imperial powers, including the British, from whose grasp the O'Sullivans had fled.

Later still, America would hold further territories in the Pacific and seek to maintain its influence in China before the Communist revolution, and later in Laos and Vietnam. What began with ambition in 1845 ended in tragedy in 1975 with the fall of Saigon. John Louis O'Sullivan's manifest destiny was a concept that changed the course of world history.

42

James Cardinal Gibbons

1834–1921

James Gibbons served fifty-two years as a bishop and thirty-five years as a cardinal of the Catholic church during a period which saw the emergence of modern America. He became symbolic of the place won by both the Irish and the Catholic church in the new, vigorous life of what had become almost inevitably the world's most powerful nation.

John Gibbons was born in Baltimore, Maryland, but at the age of three was taken back to his father's native Ireland. A decade later Thomas Gibbons died, and in 1853 his widow returned to the United States and settled in New Orleans with her children. James began his working life in a grocery store, but feeling a call to the priesthood, he entered a college in Maryland and went on to the local seminary. He was ordained in June 1861.

At first he worked as a local pastor and as a chaplain to the Civil War soldiers stationed nearby. Then, in 1865, he was appointed secretary to the archbishop of Baltimore and began his own rise to ecclesiastical eminence. In the changes after a Plenary Council in 1866, he was made a bishop (with a title *in partibus infidelium,* that is, a title to an ancient bishopric in one of those lands lost to the church by the advance of Islam, such as in North Africa) in 1868, and was placed over the new Vicarate Apostolic of North Carolina.

At that time the Catholics in North Carolina were few and scattered. Gibbons attended the Vatican Council (October 1869–July 1870) but returned to find his district suffering in the aftermath of the Civil War under the excesses of carpetbagging rule. He was appointed to Richmond in 1872 and carried almost alone the heavy burden of a difficult period in the history of the South.

From his varied experiences, in 1876 he wrote *The Faith of Our Fathers,* a simple exposition of the Catholic faith which would be of use not only to members of the church but to potential converts. This became the most successful work of its kind ever published in North America.

In May 1877 Gibbons was named coadjutor bishop of Baltimore and succeeded to the see in October. He was now in charge of the leading Catholic see in the United States. This made him at once one of the leading figures in the American Catholic church, and the world. As the archbishop of New York was a reticent personality, Gibbons stood out as *the* leader of Catholics.

Gibbons was not an initiator in a cutting-edge fashion, but once a scheme was under way he gave it all his energy. This was the case with the Third Plenary Council, and the creation of the Catholic University of America. He became chancellor of the university and was instrumental in saving it from ruin in 1904 when it fell into grim financial difficulties. These successes led to Gibbons being raised to the status of cardinal in 1886.

The last decades of the nineteenth century were ones of great change and great difficulty for America and for the church. There was a huge increase in emigrants from Europe, many of whom were Catholics from Germany, Poland, and Italy. These new Americans transformed the nature of not only American society, but the largely Irish nature of the Catholic church. Gibbons played a major role in contriving solutions to the problems of the day.

America was an industrial democracy and had needs different from the old nations of Europe, with which the officials in Rome were most familiar. Gibbons counseled against too hasty a condemnation of "secret societies" and supported the Knights of Labor, preventing that movement from being condemned. He also prevented the writings of Henry George from being placed on the Index (the Church's list of banned books), though these had been the cause of much dissension in New York, where a priest named Edward McGlynn supported George for mayor. Catholic workers were central to the growth of America, and Gibbons represented to Rome that the American way had its own protections, and that it would be harmful to the church to act the same as it had in Europe (for instance in Ireland, where many nationalists felt that Rome acted more at the behest of the British government than the Irish bishops).

"It is necessary to recognize that, in our age and in our country, obedience cannot be blind," he remarked, apropos of the church and the unions. "To lose the heart of the people would be a misfortune for which the friendship of the few rich and powerful would be no compensation."

Gibbons worked to create a sense of unity among the various Catholic nationalities, emphasizing that whatever their backgrounds they were all now united as Americans and as Catholics. Yet he also defended the church's claim to its own parochial school system (as against an imposed state system) and also against European writers who saw the emergence of a new kind of heresy in what they identified as Americanism.

Gibbons had sprung from Irish roots, but his greatest pride was in being an American. He admired the American Constitution as the greatest document ever to spring from the pen of man. A strong American patriot, he drew admiration from many other Americans such as William Howard Taft and Theodore Roosevelt. Indeed, in 1917 Roosevelt said that "taking your life as a whole, I think you now occupy the position of being the most respected, venerated, and useful citizen of our country."

His emphasis on the benefits of the separation of church and state was very American and not always echoed by European writers, but in America separation was important in creating a climate of religious tolerance in which the church could flourish. The civil government provided the protection in which the civil liberties of all could be exercised.

Gibbons died in Baltimore in March 1921, after a long and active life. He had ordained 2,471 priests and consecrated twenty-three bishops, a record which remained until the end of the Second World War. These figures alone speak of the extraordinary growth over which he presided, and the vitality which this Irish American brought to the creation of modern America.

43

John Devoy

1842–1928

When John Devoy died in Atlantic City, New Jersey, on September 29, 1928, the eighty-six-year-old Irish patriot was virtually penniless. The last of the old Fenian leaders, he had given his whole life to the cause of Ireland. In its report of his death, the London *Times* said he was "the most bitter and persistent, as well as the most dangerous enemy of this country which Ireland has produced since Wolfe Tone." He had lived to see Ireland gain her freedom, but it had brought him no reward beyond the joy of being proved right.

Devoy had been born in Kill, County Kildare, on September 3, 1842, the son of a small farmer. His father was involved in both the movement for Catholic emancipation led by DANIEL O'CONNELL [20] and in the more revolutionary Young Ireland. Their house was full of debate on the future of Ireland and what direction it should take. For John Devoy there would be no doubt: It was to be the revolutionary road.

After the famine, the family moved to the city, where his father worked in a brewery. While working as a clerk, John also attended some courses at the new Catholic University (then in the charge of its founder, the famous cardinal John Henry Newman). He joined the Fenians, and in 1861 the French foreign legion in order to learn the art of war. He spent a year in Algeria, which the French were in the long process of subduing.

Returning to Ireland in 1862, recognized as a born conspirator, he was placed in charge of the Fenian scheme to subvert the British army by placing Fenians widely throughout its ranks. Efforts were made to arrest him in September 1865, but it was not until he was captured in the aftermath of the escape of James Stephens, the Fenian "Head Center," in February 1866, that he was betrayed and sentenced to fifteen years in prison. In 1871 he was released with four other Fenians on condition that they left the British empire.

Devoy emigrated to the United States, where he and his friends were greeted warmly by the Irish community. He joined the *New York Herald* as a reporter, and rose to being in charge of the foreign desk. But in 1879 James Gordon Bennett dismissed him for supporting CHARLES PARNELL [5], whom the proprietor opposed.

In New York, Devoy worked in succession on the *Daily Telegraph* and the *Morning Journal,* and on the *Herald* and *Evening Post* in Chicago. Then, in 1881, he set up his own paper in New York, the *Irish Nation,* and became a leading figure in Clan na Gael. From 1875 to 1876 he helped to organize the rescue of the exiled Fenian prisoners from Fremantle Prison in Australia. He obtained funds from the Clan to support the work of the submarine pioneer John Philip Holland in building his *Fenian Ram,* intended to help destroy the British navy. But his greatest achievement was through his journalism and his role as a pivotal figure around which others banded.

In 1878 MICHAEL DAVITT [24] arrived to lecture in the United States. In October, he and Devoy called for a new policy for the Fenian movement, which was to be called the New Departure. This meant that the revolutionaries would rally behind CHARLES STEWART PARNELL [5] and the parliamentary party in Ireland and support the Land League. Devoy then sent a telegram to the party, offering conditional support to Parnell. He traveled to Europe, but at a meeting in Paris in January 1879 the supreme council of the Irish Republican Brotherhood rejected the notion of the New Departure as put to them by Devoy and Davitt. In April and June, Devoy and Davitt met Parnell in Dublin, and the New Departure went ahead.

Devoy reported on his mission to Europe at the Clan na Gael convention in August in Wilkes-Barre, Pennsylvania. The Irish Americans were left divided among themselves over what should be done. Their interests were now involved both in Ireland and, more complexly, in America.

In the U.S. census of 1880 the Irish were estimated at 27.8 percent of the foreign-born population. The children of Irish-born parents were estimated at 2,756,054. At a convention of the New York Irish Republicans in Saratoga, John Devoy and others planned to detach the Irish vote from the Democrats and move it, if they could, to the Republicans.

In 1882, a crucial year in Irish history, which saw the murder of the chief secretary of Ireland and one of his officials in Dublin's Phoenix Park by terrorists, and the reintroduction of rigorous measures to suppress protest and discontent in Ireland, Devoy published *The Land of Eire,* a statement of his views on the terrible past and the possible future of the country. In the *Irish Nation* he focused on trying to break the relationship between England and America, but the paper was closed down in 1885. On August 30, 1900, before the U.S. presidential election, Devoy formed with Patrick Egan and PATRICK FORD [10] the Irish-American Union to oppose the policies of the Republican William McKinley, who they saw as advocating imperialism and an understanding with Britain. Instead, they urged support for William Jennings Bryan, the Democratic and populist candidate—a reverse of what they had wanted in 1880. McKinley won.

In 1903 Devoy founded a weekly, *The Gaelic American,* which expounded the ideas of the Fenians and Clan na Gael, which had now withdrawn its support from the reunited Irish party. With Judge Daniel Cohalan, Devoy then worked in the coming decade to unite the disparate aspects of the Irish movement.

During the first years of the First World War, up to 1917, Devoy was in touch with German agents eliciting support for the Irish cause by way of guns for the Easter week uprising and defense funds for ROGER CASEMENT [94]. Yet when the new nation emerged and EAMON DE VALERA [2] visited America as president of the Irish republic in 1920, relations were difficult; the leadership of Ireland was evidently passing from Irish Americans back to native Irish. This generated a certain sense of ill feeling. However, Devoy supported the Irish Free State when it came into existence, and he finally returned to Ireland on a brief visit in 1924, the year after the civil war ended. As an American, he opposed the League of Nations and the World Court, those brainchildren of Woodrow Wilson's "new order," because he felt they posed entangling external alliances to American freedom.

He was then working on his memoirs, *Recollections of an Irish Rebel.* His collected correspondence has proved a rich source for historians interested in the details of the Irish revolutionary movements. He kept alive the old Fenian tradition, at last passing it on to a younger generation who had fought in 1916 and in the troubles. For that reason his remains were brought back for burial in Ireland, with honors from the new government, but his best work had been the creation of not only the modern Irish state, but the unity of the Irish-American community.

44

Paul Cardinal Cullen

1803–1878

At the Vatican Council held in Rome in 1870, Cardinal Cullen is said to have drafted the terms of the dogma of papal infallibility. This was typical of the man, who since he had been appointed archbishop of Armagh in 1850 had sought to impose on the Catholic church in Ireland a rigid and unquestioning obedience to authority.

Paul Cullen was born at Ballitore in County Kildare on April 29, 1803, just after the Act of Union. His first studies were at a nearby Quaker school and then at Carlow College. In 1820 he went to Rome to study at the College of Propaganda, where he was ordained a priest in 1829. His first appointment was as professor of sacred scripture and Hebrew in the college. He was then made rector of the Irish College in Rome in 1832. The influence of British diplomats was very strong in the Vatican, for the popes were, at all times, keen to secure the favor of the great powers. In Ireland this was seen as a distinct disadvantage. Cullen acted as the Roman agent of the Irish and Australian bishops in making their views, which did not always coincide with those of the British government, known to the Vatican.

One of these issues, which arose in 1840, was the question of the national school system, which the government proposed. This would have provided for a type of school in which the bishops thought that state influence might overwhelm any Catholic or Irish ethos. Cullen cautiously proposed to Rome that each bishop should be free in his own diocese to choose whether or not to join the scheme. In the end, the schools passed under the mangement of the local parish priests (or rectors in the case of those for the Protestant communities). A secularizing scheme was defeated.

Cullen, however, opposed the queen's colleges; Rome duly condemned these, and urged the Irish bishops to establish a Catholic university—an abortive project that was, however, heavily promoted.

In Rome he witnessed the excesses of the Italian revolution of 1848. When the Roman republic was established and overthrew the papal government, Cullen was made rector of the College of Propaganda. When the republican authorities ordered the closure of the college, Cullen called upon the protection of the U.S. minister to protect his American students and so saved the institution. But this experience gave Cullen an abiding distaste for revolutionary republicans of any kind.

For the rest of his life he sternly countered any revolutionary action in Ireland, while supporting the constitutional parties that respected the position of the church. He was appointed archbisop of Armagh in 1850, despite the fact that he had absolutely no pastoral or administrative experience of the country. At Thurles in 1850, the year from which the reorganized church in Ireland can be dated, he called the first synod of the church in Ireland since the twelfth century.

Cullen was the chief architect of what is now thought of as the "traditional" Irish Catholic church, with its discipline, mode of devotion, and social and political attitudes. He was often at odds with other leaders, such as John McHale of Tuam, but Cullen had the ear of Rome, and that was what counted.

His activities were varied and of consequence. He defended tenants' rights, championed poorhouse reform, advocated the creation of industrial schools, and sought to raise the quality of education. He brought Newman to Ireland to help establish the Catholic University that he had urged upon the hierarchy. Because it could not grant degrees this was a failure, though its medical school survived and flourished. He founded Clonliffe College to improve the training of Irish priests.

To generations of Irish nationalists, the theme of Cullen's whole career, to make the Catholic church the dominant force in Irish society, was one to be approved. But it has left the country with a tragic heritage. Before Cullen there had been a growing sense of accommodation between the different churches and traditions in Ireland. Cullen's extreme ultra-Montanism thwarted this and threw up barriers between them. Cullen, it has been said, had no political theories, but only the interest of his own church at heart.

"Once Ireland began to be regarded as a Catholic nation," Professor F. S. L. Lyons wrote, "there was built into this separate identity an element of puritanical exclusiveness very far from the vision of a WOLFE TONE [11], or a THOMAS DAVIS [23], of an Ireland in which the different cultures would eventually be reconciled."

Though it would have appalled Cullen to think of it, in due course his brooding influence brought about the long, quarter century of war in Northern Ireland. Seeking only to ensure the influence of his own church, he cast his country into the hands of revolutionaries merely interested in using the Catholic identity of their community as a mask for ambitions that stood totally opposed to his.

By seeking to make the Catholic church ascendant in Ireland, Cullen had contributed to its decline. His contemporaries in the United States, who sought to benefit from the protection offered by the constitution of a pluralist republican society, were much wiser.

Cardinal Cullen died in Dublin on October 24, 1878. He left a church outwardly powerful, triumphantly self-satisfied. But a century later his policies had sowed within it the seeds of its own decline.

45

Eugene O'Neill

1888–1953

The first American to win the Nobel Prize for literature (in 1936), Eugene O'Neill was also the major dramatist of the Irish community in America. All his plays, with their sense of doomed misfortune, reflect not only his own personal experience but also those of many Irish people, in Ireland and abroad.

His patriarchs and saintly mothers, the curse of alcohol—all of this was presented with an almost Greek sense of tragedy as an essential part of the human condition. After his death, *Time* magazine commented that "Before O'Neill, the U.S. had theater; after him it had drama."

The Nobel citation said that the reward was "for the power, honesty, and deep-felt emotion of his dramatic work, which embodies an original concept of tragedy." That sense of tragedy arose from his experiences as an Irish American.

Eugene Gladstone O'Neill was born in a New York hotel room on October 16, 1888. His parents sprang directly from Irish roots. His father, James O'Neill, was a prominent actor and a theatrical idol of the day; his mother was Ella Quinlan. James O'Neill had been born in Ireland in 1849 and was brought to America by his parents at the age of five. He was on the stage and getting leading roles in New York when he became typecast in 1882 as Edmond Dantes in *The Count of Monte Cristo*. Such was his success that he played the role over six thousand times. An Irish nationalist, he gave his son the second name of Gladstone out of admiration for the British prime minister who introduced the first Irish home rule bill in 1886.

Ella O'Neill was neurotic, shy, and mystically inclined, and the overemotional nature of his parents' relationship deeply affected Eugene. Both his parents were Catholics, but despite his education from the Sisters of Charity and the De La Salle Brothers, he had lost his faith by the age of fifteen and refused to go to church any longer. Religion became merely an episode of growth, but it lingered in the depths of his feelings nevertheless. Here there is a strong parallel with that other creative artist of the Irish tradition, JAMES JOYCE [25]. At this time O'Neill also learned that his mother had become addicted to the morphine she took to ease her postchildbirth pains. All his life he would struggle with a sense of the cruel nature of God, fate, or the universe, whatever it was that made people's lives hell.

O'Neill completed his early education at Betts Academy in Stamford, Connecticut, in 1906, and secured entry to Princeton University. But this lasted only a year, and he was thrown out. His only other formal education was a playwrighting course taken in 1914 at Harvard in Professor G. P. Baker's famous Forty-seven Workshop.

Between 1907, when he dropped out of college, and 1913, O'Neill did many things. For a while he lived a rakish life in Greenwich Village; he toured with his father's production of *The Count of Monte Cristo* as assistant manager, worked as a secretary, sailed as a seaman, prospected for gold in Honduras (where he suffered from malaria), and worked as a newspaper reporter. He wrote poetry, and later contracted tuberculosis. He also tried to commit suicide. If anything, these adventures gave him a wider view of life than the college classroom would have provided.

While recovering from tuberculosis, then an often fatal condition, he began to write. *Thirst,* his first play, was produced in 1916 by the Provincetown Players, and started a long association. However, it was his next play, *Beyond the Horizon,* in 1920, that confirmed the arrival of a major new American dramatic talent. It won the Pulitzer Prize, and brought recognition to O'Neill as one of America's most important playwrights.

This was followed by *Anna Christie, Emperor Jones,* and *The Hairy Ape.* All were vivid, powerful plays. Of *Anna Christie* (1921), he said, "The play has no ending. Three characters have been revealed in all their intrinsic verity, under the acid test of a fateful crisis in their lives."

He produced an immense body of work, some forty-five plays, varying from elaborate tragedies to light entertainments, and was awarded the Pulitzer Prize four times. The Nobel Prize was his final crown. During his career, in search of a deeper meaning and a broader significance to life, O'Neill moved to more symbolic and experimental forms.

Though the influence of Euripides, Strindberg, and Nietzsche can be traced through his work and outlook, there is also an important personal strain. This lies not only in the highly autobiographical nature of his plays (especially *Long Day's Journey into Night*), but in the general attempt to recreate the American experience onstage. He was the first important playwright to attempt this.

Just as important was the influence of his father, whose always popular melodramas Eugene claimed to despise. Yet he could not escape his theatrical childhood, nor could he quite escape the Catholic religion, so deeply ingrained in so many Irish Americans. His own marriage and family life was painful. He brooded on his sense of sin and guilt, but his characters find little or no forgiveness, grace, or reconciliation. They are pitted against each other in a narrow space, his themes drawn from the incidents of his own life but given no larger context. This makes his plays often seem airless and claustrophobic, but this, too, reflects much of the *inner* American experience.

Illness forced him to give up writing, and after long years of isolation, Eugene O'Neill died in a Boston hotel room on November 27, 1953. His last words reflected his sense of doom: "Born in a hotel room—and God damn it—died in a hotel room." Arthur Miller, a playwright of the new generation, said: "O'Neill was the great wrestler, fighting God to a standstill. The theater will forever need the towering rebuke of his life and his work and his agony."

In Eugene O'Neill, America possessed a great writer, one whose life and work influenced both his contemporaries and a younger generation of writers. But the heart of this American dramatist drew on the inner life of the Irish-American community, and on the dark secrets of the immigrants that success in business and politics often hid.

46

Grace O'Malley

1530–1603

Ireland has had many women heroes over the centuries, but few have been of such romantic stature as Grace O'Malley, the courageous pirate "Queen of the West." She has come down to us in legend as one of the most remarkable women of Irish history.

The western province of Connaught has always been something of a "Wild West," the last frontier which the invaders had to face. It is a place that has long lived by the sea, and Grace came from a family of seafarers. Her name in Gaelic, Granuaile, means "Grace of the Short Hair"—suggesting a manly cast of features. She was born (it is thought) about 1530, and was the only daughter of Owen O'Malley, the chief of the O'Malleys who ruled the western coast from Achill Island in the north to Inishbofin in the south.

At the age of sixteen she married Donal O'Flaherty, one of the clan who held the lands to the south of the O'Malleys in Connemara. These were lawless days, with feuds, raids, land grabbings, and piracy, though English historians perhaps made it all sound even wilder than it was. Donal was nicknamed "the Cock" due to his flashy courage in battle. He was murdered by the Joyces, who held the land to the east. Bereft of her husband, Grace did not despair. She rallied her own people and defended his castle, Castlekirke, on the shores of Lough Corrib, earning herself the title the Hen—hence the Gaelic title of the fortress, Caisleán na Circe—"the Hen's Castle."

Grace established her own base on Clare Island, one protected by a ring of forts around the shores of Clew Bay. From this lair, her fleets of ships and galleys would sail out to prey on the cargo vessels that were rounding the Irish coast en route from Spain to Scotland. She also built Carrickkildavnet Castle, which stands guard over the mouth of Clew Bay. This is an elegant sixteenth-century tower house, but was only one of her strongholds.

In 1566 Grace married again, this time to Richard Burke, the chief of the Mayo Burkes, another powerful clan. Legend has it that when she married Richard, they agreed that either of them could annul the marriage after a year. Richard had his own stronghold at Carrigahowley Castle, where they lived in what seems to the modern eye to have been very cramped quarters. A year later, when Richard returned from one of his own expeditions, she had locked the castle door. From the parapet above she called down to the unfortunate man, "I dismiss you."

In 1577 Grace was captured while looting the territory of the earl of Desmond in Munster, and was imprisoned for eighteen months in Limerick. She was released on condition that she reform her old piratical ways. Law of a new kind was coming to the west of Ireland—English law. When the viceroy Sir Richard Bingham began to enforce that law by violent means in Connaught, Grace decided she would appeal directly to Queen Elizabeth I, as one queen to another. She left Mayo to seek an audience with the queen in London, and got her wish. In September 1593 the meeting took place.

Lively Irish legend asserts that Grace O'Malley did indeed speak as one sovereign to another, and was forthright to the point of insult. She was offered the title of countess, and retorted that Queen Elizabeth had no right to think of offering such a title, for they were equals; she was no vassal. However, the reality may have been different. It is likely that Queen Elizabeth admired the powerful intelligence of the pirate queen.

Grace was allowed to return to her home in the west and to live there unmolested. She is thought to have died about 1603, though this, like other details of her life, is uncertain. Today she remains a legend of the west, and at Louisburgh in Mayo an interpretive center presents her life and legend for visitors. Her son, Tiobaid na Long, "Theobald of the Ships," was murdered in 1629 near Ballintober, where his elaborate tomb can be seen in the de Burgo (or Burke) chapel.

Whatever legend has done to enhance the life of Grace O'Malley, she remains a striking figure and a reminder that the role of women in past periods of Irish society was not always a subservient one. In the feudal society of the sixteenth century, men did not always have their way. The legendary queen became something of a model for the powerful women who ran Ireland's homes in later centuries.

The sad remains of her tower house can still be seen on Clare Island. The house was used a coast guard station in the nineteenth century, but is a ruin today. A mile and a half across the island are the remains of a Cistercian church from the Middle Ages. Here there is a tomb that is said to be the final resting place of "the Pirate Queen." The O'Malley crest is carved on the stonework, bearing the proud O'Malley motto: *Terra Marique Potens,* "Mighty by Land and Sea."

47

St. Columban

c. 543–615

In the age when Ireland was "the Island of Saints and Scholars," St. Columban was one of its leading figures, a personality of international reputation.

Also known as Columbanus, Columban was born in Leinster about 543. He studied at the monastic school of St. Sinell at Cleenish, on the shores of Lough Erne in Ulster. He then entered the monastery of St. Comgall at Bangor, which was renowned for both its sanctity and learning. Here he taught for some thirty years, wrote a commentary on the psalms, and composed poems.

About 590 he was sent by St. Comgall with twelve others to conduct a mission in Europe. He preached in Brittany and the Vosges, having been invited there by the Merovingian king Childebert. He settled in Burgundy and founded the monasteries of Annegray, Luxeuil, and Fontaines. From these three motherhouses some two hundred other monasteries were later established. (From Annegray, St. Killian later traveled to Germany to Wuerzburg and founded a monastery in 742; St. Emmeram went up into Regensburg and founded one in 739.) St. Columban also composed sets of rules and regulations for monks.

Coming from Ireland, he was dismayed with what he found in Burgundy. He thought the local clergy were degenerate, the Frankish court immoral, and some of the local customs shocking. With missionary zeal he introduced the strict Irish system of penance, which involved auricular confession—personal confession to an individual priest, an innovation which the church has maintained.

He also kept to the Celtic style of tonsure and celebrated Easter by a different calculation than the rest of the church. He had difficulties with the local bishops about this confusing matter, and tried to enlist the support of Pope Gregory I to his position. In this letter he used the term *tota Europae*, "the whole of Europe," to express the Irish concept of the West as a common cultural unit.

Columban was eventually expelled in 608 from Burgundy by King Theudric, whom he had attacked for maintaining a concubine (these Irish monks were nothing if not strict). He passed through Neustria, where he had been invited by King Clothar, and settled near Zurich in what is now Switzerland, where his companion St. Gall founded the monastery of St. Gallen. But he was driven out by the natives for his attack on their paganism.

He passed over the Alps into what is now northern Italy and founded yet another monastery at Bobbio in 612. From this new foundation his influence spread over all of Europe. He died at Bobbio on November 23, 615, and was buried in the church abbey, now dedicated to St. Columban.

Columban's letters, monastic rules, and poetry belong to the great canon of Irish medieval literature. One of these is a song of encouragement to his companions rowing against the current of the Rhine. Austere though their religion may have been, these monks found new delight in nature, and the margins of the manuscripts for which their monasteries are famous have scribbled in them delightful little verses about the birds and trees and waters that surrounded them.

They had a lasting effect on the high culture of the Middle Ages. In Ireland, the culture of Christian civilization was preserved during the long night of the barbarian invasions. It was then carried back to rekindle the civilization of Europe as a whole—the *tota Europae* of St. Columban.

His successors at Bobbio, however, ameliorated the strictness of the Irish rule he had introduced with less severe elements from the rule of St. Benedict, and exercised important influence on Western civilization. For centuries to come, the Irish monasteries, from Clonmacnoise in the west to Vienna in the east, provided Europe with its scholarship.

St. Columban's work marked the dawn of a new age and the rise of Charlemagne and the Carolingian empire, which gave Europe a new sense of its identity, to which the new European Union looks back.

48

Samuel Beckett

1906–1989

Yet another of Ireland's Nobel Prize winners, Samuel Beckett in his spare, bleak plays seems to many of his admirers to epitomize the sense of despair many felt immediately after the war, the sense of alienation and isolation, of suppressed rage with life, which characterize the modern age. In 1969, the citation by the Nobel committee spoke of "his writings, which—in new forms for the novel and drama—the destitution of modern man acquires its elevation." According to Robert Hogan, "He remains perhaps the century's most acclaimed and influential avant-garde writer."

Samuel Barclay Beckett was born in Foxrock, a comfortable, largely Protestant suburb of Dublin, on April 13, 1906. He had a comfortable upbringing in a material sense. He was educated at Portora Royal School in Enniskillen in Northern Ireland—OSCAR WILDE'S [97] old school. He entered Trinity College in the autumn of 1923, where he studied modern languages (French in particular) and took his bachelor's degree in 1927. For a few months he taught French at a Protestant school in Belfast before going to the Ecole Normale Supérieure in Paris as a lecturer.

It was in Paris that he made friends with the Irish poet and art critic Thomas McGreevy, through whom he was introduced into the circle of JAMES JOYCE [25]. Joyce was to be the greatest literary influence on Beckett's own work. He was one of a number of friends who assisted the nearly blind Joyce by reading and researching material for "Work in Progress" eventually published as *Finnegans Wake.* Beckett

was also one of the young men in whom Joyce's daughter took a romantic interest.

Beckett had literary ambitions of his own. His first publications
were a long poem called "Whoroscope" in 1930, and a short study of
Proust for a London publisher in 1931. In the autumn of 1930 he went
back to Dublin to teach French at Trinity College, where McGreevy
introduced him to JACK YEATS [26], whom Beckett deeply admired.
Indeed the later pictures of Yeats, with their isolated figures and blasted
landscapes, have much in common with Beckett's writing.

Beckett's stay in Dublin was fraught with ill health and personal
and emotional problems, especially with his demanding mother. Having
taken his master's degree, he went back to Paris in December 1931.
There he began a novel (which remained unpublished till after his
death) and a collection of stories, *More Pricks Than Kicks*, which makes
use of familiar Dublin in a unique way, pointing toward his later work.

Beckett now identified with his French friends, and during the
occupation he worked with the French Resistance, though in 1942 he
was forced to flee south to Roussillon. Later he was awarded the Croix
de Guerre. Ireland may have been neutral—Samuel Beckett was not.

On his return to Paris, Beckett settled into his major period of
production. He was now writing in French rather than English. *Molloy*
was finished in 1948, and was followed by *Malone Meurt.* By the first
months of 1950 he had finished *L'Innommable.*

But these books, when published, either in French or English,
made little impact compared with the sensation that was caused by the
production of his play *En Attendant Godot* in a theater studio early in
1953. As *Waiting for Godot,* it was successfully produced in London
and New York. Its novelty and strange atmosphere at once made it a
talking point not only among the avant garde, but the general public. It
was the beginning of the Theater of the Absurd, which many saw as
growing out of the existential philosophies of Sartre and Camus.

His earlier work came back into print, often in his own translations. In 1956 came *Fin de Partie* (*Endgame* in English). He ceased to
write novels, and his plays became briefer and more etiolated. In 1961
he married his longtime companion Suzanne Deschevaux-Dumesnil.
Though they maintained flats beside each other in Paris, much of their
time was spent in the country or in North Africa. In July 1989 Beckett's
wife died, and he himself passed away on December 22.

The following year one critic observed that "by the year 2000 Beckett criticism will equal that of Wagner and Napoleon, who are the most written about personae in history." Beckett himself was an obsessively private person, and his biographers have not even yet fully plumbed the depths of his experiences. It is clear now, however, that though he wrote in French and published in Paris as a European author, much of his initial inspiration draws on his early experiences in Dublin. Indeed, it was the ambition of the actor Peter O'Toole to film *Waiting for Godot* in the bleak rocky district of the Burren in the west of Ireland, as its windswept acres seemed to echo the barren isolation of the play. Like Joyce, who influenced him greatly, Beckett never escaped from Ireland, and a haunted childhood and illness were major matters in his life. Many would now regard as his best work not the later briefer items, but the more closely grained world of his novels and early plays.

When the Nobel committee spoke of destitution, they seemed to be thinking of the bleakness of life and soul which his work reflects, and thinking how appropriate this was for an era threatened with annihilation at a moment's notice. Personal courage would have no place in an atomic war, but for Beckett, waiting for the end had become intolerable, while life itself was even more so.

Quite how his work will wear with time is still a matter of controversy, but his influence on the literature of the late twentieth century was very great. "Beckettian" is an adjective that everyone understands the meaning of, even if they cannot understand the meaning of Beckett.

49

George Bernard Shaw

1856–1950

In contrast to SAMUEL BECKETT [48] and EUGENE O'NEILL [45], George Bernard Shaw epitomizes a sense of optimism about man and his achievements. He was another of the Irish artists to be awarded the Nobel Prize for his work, "which is marked by both idealism and humanity, its stimulating satire often being infused with a singular poetic beauty."

These comments provide an insight into the work of one of the world's most important dramatists, who was born in Dublin on July 26, 1856, a decade after the famine, and lived to see the arrival of the atom bomb. His family was middle-class, decayed gentry, in financial difficulties. A poor student at school, Shaw found work in a real estate agent's office, but did not find the work agreeable.

In 1876 he migrated to London to join his mother and sister. There he found desultory work as a journalist. He attempted to write novels, but these were either failures or sold badly. But he was tenacious. He later commented that poverty threw his mother into a struggle for survival, and vowed never again to do "an honest day's work." He thought his later success validated this early decision to disregard "all the quack duties which lead the poor lad of fiction to the White House."

From his mother he had inherited a love and knowledge of music; music, indeed, had been the constant factor in his upbringing. And it was as a music critic, and then an art critic for the newspapers, that he began to be better known. He then added drama critic to the list.

Having commented on the work of others, he thought that he might do better.

Since 1884 he had been a socialist and member of the Fabian Society, a group of socialists who worked for the evolutionary improvement of society rather than immediate revolution. He had been converted to socialism after hearing the American Henry George speak in London. He was deeply involved in the society, editing *Fabian Essays* in 1889. For many years he was also involved in municipal politics.

For thirteen years Shaw wrote for a wide range of newspapers and magazines, his views on art and drama proving effective in their impact on taste. Influenced by Henrik Ibsen, he railed against the settled, comfortable nature of London theater. He was also a champion of Wagner. His strong opinions about art, society, and politics proved from the beginning to be the material for his plays.

Between 1885 and 1913 he wrote some twenty-five plays, of all lengths. Over the length of his career, up to 1939, he wrote an average of a play a year. These were not only produced, but were published as books, equipped with long prefaces treating not only the plays, but their subject matter and background, some of which dealt with medicine, housing, religion, and so on. These were published by the author himself, his ostensible publisher being his agent, so that Shaw could control all details of their production.

His first play was *Widowers' Houses*, which attacked slum landlords. This was followed by *Arms and the Man* in 1894, which lampooned the romance attached to soldiering, especially in the British Empire and America. *Mrs. Warren's Profession*, which dealt with a prostitute of great capacity who runs a series of brothels, continued his attack on social problems. It was so shocking that it was banned by the censor and not produced until 1902.

His plays have little in the way of mere mechanical plot. They are dramas of conflict and debate, the clash of the old and the new, the young and the aged. He remained at work until the age of eighty-three, when he wrote *In Good King Charles's Golden Days*. Mentally he remained alert and caustic till the end of his life.

In 1898 Shaw married Charlotte Payne-Townshend, an Irish heiress. Though he maintained a London flat, in 1906 they moved to "Shaw's Corner" at Ayot St. Lawrence in Hertfordshire.

In old age Shaw became one of those public figures whom the newspaper could rely on for comments on everything from nudism to the atom bomb. To a vast public unacquainted with his plays and books, he became best known for *My Fair Lady,* a musical based on his play *Pygmalion.* The estate of this strong-minded socialist benefited by many millions of dollars.

Eccentric to the end, he had also left money for alphabet reform, another one of his quirks. A novel revision of the alphabet was eventually awarded a prize, and a version of *Androcles and the Lion* was published, using the new forms—but the Shaw alphabet failed to gain acceptance.

Stripped of all its merely ephemeral details, Shaw's career is still an extraordinary one. His plays are still alive on the stage. Though many of the issues which he addressed are now dead ones, his hatred of hypocrisy and cant is still very much alive. He was, in the eyes of many of his admirers in Europe and America, the greatest dramatist of the twentieth century, and a rival of merit to William Shakespeare.

Shaw had hated his youth in Dublin and was glad to leave it, but he and his wife and family had financial interests there. The perennial problems of Ireland came under his review in *John Bull's Other Island,* which dealt with the mental barriers between the natives of both islands. Here, the Englishman Tom Broadbent is mystically enchanted with Ireland's romantic past, while his friend Larry Doyle is a realist, intent on transforming the dying, dreaming nation. In this debate Shaw's own mouthpiece is the former priest Peter Keegan, whose middle way is an ideal state, a Shavian socialist commonwealth. The play was written for the Abbey Theatre in 1904 but rejected by them, and only performed in Dublin in September 1916, a year which had seen other kinds of dreamers at large with guns on the Irish streets.

In her will, his wife left her money for an institution to improve the manners of Irishmen—perhaps a comment on her husband's own abrasive nature. When he died Shaw left part of his estate, later enriched by royalties from *My Fair Lady,* to the National Gallery in Dublin, where he had spent so many happy hours as a young man. It was from the great European masters of that collection that he gained his first hint that the ideal of the artist was "to shew us to ourselves as we really are."

As Shavian scholar William F. Feeney put it: "Shaw, young man of Dublin, senior citizen of the world, continues to stand before us on his soapbox, Mephistophelian, nimble, provocative, outrageous, teasing, or browbeating us to hear him out."

50

Finley Peter Dunne

1867–1936

Finley Peter Dunne, the creator of Mr. Dooley, one of the most famous Irish characters of all time, was born on July 10, 1867, and reared among the Irish of Chicago. His parents were Irish immigrants who had come to America as children. His father's sister was a prominent educator in Chicago, while a cousin was archbishop of San Francisco.

Dunne was educated at a public school in Chicago. When he left school in 1884, he went to work as messenger boy at the *Chicago Tribune,* which was his introduction to the hectic life of the newspapers. He was promoted to reporter, and by the age of twenty-one, the talented young man was city editor of the *Chicago Times.* He was also a staff man on the *Chicago Evening Post* (1892–97) and editor of the *Chicago Journal* (1897–1900).

From 1892 he had been writting short humorous pieces for the *Post* in the Irish brogue. It was only when he began writing for the *Journal* a series featuring the observations of life and current events by a tavern keeper, Mr. Martin Dooley, that he achieved fame. These were republished widely, and even in England the Newnes press, and publishers like Routledge and Grant Richards, brought them to the attention of the British and Irish public.

The first collection was called *Mr. Dooley in Peace and War* (1898)—the war being the controversial Spanish-American War. It was Martin Dooley's ironic commentary on that imperial enterprise that made Dunne even more famous. His influence over foreign policy was recognized, and one of his biographers, Elmer Ellis, called him "the wit and censor of the nation."

Dunne was on friendly terms with Theodore Roosevelt, Elihu Root, and William C. Whitney, politicians then as now being careful to cultivate influential columnists. Many other collections followed, leading up to *Mr. Dooley Says* (1910). These widely read and influential books made Dunne world famous as the creator of a truly original character, and a humorist with a sharp eye.

At the turn of the century he moved to New York City to edit the *Morning Telegraph*—this was when New York had a wide range of papers. He married Margaret Abbott of Boston, by whom he had four children. In New York he rose to become part owner of the *American Magazine,* and later still editor of *Collier's Weekly.* In these journals he wrote nondialect columns which were acute and witty, but did not achieve the same universal fame as the Mr. Dooley pieces.

As is so often the case with creative talents, the money he received (more than a million dollars) snuffed out his talent as a writer. After 1920 he wrote very little, though in 1936 he wrote some autobiographical pieces which his son Philip eventually edited as *Mr. Dooley Remembers* (1963). He died in New York City on April 24, 1936.

Aside from his journalism, the only books Dunne published dealt with the musing of his saloon keeper philosopher Mr. Dooley. There were ten books in the series, nine of which appeared before his retirement.

Philip Dunne saw his father's writings as being in the American rural cracker-barrel tradition of the humor of Poor Richard, Hosea Biglow, Artemus Ward, and Mark Twain. But they had been rural writers, humorists of America's frontier experience. Dunne was something new, an urban humorist, perhaps the first of a long line of Irish, Jewish, and Italian humorists in the twentieth century. The dialogues of Mr. Dooley are written in what native Irish writers might regard as a stage-Irish idiom, and they derive in part from the popularity of the Irish comic on the contemporary American stage. But the language was in fact close to that actually spoken on the broad walks of Chicago and New York.

Mr. Dooley represents not only the fey whimsicality of the Irish temperament, but also all the solid common sense of the race underlying it, which had taken on the American ways, and won the fight.

At an earlier time Mr. Dooley would have been rejected. His popularity derived in large part from the prominent, indeed, essential role which the Irish had begun to play in the life of urban America. In a sense, Chicago and New York were *Irish* cities.

Dunne, too, represented the gift of the Irish for language and storytelling, skills beyond their more taciturn neighbors in the cities, both American and immigrant. Like JAMES JOYCE [25], Dunne was a bravely experimental writer who realized the full potential of the Irish brogue.

The city is "where there is nawthin' to eat but what ye can buy," says Mr. Dooley to a friend. "Where the dust is laid be th' sprinklin' cart, where th' ice-man comes reg'lar an' the roof garden is in bloom an' ye wake not by th' sun but by th' milkman, I says. I want to be near th' doctor whin I'm sick an' near eatable food whin I'm hungry, an' where I can put me hand out early in th' morning an' hook a newspaper. Th' city is th' on'y resort fr a man that has iver lived in the city."

The Irish had come as immigrants, but by the turn of the century policy was turning against immigration. Mr. Dooley had his comment on this as well. As his son later pointed out, Dunne's humor "always had a social purpose. Mr. Dooley was a weapon against hypocrisy and cant, the pompous and the predatory, in politics, business, and society in general."

Mr. Dooley's "philosophy" was widely shared by his Irish compatriots, many of whom lamented his later silence. It coincided with the emergence of a modern Ireland with new notions, where the city was rejected. Here in part was the emerging difference between Ireland and her exiled American children.

51

Archbishop Daniel Mannix

1864–1963

During a long and remarkable life, Daniel Mannix saw the transformation not only of Ireland, but also of Australia, his adopted land, from a frontier country into a leading nation of the world. His was a crucial presence in the development of the Irish community in Australia.

He was born in Charleville (now Rath Luirc) in County Cork in March 1864, the third son of a family of four boys and a girl. He was educated by the Sisters of Mercy and the Christian Brothers in Fermoy, and then went on to study for the priesthood, like so many clever young men in those days. He was ordained at Maynooth in 1890, becoming professor of theology in 1894, and president of the college in 1903.

This would have been an important enough career, but in 1912 he was named coadjutor (or deputy) to the archbishop of Melbourne, eventually becoming archbishop himself in May 1917.

He arrived in Australia in 1913. During the crucial years of the First World War he came to the fore as a leader of the Irish community's opposition to conscription for overseas military service (not always seen as a patriotic position, however, by other elements in Australian society, where the returned servicemen's organizations are very powerful). After the Easter Rising he also supported Ireland's claims for independence.

He also fought for the independence of Catholic schools within the Australian system, an echo of a struggle that had gone on in Ireland and the United States. He supported the creation of Newman College at the University of Melbourne, and Corpus Christi College at Werribee.

In 1920 Mannix had to visit Rome to make a periodic report to the pope in person. He traveled to Europe by way of the United States, where he was met with great enthusiasm from Irish-American communities from San Francisco to New York. On the way he made inflammatory speeches. "All that Ireland asks of England is this—take one of your hands off my throat and the other out of my pocket."

The ship he was traveling on was met by a British warship off the coast of Cornwall, and he was arrested by order of Prime Minister Lloyd George "in view of his disloyal statements." Mannix was told that he was free to stay in England, but he was not to visit Liverpool, Glasgow, or Manchester, the Irish population centers. Instead he stayed in Leeds. He could not go to Ireland, and was also forbidden to speak in England. Inevitably, this left him with a tremendous reputation as an Irish patriot.

He served for forty-seven years as archbishop, establishing new parishes, building schools, and opening colleges. There had been sixty parishes and 180 churches in 1917; by 1963 there were 176 parishes and three hundred churches. He also promoted Catholic Action, the movement for Catholic engagement in politics, and encouraged the Catholic press and Catholic social service. In 1937 he established the National Secretariat of Catholic Action and assisted in the creation of the Catholic Social Movement in 1941. Since his elevation he had opposed the influence of communism in Australia, and when the great labor split occurred in 1955 he supported the Australian Labour party's anti-communist Industrial Groups.

Theologically and liturgically he was very conservative, like many other Irish bishops, but so also was the community he led. He died in Melbourne in November 1963, on the eve of the vast changes in the church which were to be wrought by the Second Vatican Council. By this time the Irish community in Australia had moved to a central position—immigration from nonwhite countries was beginning. Though the rhetoric of the Australian Irish might often sound revolutionary and radical, as in the Labour party, it was also imbued with the same deeply held conservative views that marked Daniel Mannix.

Mannix had many characteristics. In Irish-Australian folklore he was a great patriotic hero. He was also the subject of many humorous anecdotes. Every day he would walk four miles from his home to the cathedral, and so came to know many of the city's poor. Giving money to a drunk, Mannix warned him not to spend it in the next hotel. "No, Your Grace. Well then, which one *would you* recommend?"

His most important contribution was his public leadership. He derived his public style from the Irish examples of John McHale, archbishop of Tuam, and Thomas Croke, archbishop of Cashel, men who identified the Catholic church with the national aspirations of the Irish people. It was a tradition (found elsewhere, of course) of combining ecclesiastical position with public leadership, championing the national cause against spiritual and political oppression.

This was not the only style. There were other bishops who supported British rule, and those like PAUL CARDINAL CULLEN [44], who concentrated on the interests of the church alone. To Australia Mannix brought the experience of Irish history, the role of the Catholic clergy in Irish communities, and shaped a course which still influences the public life of the southern continent.

In 1917 Mannix had seen that there was an emerging Australian interest which was not to be identified simply with the interests of the British. Though this was controversial then, it has become the state of things today, when Australia finds itself having more in common with its own part of the world, and with the United States. Mannix was one of the important influences on the emergence of an Australian national identity in the twentieth century.

He had helped to mold the Irish-Australian community, but that community would have to face great changes, such as the rise in Asian immigration, which their English-speaking emigrant background made them unfamiliar with. By the time he died, a new Australia was emerging, racially mixed, increasingly democratic, which would provide many new challenges to the old faith of the Irish.

52

Maud Gonne MacBride

1866–1953

Constance Gore-Booth, the Countess Markievicz

1886–1927

Given that Irishmen have, in general, a reputation for being male chauvinists, it is all the more remarkable that women have played major parts in all national movements. Among the most remarkable and charismatic were Maud Gonne and Constance Markievicz. Even more remarkable was the fact that these champions of the poor and the oppressed came from socially privileged backgrounds.

Constance was born Gore-Booth, of a Sligo landed family (members of which still serve in the British foreign service). She was presented at court in 1887 and hailed as "the new Irish beauty." She wished to become a painter, and was already a friend of W. B. Yeats and others in the Irish literary revival which was causing such a creative ferment at the time. In pursuit of her ambitions as an artist she went to London, and later to Paris.

In Paris she met and married Casimir Markievicz, a Polish nobleman by whom she had a daughter. Though he had extensive estates in the Ukraine, they returned to live in Dublin, where they involved themselves in many artistic movements. The count was a genial man, and with his wife helped to found the Dublin Arts Club.

Constance, however, became interested in Irish nationalism and joined her friend Maud Gonne in her organization, the Daughters of Eireann, the feminist side of the nationalist cause. In 1909 she established her own group of boy scouts, Na Fianna Eireann, who were taught the use of weapons as well as woodcraft. Her husband did not find these activities quite so appealing, and returned to the Ukraine. She never saw him again.

She was involved in the lockout of 1913, running a soup kitchen for the workers, who were verging on starvation. She also took part in the Easter Rising, commanding the garrison which was installed in the College of Surgeons in St. Stephen's Green. She was sentenced to death, but reprieved because she was a woman.

In the general election of November 1918, she was elected from a Dublin constituency, the first woman ever elected to the British Parliament—itself an historic achievement. It might have been more notable if she had entered Parliament, but along with the rest of Sinn Fein, she refused to take her seat in London, and instead was one of those who met in Dublin in January 1919 and proclaimed the independence of the Irish republic to the world.

She was minister of labor in this government, which existed underground during the troubles. When the war with the British came to an end, she opposed the treaty settlement and supported the republican cause. She continued in politics, being elected again in 1923 after a defeat in 1922. Arrested, she went on a hunger strike. A founding member of Fianna Fail, she was reelected to the national assembly in 1926, but by now her activities had undermined her health, and she died on July 15, 1927.

Maud Gonne, another social beauty, the daughter of a British army officer, was also the beloved of WILLIAM BUTLER YEATS [8]. But she refused to marry him, and instead devoted her life to the cause of Ireland. Her love life was centered on a French politician, Lucien Millevoye, a ultra-nationalist supporter of General Georges Boulanger, whom she met in France in 1887 while recuperating from a serious illness. They became lovers but never married. By him she had two children, a boy who died, and a girl, Iseult (later Mrs. Francis Stuart), who was described for many years as her niece, and whom Dublin gossip saw as the daughter of Yeats.

In Paris she edited a paper which supported Irish extremists and broke with her lover because of his failure to support her cause after

Boulanger committed suicide. She played the role of an active gadfly of the period, eventually founding the Daughters of Eireann, mentioned above, in 1900.

When Queen Victoria visited Dublin in 1900 to thank the Irish for their support of the Boer War, Maud Gonne organized a countercelebration. She was still involved with literary matters—she acted in Yeats's play *Cathleen ni Houlihan* in 1902. She married Maj. John MacBride, who had commanded a Boer unit, and by him had two more children. However, MacBride was, in Yeats's words "a drunken vainglorious lout," from whom she soon separated. He was one of those executed in 1916.

Maud worked for the White Cross and ambulance service during the troubles and opposed the treaty. To the end of her life, she and her family remained deeply involved in republican activities. She wrote an account of her life, *A Servant of the Queen,* in 1938—the queen in question being Ireland rather than Victoria.

Maud died on April 27, 1953, by which time her son Sean MacBride had risen to be foreign minister for Ireland, after a controversial career in republican politics. It was his government that finally declared Ireland a republic and took it out of the commonwealth. Her funeral was attended by huge crowds, gathered not only to see the passing of the grand dame of Irish politics, but the woman whose beauty in her youth had captured the heart of Ireland's greatest poet, W. B. Yeats.

These two women, in very different ways, are representative of thousands of others who were involved with the labor and republican causes in Ireland and America. At a time when women were seen as secondary figures, they created their own organizations and gathered their own followers. For a while they were a significant force in Irish life and politics, and generations of women after them were less content with their conventional roles. The Irish constitution of 1937, which recognized the special place of women as being in the home, seemed to many radicals to be a snub to the achievements of gallant women like Maud Gonne and Countess Markievicz, with men once again claiming the political arena exclusively for themselves. When the women's liberation movement came to Ireland in the late 1960s, however, it was to Maud Gonne and Constance Markievicz that it turned for role models. They remain icons of the women's movement to this day.

53

John O'Donovan

1809–1861

Eugene O'Curry

1796–1862

A nation's identity depends on more than patriots and politicians. A crucial ingredient is a knowledge of its past and its traditions, and those traditions are bound up in many ways with the nature and history of the land itself. In Ireland these had almost been lost when the appearance of the scholars John O'Donovan and Eugene O'Curry saved the remnants of the past and helped to create an idea of Ireland and her past that remains influential to this day.

John O'Donovan was born on July 9, 1809, at Attateemore in rural Kilkenny. His father died when he was a child, but he was educated in Dublin, thanks to the care of his uncle, Patrick O'Donovan. Patrick proved to be an influential figure in the boy's career, for he was a native Gaelic speaker and loved all aspects of the old Gaelic culture, and he taught the boy about these.

In 1826 John O'Donovan began his working life in the Irish Record Office, filing and translating Gaelic manuscripts, working on old law tracts, and assisting in the research for Peter O'Connell's English-Gaelic dictionary. In 1829 he moved to the Ordnance Survey, which was then engaged with the first full-scale survey and mapping of Ireland. In preparation for this O'Donovan traveled the country, visiting every townland (the basic land division of which there would be several per parish), to record and investigate locally and in manuscript sources the history of the place names. He reported back to the head office in a series of letters that later filled fifty edited volumes. At the time, however, only the first survey, relating to Derry, was published before the project was suspended. The British authorities feared that the recording of the actual history of the places of Ireland, a record of dispossession and eviction, was not appropriate. (This work lies behind Brian Friel's play, *Translations*.)

With Eugene O'Curry he established the Irish Archaeological Society, which undertook the publication of a long series of scholarly works by both writers. The greatest of O'Donovan's wide-ranging achievements was the editing and translating in seven volumes of the *Annals of the Four Masters* between 1848 and 1851—a remarkable feat of applied industry and scholarship.

At this time he contemplated emigrating to America, but in 1852, when the Brehon Law Commission was established, he was employed there at a much improved salary. These laws were the old Celtic legal system, which had been supplanted by feudal and statutory law but which was vitally important for understanding all aspects of ancient Irish culture.

His work was recognized with an honorary doctor of laws degree from Trinity College, but his real fame has come in the praise which later generations have heaped upon his skilled pioneering research into the manuscripts of ancient Ireland. O'Donovan had lived in difficult circumstances all his life, and his health had never been good. He died in 1861, before the appearance of the materials he had been working on. He was only in his middle fifties, and left a widow, six children, and an estate valued at a mere £570.

Eugene O'Curry was also born in rural Ireland, at Dunaha in County Clare, in 1796. He was never formally educated, but his father had a vast store of knowledge about the traditions and antiquities of Ireland and ancient Irish literature. This he passed on to his son, and it was an education in itself.

O'Curry worked on the small family farm and then struggled for four years to earn a living as a teacher. With his brothers he moved to Limerick about 1824, and worked as a laborer and later a ganger. He then managed to get appointed warden of the Limerick mental home. Here his own scholarly skills were recognized, and he was invited to join the staff of the Ordnance Survey in 1835.

He was employed on the survey with John O'Donovan, working with him on the survey of Clare, and when this project ended, in 1837, he was employed to catalog and arrange the ancient Irish materials in the Royal Irish Academy, Trinity College, and the British Museum in London.

The important person in the survey was George Petrie, an artist who became a member of the council of the Royal Irish Academy in 1829, and instigated the collection and recording of Gaelic manuscripts. So O'Donovan, O'Curry, and Petrie came together. O'Curry then began the even larger task of editing and publishing some of these manuscripts.

When John Henry Newman established the Catholic University in Dublin, O'Curry was hired as the professor of Irish history and archaeology in 1854. This was the first professorship of archaeology in the world. His inaugural lectures, published in 1861, covered the whole range of Irish manuscript materials. Though he died on July 30, 1862, a further set of lectures, *The Manners and Customs of the Ancient Irish*, appeared in 1873.

The importance of the pioneering work undertaken by these two relatives (O'Donovan was married to O'Curry's sister-in-law) cannot be overestimated. It laid the foundation for all further inquiry and research in what they revealed to be one of the most ancient cultures in the Western world, even older than Greece in some respects.

What Patricia Boyne, the recent biographer of O'Donovan, wrote about the one, applies to both: "His work was responsible for the marked growth in the study of Irish language, history, folklore, and poetry in the second half of the nineteenth century. It promoted an awareness of the significance of the Irish language and of Irish antiquities, and of their value to the Irish people. It also proved seminal to the great upsurge of drama and poetry manifested in the Irish literary revival."

A writer of an earlier generation, Patrick McSweeney, saw the matter in a more nationalist light: "In the battle for intellectual freedom it is true to say that O'Donovan, O'Curry, and Petrie are national heroes. They loved Ireland and the Irish people with a lasting love. They cherished the Past of Ireland, they reverenced it; and they believed in it. They determined that the Ireland of the Future should be bound to the Ireland of the Past by the links of knowledge and of love. They forged these links in the white heat of patriotic research. They were, in every true sense of the word, Nation-builders; and we, their heirs, must not forget them."

Today their pioneering work is continued by scholars in university departments and institutions around the world, but especially in Ireland and America. The true value of what they did lies in the love of many millions for the ancient culture they uncovered.

54

Horace Plunkett

1854–1932

Though he was born and died in England, Horace Plunkett was a scion of the Dunsanys and passed much of his early life at Dunsany Castle, the ancient family seat of the Plunketts, in County Meath. He was born in Gloucester on October 24, 1854, and was a son of the sixteenth Baron Dunsany and the uncle of the well-known writer, Lord Dunsany (a family in whose ancestry lay the Irish saint, Oliver Plunkett).

Having been educated at Eton and Oxford, he was sent to Wyoming in 1879 to recover his health, and remained there for a decade. It is often forgotten just how large the investment of Britain was in the cattle lands of the American west in the late nineteenth century.

In 1888 he published an article on the value of cooperative stores for Ireland. When he came back to Ireland in 1889 he threw himself into the cooperative movement, which aimed at improving Irish agriculture for small farmers. By 1891 some eighteen societies had been formed by over a thousand farmers. From 1894 to 1899 he was president of the Irish Agricultural Organisation Society, which he founded. He was appointed to the Congested Districts Board, where he served from 1891 to 1918, and was elected MP from South Dublin in 1892 as a unionist. Until 1900 he was a staunch advocate of the claims of Irish agriculture in the British Parliament.

He was largely responsible for achieving the establishment of the Department of Agriculture and Technical Instruction in Ireland. He employed the poet George Russell to edit the movement's paper, the

Irish Homestead, in which JAMES JOYCE'S [25] first stories from *Dubliners* appeared.

Plunkett was convinced that the solution to the social and economic problems of rural Ireland depended on a mixture of self-help and state aid, but he had to fight long for his cause against the lethargy and opposition of vested interests. Nor did he believe in "compulsory cooperation"—the Marxist solution.

The Irish Agricultural Organisation Society was one of the most influential agencies in the remaking of modern Ireland, and its influence can still be felt through the giant cooperative dairies which flourish all over Ireland and are now among the biggest businesses in the country. He was elected a fellow of the Royal Society in 1902, and was made a knight commander of the Victorian Order in 1903.

His book, *Ireland in the New Century,* published in 1904, caused immense controversy, as he claimed that one of the drags on social and economic development in Ireland was the Catholic church, which stifled any sense of personal enterprise. This was angrily rebutted by Catholic apologists. As a Protestant, Plunkett may have exaggerated the power of the church, for later it would be unable to hinder Irish rebels undertaking often radical reforms. The inertia lay in the poor education and traditionalism of the farmers themselves.

The controversy may well have damaged Plunkett in the eyes of the rising generation of Irish nationalists. However, he was a unionist in politics, and hoped to keep Ireland whole under one government. He was strongly opposed to the partition of Ireland in 1922. Like many, he saw the development of Canada and Australia as having relevance to Ireland. He founded the Irish Dominion League to keep the Irish Free State within the British Commonwealth, but Irish nationalists were intent on full independence.

He was a senator in the Irish Free State in 1922 and 1923, but republicans burned his house down and he left Ireland in some bitterness to pass the rest of his life in England, where he continued to promote the cooperative movement worldwide. In 1924 a major conference on agricultural cooperation in the British Empire was held in London, over which he presided. He visited South Africa in 1925, and in 1927 made a special study of the benefits of cooperation in India.

In 1919 Plunkett endowed a trust under his name which encouraged the development of agriculture through cooperation. He published other books, and to the end of his life was active in the causes to which he had devoted himself. He died in Weybridge, in Surrey, on March 26, 1932. He never married, but for much of his life retained a strong affection for Daisy Fingall, with whom many thought he was in love.

Though Plunkett's enthusiasm might not have endeared him to the rich graziers and strong farmers of Ireland, the country, as a whole, has done well due to cooperation. Some co-ops were tiny operations to begin with. In the early days, perhaps the most famous co-op was at Templecrone in Donegal, largely the creation of Patrick Gallagher. But since 1906, when that enterprise was founded, co-ops have grown into immense operations. Small farmers were able to sell their milk or pigs into the co-op facility, where they could take their share of the profits through a monthly or even weekly check. The co-op check became an essential feature of Irish rural life from the 1930s onwards. The driving force behind the enterprise would often be a local priest, though today the co-ops have almost disappeared.

The transformation of Ireland that Plunkett had hoped for has been achieved, and it brought just the social changes he had hoped for. Horace Plunkett was one of the great men whose services Ireland lost through the narrow and sectarian action of political extremists, but his vision has survived all opposition.

55

Sean O'Casey

1880–1964

Sean O'Casey is among the most famous Irish dramatists of any century, largely due to his set of plays about the Irish troubles. His life was a long and controversial one, and he affected life and literature in many other ways.

He was born in Dublin on March 30, 1880. His family had been upper-working class, but with the early death of the father, their social fortunes declined. As an infant, Sean developed trouble with his eyes, an affliction which was to haunt him all his life. The first volumes of his autobiographical series, *I Knock at the Door* and *Pictures in the Hallway*, describe these early years in vivid if often overcolored detail.

As a young man O'Casey combined hard manual work with omnivorous reading. Like so many working-class writers, he was largely self-educated. He delighted in all kinds of writers, from Shakespeare to Shaw. He was also an energetic churchman, involved in the parish of St. Barnabas. He was an early and enthusiastic member first of an Orange lodge, then of the Gaelic League, and finally he joined the IRB.

He was a follower of JAMES LARKIN [37] and was involved in the founding of the Irish Citizen Army (of which he wrote the first history), though he had broken with it before his comrades took part in the Easter Rising. His early reading of Marx and Engels had convinced him that their social analysis was correct, or at least true to his experience. For the rest of his life he remained a Communist, or at least a Communist supporter, if not a party member.

His ambitions as a writer were encouraged by Lady Gregory, and eventually, after several rejections, his first serious play, *The Shadow of a Gunman,* was produced to great success in 1923. This was followed by *Juno and the Paycock* (1924) and *The Plough and the Stars* (1926). If J. M. Synge had been a triumph of the Abbey Theatre's early years, O'Casey was the counterpart of its maturity. His plays were both critical and commercial successes.

He was now able to give up his life as a laborer, and moved, temporarily he thought, to London, where he married a young Irish actress in 1927. But that year his next play, *The Silver Tassie,* about the First World War and its aftermath, was rejected by W. B. YEATS [8] and the Abbey management, largely for ideological reasons. Nevertheless, the play had some success in London in 1928. It has been revived several times since, and is viewed by some as the necessary conclusion to the earlier trilogy, bringing the experience of another war, which half a million Irishmen shared in, home to Dublin.

O'Casey then vowed to stay out of Ireland, and never returned to Dublin. He wrote many other plays, and remained a controversial personality into his old age. These later works never achieved the stature or success of the early ones set during the years of revolution. The plays of the late 1930s received only lukewarm critical praise and were commercial failures. They were colored by a vigorous anticlericalism and an overheated political view.

However, for many of his admirers, his six-volume autobiography, which he began publishing in 1939, is a far greater work than his later plays. Having left Ireland, O'Casey cut himself off from his roots. His memory of a lost era in Dublin life sustained his creativity, and he was one of the most admired writers of the Irish literary revival, especially in America.

He and his young wife were settled in Devon with their three children, where he remained for the rest of his life. His new plays, such as *The Star Turns Red,* were produced by small companies; he was no longer a feature of the commercial theater. Two of his plays, *The Bishop's Bonfire* and *The Drums of Father Ned,* were produced in Dublin, and both caused delightful rows of a peculiarly Irish kind.

By now he was becoming of increasing interest to academic writers. With the completion of his autobiographical series in 1954 his reputation began to climb again. This was due in part to the appreciation of the autobiographies as works of art in their own right.

O'Casey remains a figure of controversy, yet there is no doubt that the story of his own life and his early plays had shaped a view of Irish life, in all its tragedy and comedy, which has come to be better known outside Ireland than its real history. When many think of Ireland's troubled past they think of it as Sean O'Casey showed it.

He died at St. Mary's Church, near Torquay, in Devon, on September 18, 1964. Whatever the final verdict of history will be, he will remain one of Ireland's, and the world's, greatest dramatists.

56

William Cosgrave

1880–1965

Though he had taken a large part in the Irish revolution, to W. T. Cosgrave fell the harder task of establishing the new Irish state in 1922. That modern Ireland is an open, stable democracy is largely as a result of his work and it remains his greatest memorial, whatever the claims of other figures such as MICHAEL COLLINS [3] and EAMON DE VALERA [2].

Born in 1874 in the shadow of the Guinness brewery on St. James Street, from his earliest years he was involved in nationalist activities. He was educated by the Christian Brothers, then a certain way of being introduced to the notion of Ireland's special destiny. His father, Thomas Cosgrave, had at one time been an elected town councilor and a poor-law guardian, these being the main posts of local government in Dublin.

W. T. Cosgrave entered the grocery trade as a lad and seemed set to follow that mundane vocation. But perhaps due to his education he was attracted to Sinn Fein, which after 1904 became the most attractive political group to the younger generation in Ireland. In 1913, that significant year, he won his own seat on the Dublin Corporation for Sinn Fein. From his business background he had a sound grasp of finance, and in 1916, another significant year, he was elected chairman of Sinn Fein's finance committee.

In 1913 he joined the Irish Volunteers, which had been formed that year. When the volunteers, who then numbered about one hundred thousand men, split in August 1914 over the issue of the First World War, he was one of the ten thousand who refused to follow the lead given by William Redmond. When the uprising was under way he was one of those who followed Pearse and Connolly, disobeying the order of Eoin MacNeill to stand down. Only 600 men, a very small fraction of the Volunteer movement, took part in the Easter Week rebellion. He was arrested after the uprising and interned at Frongoch in North Wales until July 1917, when most of the prisoners were released.

In 1917 Cosgrave was nominated to stand in the Sinn Fein interest in a by-election in Kilkenny. By now Sinn Fein had moved from its original nonviolent espousal of a dual monarchy for Ireland to being a republican party. In the December 1918 postwar election he was elected from Kilkenny County. He was a member of the first Dail that met in Dublin in January 1919 and declared the Irish republic. He was appointed minister for local government in the underground administration because of his own experience in that area.

During the troubles his main task was to coordinate the refusal of local authorities in Ireland to cooperate with the British authorities at Dublin Castle. All this time he was on the run, and was more than once imprisoned.

When the treaty was signed in December 1919, it split the movement again. In the Dail treaty debates, Cosgrave's speech was one of the very few that attracted widespread comment. In the government of Arthur Griffith and Michael Collins, he was once again minister of local government, now charged with easing the transition from the old administration to the new without a hitch.

In the summer of 1922, when tensions were building toward the outbreak of the civil war, Cosgrave was appointed Griffith's deputy while he was in London discussing the administration of the treaty. On August 12, 1922, Griffith suddenly died. In his place, Collins was chosen as president of the provisional government. Cosgrave was now acting chairman of the provisional government. Ten days later, Collins was also dead. These two strokes of ill fortune placed W. T. Cosgrave, the straightforward Dublin man of business, into the chief place in the government of the Irish Free State. Griffith had been a national figure since the turn of the century. Michael Collins was the adored hero of the masses. Cosgrave was almost unknown in comparison.

Troubled times need heros, but stable administration needs something else. When the government came together again, Cosgrave made it plain that what was now required to run the country was not the clash of personalities, but effective teamwork. There was a newly drafted constitution to be passed by the Dail, a military campaign to finish, the cost of the civil war—estimated at the then astonishing sum of £7 million—

as well as all the normal business of good government. Some of his cabinet, such as Kevin O'Higgins, were strong men in their own right, but Cosgrave held them all together. But more than that, he managed, through the appointment of Protestants and former unionists to the Senate, to bring the Protestant minority into the councils of the free state. The appointments to the civil service, the judiciary, and the Senate reflected merit rather than friendship, religion, or politics.

The civil war petered out and ended. In September 1923 Cosgrave was welcomed to the League of Nations as the representative of the Irish Free State, and the following month he attended a conference of the Dominions, those self-governing states, such as Canada, South Africa, and Australia, that formed what later became the British Commonwealth.

With the end of the fighting, order returned to Ireland and the task of rebuilding began. Finances were a pressing concern, and these were handled in a careful, even mean manner. But after the government had decided to keep the size of the military in line with peaceful conditions some army officers mutinied, and Cosgrave faced down what might have been a very serious threat to the new democracy from the military and the right wing. A few months later another minister took over his role without a fuss. Unlike Collins or de Valera, Cosgrave had no messianic ambitions, but his steady course and good sense won overseas admirers of the new state.

It was under Cosgrave that the great task of building the Shannon hydroelectric plant was begun. Though the taxes were high, the government spoke of free electricity in a decade, a promise it failed to keep.

Cosgrave's party in the Dail faced opposition only from the Labour party and some smaller groups. The main body of the real opposition, de Valera's party, and the other republicans, was outside the Dail. This was not a healthy situation and could not long continue. In August 1927 the minister of justice, Kevin O'Higgins, identified by many as the real strongman, was assassinated by a republican splinter group. Legislation was passed that forced anyone standing for election to take their seat if they won. This forced the hand of de Valera and Fianna Fail; they came in out of the cold. In October an election left Cosgrave's party the largest. But a coalition of other parties could now outvote the government. With the support of the Farmer's party he maintained a narrow majority.

In early 1928 Cosgrave paid a state visit to the United States, where he was received with great warmth not only by the Irish-American community, but also by President Calvin Coolidge. He addressed the Senate and then went on to visit Canada before returning in triumph to Ireland. He had achieved a recognized place for Ireland in the community of nations. It was his greatest moment.

In the election of 1932 de Valera gained a narrow majority, which he improved by quickly calling another election in 1933. Cosgrave, however, remained the leader of his party, but these were to be troubled days. His was by nature a conservative party, but it harbored within it a right wing that cast admiring glances at developments in Europe. A fascist group under General Eoin O'Duffy, popularly called the Blueshirts, came into existence out of the Army Comrades Association, an anti-republican group. There were street clashes between them and the republicans, by now a Communist-influenced group.

De Valera acted with decision to deal with these elements. Cosgrave split with O'Duffy, and something approaching normal politics was restored. Ireland had had a very close brush with fascism and communism, but thanks to the leadership of de Valera and Cosgrave, avoided disaster.

Cosgrave was still party leader when the war broke out in September 1939. He supported the measures of national unity, which the war entailed, until he retired from politics in 1945.

His son, Liam Cosgrave, was the leader of Fine Gael, the successor party to his father's. W. T. Cosgrave died in 1965, having lived to see the old divisions of the civil war effectively buried in the progress of the new Ireland. That nation owed him a debt which the perspective of history will only enhance. Though naturally cautious and careful, he carried his nation through a perilous period, succeeding where a lesser man, or a more headstrong personality, would have failed. For a quiet man, it was a great triumph.

57

John Hume

1937–

In 1998 John Hume, along with the Ulster unionist leader David Trimble, was awarded the Nobel Prize for Peace. Since 1969, during the long purgatory of the Northern Ireland troubles John Hume, as leader of the largely Catholic Social Democratic and Labour party (SDLP), has carried the burden of the majority of the nationalist community. He has tried to reach a permanent and just settlement in the face of unionist determination to retain the tie to Britain on the one hand, and the terrorism of the IRA and the demands of Sinn Fein for a united Ireland on the other. He has sought to achieve reform, reconciliation, and, eventually—very eventually—reunification. Hume has proved very important to the breaking of the mold into which history has cast the politics of Ireland as a whole.

John Hume is a Derryman, a native of a city that plays a large part in the imagined history of Northern Ireland. To Catholics, Derry means Doire, the monastery founded by the great ST. COLUMCILLE [58]. To unionists it is Londonderry, the brave city that closed its gates against the army of James II and resisted a long siege in the cause of William III. Though its people share a common soil, they live in different countries. Derry's politics have always been volatile, though it lacks the wealth of Belfast and was cut off by partition from its natural hinterland in Donegal.

John Hume was born on January 18, 1937, the son of Samuel Hume, of Derry. He was educated at St. Columb's College in Derry, and at St. Patrick's College in Maynooth, taking a master's degree from the National University of Ireland. He married Patricia Hone in 1960. They live in Derry, where they have reared a family of two sons and three daughters.

John Hume was of the first generation of Ulster people to benefit from free secondary and university education provided by the Education Act of 1944. He worked first as a teacher in Derry, but emerged into public life initially as a community leader, involved especially in the credit union movement, which was so important in working-class areas of Ireland, and served as president of the Credit Union League of Ireland from 1964 to 1968.

With these strong roots in the community, he was inevitably drawn into a full-time political career, being elected MP to the Northern Ireland parliament from Foyle in 1969. This was the year that the present troubles began, though for nationalists there had been troubles as far back as the 1880s. When Stormont was dissolved by direct rule from London, Hume was elected to the British Parliament from Londonderry, now Foyle. He was minister of commerce in the short-lived power-sharing executive of 1974. He has also been a member of the European Parliament since 1979.

Hume was a founding member of the Social and Democratic Labour party, serving as its deputy leader from 1970 to 1979. He was elected leader in 1979, and since then has played a central and increasingly influential role in the resolution of the Ulster problem. The party was intended to provide Ulster politics with a new beginning. The old nationalist party was hopelessly out of touch with the new situation, and the resurgence of Sinn Fein posed as much of a threat to Catholics as to unionists. The SDLP was intended to provide a party which was social democratic, would cross community boundaries, and provide a common party for the working-class voters of all traditions.

Inevitably, however, it developed as a largely Catholic party due to the nature of community politics in Northern Ireland. But the party has never lost its initial aspiration, and remains involved in the worldwide social democratic movement. John Hume himself served on the bureau of the socialist group in the European Parliament—the largest political grouping in that body.

But the European dimension that has affected the lives of all Europeans could not eradicate overnight the long and tangled history of Hume's homeland. That is where John Hume's real purpose in life was to be. The settlement in Northern Ireland, reached on Good Friday 1998, was owed largely to his patience in drawing Sinn Fein and the IRA into a more conventional form of politics.

Ireland has now moved on. The Good Friday Agreement, representing the first time since 1918 that the whole island voted together on one issue, has hopefully provided a new way ahead. The claims to a mandate by the IRA and the other terrorists groups have been shown to be empty. A new way of dealing with the relations between the communities in the north, and the governments, north and south, east and west, may be developing. Despite many setbacks, the Northern Ireland Assembly, the best hope for peace in Ireland, has proved workable. Arms decommissioning by tenants groups may still be achieved, as the majority hope.

If this is so, Ireland as a whole owes John Hume an unrepayable debt. He and his party have brought about a sea change, but as is ever the case, the future is not always in the hands of good men. In the autumn of 2001 ill health finally took its toll, and John Hume resigned the leadership of his party, which passed to a younger man. Northern Ireland remains among the troubled places of the world.

58

St. Columcille
521–597

Along with St. Patrick [1] and St. Bridget, Columcille (also known as Columba of Iona) is one of the three patrons of Ireland, whose life's work was critical in the formation of early Christian Ireland. The year of his death coincided with the arrival of the mission of St. Augustine, in Kent.

The two aspects of Western Christianity, the Celtic and the Continental, clashed for many decades until the Synod of Whitby extinguished the Celtic customs. But the mission of Augustine was largely a failure. The long Christian tradition of Scotland and England owes much more to the determination and courage of Irish missionaries such as Columcille than is often realized.

He was born at Gartan in Donegal on December 7, 521, of aristocratic stock, being one of the clan of Conall, and an O'Donnell, who were the princes of Donegal. He was educated at the monastic centers of Moville by St. Finnian; at Clonard, where he was a pupil of another and greater St. Finnian; and later at Glasnevin, in Dublin. In 544 a plague forced his return to Ulster.

He was ordained a priest in 541, and established his own monastery at Derry in 545. He spent some fifteen years founding monasteries throughout Ireland, at Derry (545), Swords (circa 550), Durrow (about 553), and at Kells (about 554).

He was accused of being responsible for the bloody battle of Culdrevy in 561 between his own people, the Dalriada Scots, and King Diarmid, the overlord of eastern Ireland. Taking his doubts to his own confessor, he was given the penance of going into Scotland to spread the gospel there.

In 563 St. Columcille went into exile with twelve followers as a missionary among the pagan Picts of Scotland. The Irish had already carved out a kingdom along the western coast of Scotland. (At this time the Irish were called Scots.) He established a monastery on the island of Iona in Argyll, which was presented to him by his kinsman Conall. From there he and other missionaries set out to spread the faith among the Picts of northern Scotland. These journeys are described by his early biographer, Adomnán. (On one of them he became the first person reported to have encountered the Loch Ness monster.)

The important result of this mission was not just to convert the Picts to Christianity, but to provide the ground on which the Scots and Picts could unite, and so create the nucleus of the modern kingdom of Scotland. He revisited Ireland itself on only two occasions, and (according to legend) acted as a mediator at the convention of Druim-Cetta in 575. He was the supposed author of poems in Latin and in Gaelic. The oldest surviving manuscript of the Gallican Psalter, the so-called *Cathac,* is said to be in his own hand. The record of his life by Adomnán gives a good account of the rule he established, and this too was also widely influential in the church.

His ascetic way of life often led to him withdrawing from his companions and into the woods to pray and fast. He impressed everyone with his holiness.

Among some Protestant writers, the independence of the Celtic church has been overemphasized, while its essential loyalty to Rome was overplayed by Catholic writers. In many ways, the atmosphere of this church was similar to the Ethiopian church; both worked beyond the bounds of the old Roman Empire among pagan tribes and out of direct communication with more metropolitan centers.

Iona was also a scholarly center. The Celtic church, however, developed its own extraordinary culture, especially in illuminated books, many of them produced by the monasteries with which Columcille was associated. A key figure in the development of Scotland, he was thus a seminal person in the development of Western European civilization. As Toynbee and other historians have pointed out, these monks were an essential link in the transmission of the older classical cultures of Greece and Rome, through their revival during the Middle Ages, following the Dark Ages, which fell upon most of the continent after the barbarian invasions.

According to an old tradition, Columcille died while kneeling before the altar of his own church on Iona in 597. He was buried on the island, but his remains were later removed to Kells in Meath, and some to Dunkeld. The famous Stone of Scone, on which the ancient kings of Scotland, and later the kings of England, were crowned is thought by some to actually be the pillow of St. Columcille.

The anniversary of his death in 1997 was the occasion of pilgrimages from all over the Britain and Ireland to Iona. As Scotland prepares to reestablish its own parliament once again, it is now appreciated that Columcille's mission marks the beginning of the history of Scotland and the Scottish people.

59

John Scotus Eriugena

c. 810–877

The first Irish philosopher to attain universal fame, John Scotus Eriugena was a figure of controversy. He was, as John O'Meara pointed out, "the most considerable philosopher in the Western world between Augustine and Thomas Aquinas and the greatest Irish philosopher (with the possible exception of Berkeley) ever."

John Scotus Eriugena (not to be confused with Duns Scotus, as he often is) introduced a radically new view of the universe, anticipating Copernicus by six hundred years; and of Heaven and Hell. Despite this eminence, Ireland has taken little interest in a man, of whom another scholar wrote, was in the eyes of some merely a boozy Irish monk given to sitting up and talking through the night.

The date of his birth and his family background are unknown, though it seems certain that he was born in Ireland (for that is what the name Eriugena means), and that his formidable learning, which included Greek and philosophy, was gained there.

The year 847 found him in the Paris court of the West Frankish king Charles the Bald, where he was in charge of the palace school. But he had been trained as a theologian, so he also took part in the learned disputes arising from the doctrines of Gottschalk, a monk from Soissons, who had become indoctrinated with an heretical view of predestination and died in prison in 868. There is, however, no real evidence that Eriugena was himself either a priest or a monk.

He wrote a treatise, *De Praedestione*, which was condemned by the Council of Alence in 855; his ideas were called *pultes scotorum*,

"Irish porridge." At the request of Charles the Bald, he translated the works of Pseudo-Dionysius the Areopagite into Latin; afterward, these were to have a tremendous influence on the future development of medieval thought.

Eriugena's own chief work was called *De Divisione Naturae,* which was condemned by Pope Honorius III in 1225. As late as 1658 it was seen as a danger to faith and morals, and was placed on the index of prohibited books by the Catholic church. He was not a scientist in the modern sense of the word—he did not make measurements or conduct experiments—but was more what the eighteenth century might have called a natural philosopher.

In his system Eriugena placed the sun at the center of the universe at a time when others believed (with Ptolemy) that the earth was at the center. He came to the conclusion that God and Heaven did not need to be physically above the stars, as was commonly conceived, nor was Hell located underground (as Dante was to imagine). For these radical ideas Eriugena was accused by another theologian of being a pantheist—of identifying God with the material world. But he was not in fact a pantheist. As a rational person, he thought with firm logic and dismissed many superstitions. On the evidence of Eriugena and his learning, the Dark Ages, so called, were not really quite so dark after all.

After Charles the Bald died in 877, Eriugena was forced to leave France, suspected of being a heretic. Some scholars assert he never left Europe and died there that same year. But an early tradition asserts that he was called into England by Alfred the Great and was made abbot of Malmesbury. Having lived by the pen he died by it, for he was put to death by his students—a fate wished upon many teachers, one suspects. They stabbed him to death with their writing implements.

Yet Eriugena's theories, neglected for so long, now appear to modern scholars fresh and newly relevant.

60

Fr. Charles Coughlin

1891–1979

In a world seemingly dominated by television, it can be forgotten what a powerful force radio once was in the United States—and still is in other parts of the world. As the Canadian media guru Marshall McLuhan observed, it is a hot medium, ideal for the broadcasting of powerful nationalistic or political messages, and it remains much favored by demagogues of the third world.

One of the earliest exponents of the power of radio was Fr. Charles Edward Coughlin, "the Radio Priest" whose views dominated the public affairs of America in the days of the New Deal. To a modern medium he brought the enthusiasm and passion of his Irish ancestors.

He was born in Canada, in Hamilton, Ontario. His father, Thomas J. Coughlin, was a sailor on the Great Lakes waterways and also a church sexton. Thomas Coughlin was a U.S. citizen, while Mrs. Coughlin, Amelia Mahony by birth, was a Canadian.

The Irish-Catholic culture was strong in Canada, and Coughlin was reared in a very traditional way. He was sent first to St. Mary's Elementary School in Hamilton, and then to St. Michael's High School in Toronto. His best subjects were math and athletics. He went on to St. Michael's College, where he played rugby—too often seen as an upperclass sport—and made a name for himself as a speaker.

His religious upbringing prompted a vocation for the priesthood, and in 1911 he entered the novitiate for the Basilian order who ran St. Michael's. He was ordained in 1916—the year of the Easter Rising—and sent to work at Assumption College in Windsor, Ontario. Though his productions of Shakespeare were popular, he also taught English, psychology (from a Catholic point of view, a new, and potentially dangerous subject), and logic.

Though Canadian, Windsor is near enough to Detroit to be heavily influenced by the culture of the United States. When the Canadian Basilians separated from their French parent order, Coughlin became a priest under the rule of the archbishop of Detroit. Like all the northern industrial cities, Detroit had a significant Irish population. Fr. Coughlin worked in the parish church of St. Leo's, where his outspoken sermons became popular. The local bishop, Dr. Michael Gallagher, selected him to establish a new parish in the suburbs of Royal Oak.

Though the Irish might have been well represented in the cities of Michigan, in the country it was different. Fr. Coughlin was welcomed into Royal Oak by the local Ku Klux Klan burning a fiery cross on the presbytery lawn. Aside from this Protestant intolerance, typical of attitudes toward Irish Catholics at the time, there were few actual parishioners.

For the masses, radio, literally broadcasting, was new. The British Broadcasting Corporation had been established in 1922, and commercial radio was only getting under way in America. In the northern cities many people were of European origin, and though they spoke and understood English they could not read it. Coughlin hoped to reach them through radio. On October 17, 1926, he made his first broadcast over WJR, the Detroit station. He was an immediate hit, and soon his on-the-air sermons were being relayed to many other stations. At first his message was purely a religious one, and he talked about the gospel message of Christ's life and told simple parables extolling traditional Christian values. It was a very typical God-spot routine, as broadcasters of today would call it.

But the times were changing. In 1930 he began to attack bolshevism and socialism, which were making their way through the immigrant communities of the United States. From this external threat of the new, godless philosophies, he moved on in 1931 to attack President Herbert Hoover for his failures to counter the rising unemployment of the Great Depression that was now sweeping the United States. In Europe, the economic downturn was a fertile ground for the rise of Communist and Fascist parties.

The message proved a popular one. Fr. Coughlin received over a million letters from listeners supporting his views. He had touched a nerve, and though to some the departure of a priest into the hurly-burly of politics seemed improper, his radio "sermons" from then on dealt with political, social, and economic matters.

To his critics, he could point to the church's own concern with these matters, through the teachings outlined in *Rerum Novarum* (New Things), the famous and forceful papal encyclical of Leo XIII. The church's social program, and its care for the needs and legitimate aspirations of workers, was based on this document. The pope had emphasized the duties of the capitalists to the workers whose labors created their fortunes. This was not always a popular message, and Coughlin went further. His enemies were the international bankers, those scapegoats of so many radicals and reformers between the wars. By manipulating capital and credit they were controlling the world. Real power lay not with the citizen, but with the shadowy men behind board-room doors.

Coughlin had used contributions from those millions of listeners to build a church in Royal Oak, Michigan, called the Shrine of the Little Flower—the cult of St. Thérèse of Lisieux was then a popular one. He broadcast on Sunday afternoons, the radio signals going out from a high granite crucifixion tower beside the church.

These colorful activities made good copy. Soon newspapers and magazines were running stories about the Radio Priest and his views. The first edition of his complete radio sermons became a mammoth bestseller, selling a million copies in 1933. By the following year he was getting ten thousand letters a day, many with contributions in cash. He had four secretaries and a staff of over a hundred. The simple sermons had become big business, and with size came influence.

Personally, Coughlin was a charming and convivial person. He had that special confidence of the born preacher and exuded a certainty that he had all the answers for an increasingly worried nation. He was also a broadcasting genius; his firm voice with the slight Irish intonation was said to be "without doubt one of the great speaking voices of the twentieth century."

In 1932 he had become an active supporter of Franklin D. Roosevelt. His support, he thought, had been partially responsible for bringing FDR to the White House—a large claim. He insisted that "the new deal is Christ's deal," and it was "Roosevelt or ruin." But the wise president kept his distance from this overzealous support.

The Columbia Broadcasting System, of which the Detroit station was an affiliate, had already asked Fr. Coughlin to calm his rhetoric. In the course of a broadcast in January 1931 he exposed their efforts to "censor" him, and the network bosses were deluged with letters in support of Coughlin. The priest now felt he could say what he wanted, with no regard to the church or capitalism. CBS cancelled his contract.

Coughlin was unfazed. He put together a network of forty stations, crossing the continent from Maine to California. His sermons, if they could still be called that, were heard at times by the largest radio audiences in the world, sometimes as many as forty million people. He was the father of the radio and television evangelists which are now such a feature of broadcasting in North America and elsewhere.

FDR was conscious, as all presidents must be, of the Irish-American and Catholic vote. Coughlin's own solution to the Great Depression was to put more money into circulation, and he claimed that FDR was planning to do this. Such inflation would have been ruinous; it had undermined democracy in Germany, and many felt it could do the same in America. This was not to be the policy of the New Deal, and Coughlin began to call for the nationalization of credit, money, and the Federal Reserve.

From broadcasting, Coughlin's ambitions moved to actual politics. In 1934 he founded the National Union for Social Justice. This was not claimed to be a political party, but a movement to protect the rights of the workers. It ran a newspaper, *Social Justice,* to carry its message. Its one victory was a campaign to prevent the United States from joining the World Court, which he saw as undermining national sovereignty. Though its membership rose to five million, it never again achieved the same impact as it had at its beginning.

Now anti-Roosevelt, Coughlin established the Union party to fight in the election of 1936. But third parties never do well in the United States, and their candidate polled only a million votes, even though it had drawn together the fragments of other political movements on the radical right.

Failure left Coughlin undaunted. He only moved further to the extreme right. He reprinted the bogus "Protocols of the Learned Elders of Zion" in his paper, and accused the Jews and international Jewish financiers—those bogeymen of the right and left—of being responsible for America's problems. Here he had the sympathies of some, like Henry Ford, who should have known better. He said the Jews were behind communism and began to defend the Nazis.

Some of his sentiments were shared widely in society, both in the United States and in Ireland. In August 1938 he organized the Christian Front as an anti-Communist movement, but his young supporters spent their time attacking Jews. Though he might defend this, using the example of Christ and the moneychangers in the temple, it was bringing the street politics of Europe into America. His enemies now confronted him.

At last, in 1940, his broadcasts were largely eliminated by the National Association of Broadcasters. Never again would a demagogue have free access to the airwaves of the United States in the unrestricted and unregulated way that Coughlin had had in the 1930s.

Pearl Harbor and the entry of the United States into the war brought his career to an end. He was silenced by his bishop in May 1942, and his papers were banned from the U.S. mail. He remained the parish priest at the Shrine of the Little Flower until he was forced to retire in 1966, and then lived privately in Birmingham, Michigan, until his death on October 27, 1979.

He was, notes Francis R. Burns, "undoubtedly one of the most powerful figures outside the government during the Depression era." The influence he exerted over the American people was powerful and immediate, but in the end the institutions of both church and state were stronger than the voice of a demagogue. At one time he was the most influential Irishman in the world, but in the end the will of the people prevailed.

61

Ian Paisley

1926–

Since the middle of the 1960s, the bulky figure of Ian Kyle Paisley has dominated the politics of Northern Ireland, causing concern in both Britain and America, as his fiery rhetoric has contributed to the dangerous situation there. But Paisley's opinions are not now his alone. He represents the culmination of a long tradition of Presbyterian independence, and his religious views are widely shared all over the world.

He was born in Armagh on April 6, 1926, the son of the Rev. J. Kyle Paisley, a Baptist minister who had been a member of Carson's Ulster Volunteers in 1912. But as his name suggests his cultural connections are with Scotland and the United Kingdom. It is these connections he has worked much of his life to maintain.

When he was two his family moved to Ballymena, where he was reared on the vivid prose and sensational illustrations of *Foxe's Book of Martyrs*. He was educated at Ballymena Model School, Ballymena Technical High School, and the South Wales Bible College in the Rhondda Valley. His further studies were at the Reformed Presbyterian Theological Hall in Belfast, though his honorary doctorate in divinity came from the Bob Jones University in America, in 1966.

He was ordained a minister of the Free Presbyterian Church in 1946, and was elected its moderator in 1951. Since 1946, his own ministry has been at the Martyrs Memorial Free Presbyterian Church at Ravenhill in Belfast, which he erected. He is also a director of the *Protestant Telegraph* (founded in 1966), a newspaper which expounds his views, and president of the Whitefield College of the Bible. He is married to Eileen Emily Cassells, and has twin sons and three daughters (one of whom, Rhonda, has written a warmly affectionate account of him as a family man).

As befits his public life, Paisley is interested in history (who in Ireland is not?), and in collecting antiquarian books, especially of religious interest. "One of the worst contributions that the other media have made is take people away from the art, the pleasure, and the gain of literature," he told his daughter. He is also, surprisingly, a fellow of the Royal Geographical Society—as a boy he had ambitions to be a sea captain. He is a humorous and jovial man—though not all his fellow citizens would appreciate calling his pet collie "Bishop."

His political career only started in the mid-1950s in answer to, he claimed, "the call of the people." He founded the Ulster Protestant Volunteers—harking back in title to the heady days of Ulster revolt before the First World War in the summer of 1914. He was imprisoned twice for his street politics, once in 1966 and again in 1969. This activity was all before the present renewed IRA campaign. His street corner speeches were one of the factors that contributed the real sense of fear felt by besieged Catholic communities in Belfast and Derry, and to which the Provisional IRA was an initial response.

In due course Paisley was elected to the Stormont, as the Northern Ireland assembly was called, and campaigned for the assembly to be restored after it was suspended by the British government following the imposition of direct rule on the troubled province by Westminster, in 1972. He was elected to the United Kingdom Parliament in 1970 as the MP for North Antrim, a largely rural and agricultural area with strong conservative traditions.

His original political vehicle had been the Protestant Unionist party, but in 1971 he and other leaders came together to create the Ulster Democratic Unionist party, which he still leads today (1999). He was reelected as a member of the European Parliament in 1979, a post he still retains. He is the highest polling politician in Northern Ireland, but in the fractured politics of Ulster, he still represents a minority view. Among his own constituency, he wins over 50 percent of the votes.

He made a symbolic resignation from his North Antrim seat in 1985 as a protest over the Anglo-Irish Agreement, which has been the basis for what political progress Ulster has made. He saw the agreement as a step toward a united Ireland, which allowed the government of Ireland a say in the affairs of a portion of the United Kingdom. In reality, the government and people of Ireland no longer have ambitions for a united Ireland; what they want is peace, and they are fearful that the turmoil of Northern Ireland could be imported into the south. However, the government of Ireland is bound to give support to the nationalists in the north. Paisley was reelected to the seat in 1986. Talks on the future of Northern Ireland proved inconclusive in 1991, but since then, largely through the work of many others, the affairs have moved on to the Good Friday Agreement of 1998. But Ian Paisley remains firmly committed to the maintenance of the union, so the road ahead will still be rocky.

As a local MP, Ian Paisley has a good reputation, and in Westminster, he works hard to obtain all that he can for his own constituents, and for Ulster in the councils of Europe. In this area he does not regard people's religion. Nevertheless, belonging as he does to the extreme wing of Presbyterianism, he still believes that Roman Catholics are damned to perdition, that the pope in Rome is the anti-Christ spoken of by St. John the Divine, and that only through the retention of the union can the Protestant faith of Ulster be retained. For him, personal and religious freedom are intertwined.

For Ian Paisley, salvation is a gift, and only Christ can mediate between God and man. This places him in opposition not only to the majority of Irish people, but to the majority in Britain. Nevertheless, his views are those espoused by many millions across the United States. Just as Irish nationalism has found rooted support in the cities of the north, so Ian Paisley finds support in parts of Canada and all across the southern states.

Though presented as an ogre by the media, to many who meet him or hear him preach he expresses the fundamental truth. He has carried into his politics the sense of personal witness he feels in his religion. That courage has made him one of the most powerfully influential men in Irish history.

62

Bernardo O'Higgins

1778–1842

The apostle of Latin American independence was the natural son of Irish-born Ambrose O'Higgins, who was governor of Chile and viceroy of Peru. Ambrose had been born near Dangan Castle, in County Meath, in 1720. He was sent to Cadiz, Spain, to be educated by a Jesuit uncle. However, he found he had no vocation for the church, and went to South America. Landing in Buenos Aires, he later went on to Lima, Peru. He first worked as a peddler, then as a road contractor. He eventually joined the army and rose to the rank of brigadier general. In 1786 he was made intendant of Concepción, and was enobled. He was governor general of Chile and later was made viceroy of Peru, a country he defended against the British during the war of 1797. But he died suddenly in Lima on March 18, 1801.

Bernardo's mother was Chilean, and he was born at Chillán, on August 20, 1778. When he was fifteen he was sent to Europe to complete his education. For three years he lived in Richmond, outside London, attending a Catholic school. There he met Francisco de Miranda and other Latin American revolutionaries. He joined a Masonic secret society dedicated to undermining the rule of Spain and the Catholic church in Latin America. In 1802 on inheriting his father's estate, he returned to Chile, becoming mayor of Chillán. He also remained deeply involved in the plots against Spain. Their opportunity came in 1808, when Napoleon invaded Spain and overthrew the royal house. In September 1810 the revolution began, and the National Congress of Chile was called in April 1811.

O'Higgins and his reformist ideas stood out, while the Chilean patriots ineffectually argued among themselves. In September 1812, José Miguel Carrera declared himself dictator. O'Higgins became a member of the junta, but resigned to care for his farms. Though the revolutionaries had been inspired by the American example, their revolution was taking a different course. At this time O'Higgins was ill, and was planning to leave Chile when the Spanish imperial forces arrived in 1813. Faced with this new danger, he returned to public life.

He was given the rank of colonel and fought at San Carlos, Chillán, and El Roble. His battlecry, which urged on his troops, was "Let us live in honor or die in glory." He was promoted to army commander, but had to come to terms with the Spaniards in May 1814. However, the agreement was accepted by the viceroy in Peru, and the government that made it was overthrown by Carrera. The war went on, and O'Higgins, though he disapproved of the coup, joined Carrera. The Chileans were defeated at Rancagua in September 1814. In the first days of October, O'Higgins's escape from the town square, by opening a path through the barricades with the help of some soldiers, was a moment of epic heroism in his life.

O'Higgins fled to Argentina, where the government gave him a command in an army which San Martin was organizing to cross the Andes, invade Chile, and defeat the Spanish. The campaign went ahead and the Andes were traversed. On February 12, 1817, the Spanish were defeated at the battle of Chacabuco. Soon afterward the capital was seized and O'Higgins was proclaimed dictator of Chile.

A further victory by the patriots at Maipo, in April 1818, secured Chilean freedom. In 1820 O'Higgins began to organize a naval expedition to attack Peru, but the campaign did not go well. He promulgated two political constitutions, intended to reinforce his position. O'Higgins lost support, largely because he had lost the confidence of the conservative elements in Chilean society, though he gave ample evidence of his abilities as an administrator. He attempted to inaugurate land reforms, educational advances, and restrictions on gambling and bullfighting. These seemed to threaten the landed class and the macho style of Latin American life. Distrust of his liberal policy led to revolution in Chile in 1822. Early in 1823 O'Higgins was forced into exile in Peru, where he lived until his death in Lima on October 24, 1842. His ashes were brought back by the Chilean government and interred with state ceremonies in 1869, and in 1872 an equestrian statue of O'Higgins was dedicated in Santiago. (Bernardo's son, Demetrio O'Higgins, a rich estate owner, died in 1869.)

O'Higgins is representative of the many Irish people who lived and worked in Latin America, some in the days of the Spanish Empire, others in more recent centuries. Like O'Higgins, these people brought to their new countries a love of freedom and courage. Having often left Ireland and great hardship, they sought to build a new life in a new continent. Yet their experiences were not as happy as in the United States or Australia, and Irishmen were always to be found among the small vanguard that kept liberal ideas of freedom alive in the republics of the south. Their pervasive influence was, and is, of great importance.

63

Bob Geldof

1954–

Though he first made his name in the field of music, Bob Geldof was nominated for the Nobel Peace Prize for an extraordinary feat of organization which both astonished and delighted the world.

Though Geldof himself seems essentially Irish in his outlook and attitudes, his grandfather was a Flemish pastry cook who ended up in Dublin. He was born in middle-class Dublin. His mother died when he was only seven, leaving his rearing largely to an older sister. His father was a businessman, which meant they were at least well off.

He was educated at fashionable and elite Blackrock College, where he did not, he thought, do well. Youthful rebelliousness took him away from home to England and then to Canada. He took a series of jobs, as a truck driver, factory hand, street entertainer, and English language teacher. He also did a stint as a pop music journalist on a newspaper in British Columbia called the *Georgia Strait*.

However, his break came when in 1975 he returned to Dublin to start his own free community paper in the city, and with others set up a rock group called the Boomtown Rats, of which he was the lead singer. Their main gimmick, aside from their songs, was to release live rats fed on liver from the stage into the crowd. The band quickly achieved a certain local fame in their native city, due in part to Geldof's own personality and flair for publicity.

In March 1977 they went to London, where they were signed by a record company. They had two important hits, "Rat Trap" in 1978 and "I Don't Like Mondays" in 1979. The early albums also sold well, but the band depended on Geldof, whose range was never wide, and the band began to fade in the early 1980s. This was due largely to Geldof's own attitude to the music business, which he saw with refreshing cynicism. In San Diego, in 1979, when they were playing a showcase gig that would have launched them onto U.S. television and radio, he urged the crowd of youngsters to boo and heckle the radio company bosses sitting in the balcony. The albums, not unnaturally, had their playtime cancelled. This penchant for speaking his mind made him many enemies, though many others found him friendly, frank, and engaging.

Geldof returned to London. In October 1984 reports of the famine in Ethiopia appeared on British television; indeed, they were said to have contributed to the overthrow of the Emperor Haile Selassie and the installation of the Communist regime, which was equally unable to cope with an increasingly dire situation. Children and adults were shown dying of starvation on the nightly news. Many were affected, but Geldof decided something must be done.

He organized his friends in the music business, and to aid Ethiopia they recorded and issued a single called "Do They Know It's Christmas?" The group was called Band-Aid, and that season the song became the biggest-selling single in British history, making over £8 million for the appeal.

This was success enough, but Geldof was on a roll. He now pulled in even more favors and from his base in London organized the Live Aid Concert, held simultaneously in both London and Philadelphia on July 13, 1985. The show was a huge success, and was broadcast live around the world to an audience said to have numbered more than one and a half billion viewers. It raised some £50 million, and a further effort in 1986 called Sport Aid raised yet another £50 million. Geldof was chairman of the Ethiopian appeal, and for some years was actively involved in the distribution of the monies raised. It was recognized that this achievement was due very largely to Bob Geldof's nerve and determination. Whatever he had not been taught at school, he had been taught not to turn back.

In 1986 he published his autobiography, *Is That It?*, which became a bestseller in Europe and America. By now, however, his own musical career was dead. His talent and drive were harnessed to various projects and companies in television. A relationship with the entertainer Paula Yates ended in separation, and was later followed by her tragic death.

Heroes in the past had often been held up as being all of a piece, people of exemplary virtue in every way. Geldof showed this was not the case. He remained his snarky and abrasive self, despite receiving an honorary knighthood from the queen of England in July 1986.

Yet he had shown what could be done on an universal scale to aid those unfortunate victims with which the modern world is filled. No one expected him to become a saint, and he didn't. His personal life has been fraught with disasters and disappointments, particularly the death of his former wife Paula Yates. In the autumn of 2001 he released a new album, *Sex, Age and Death*—his creativity had at last encompassed after eight years, his continuing experience of the human condition. But he had given an example of what could be done with enthusiasm and passion when the right man met the right cause. He had found that rock 'n' roll was not enough—even rock stars have to grow up.

For anyone reared in Ireland, famine has a special meaning. From the grim days of the Great Famine in the 1840s the Irish have been inspired when they can help the less fortunate through development aid and missionary work. The efforts of Bob Geldof carried this national aspiration through the most spectacular ultimate achievement. For a few days he enabled the whole world to feel as one.

64

Archbishop James Ussher

1581–1656

Though his name may not be widely known today, James Ussher, the Church of Ireland archbishop of Armagh in the early seventeenth century, is among the most influential men who ever existed. For millions of Bible Christians, he is the one who settled the date of the creation of the world, which they find printed in the margins of their King James translation of the sacred scriptures.

Though most people today accept that the world is many millions of years old, for those who hold a literal, fundamental view of the Bible, the date of 4004 B.C., which he put forward, is not to be gainsaid.

James Ussher was born in the parish of St. Nicholas, in the city of Dublin, on January 4, 1581, a generation after the Reformation had begun. From an early age his education was keenly Protestant. He was sent to a school which had been set up in the city by two political agents of James VI of Scotland, the heir apparent to the English throne. His education continued at Trinity College, then an almost new establishment, which had been founded with the blessing of Queen Elizabeth I by his uncle Henry Ussher, archbishop of Armagh. He entered the college at the age of thirteen.

He was admitted as a fellow of Trinity in 1599, earning his master's degree in 1600, and was ordained both a deacon and Anglican priest in 1601. In 1607 he was given his bachelor in divinity. He was chancellor of St. Patrick's Cathedral and rector of Finglas, just outside the city. In 1607 he was also appointed regius professor of divinity at Trinity, and received his doctorate in 1614.

His education had filled him with enthusiasm for the Reformation, and he began an extended and intensive study of the Scriptures and the Fathers of the Church (such early scholars as St. Augustine and St. Jerome) in order to defend its positions. In 1613, his first publication, though not his first composition, was a history of the church between sixth and thirteenth centuries.

He was vice chancellor of Trinity in 1614 and 1617. During a two-year period in London he was presented to King James (now monarch of England as well as Scotland), was appointed bishop of Meath, and preached before the House of Commons at Westminster. In 1625 the king transferred him to Armagh as archbishop and primate of all Ireland.

Ussher was bitterly opposed to Catholicism. In 1626 he prevented the viceroy from granting Catholics partial relief from the penal laws. He objected to the use of Gaelic in the services of the established church, which was being promoted by William Bedell, who had made the first Gaelic translation of the Bible to be printed. He was largely responsible for the Calvinistic canons drawn up for the Church of Ireland in 1634, though these were never accepted. But he was also opposed to efforts to make the Church of Ireland conform in all points of teaching with the Church of England, which he felt was still tainted with Catholic ideas. He was perhaps largely responsible for the austere outlook of the Church of Ireland, which was faced with a largely Catholic population in Ireland.

He had a European reputation as a scholar and Protestant theologian. He made many trips to England, searching out books to build up the library at the new Dublin university. He was on friendly terms with such scholars as Sir Thomas Bodley, Sir Robert Cotton, and the antiquarian William Camden. While Ussher was in England on a scholarly research trip the Great Rebellion broke out. This was in 1641, and Ussher never returned to Ireland again. During the rebellion he lost his house and property in the city of Armagh. He had pleaded with Charles I not to abandon Strafford, but in vain. He remained in England, and to compensate him for the loss of Armagh, he was given the monies from the vacant See of Carlisle. He refused a seat in the Assembly of Divines at Westminster in 1643 and never held office again, but spent his time preaching and writing.

During the civil war he left Oxford and sought refuge in Wales. He returned to London in 1645, and in 1647 he was appointed preacher to the lawyers at Lincoln's Inn. In 1648 he discussed the question of the episcopacy with Charles I on the Isle of Wight, but the following year he witnessed the execution of the king at Whitehall.

His greatest scholarly achievement was his work on the epistles of St. Ignatius of Antioch. In 1644 he edited an authentic text of the seven genuine surviving letters, eliminating the spurious ones and later interpolations.

By temper, Ussher was a Calvinist. As a young man, his association with Walter Travers, the provost of Trinity, had given him a Puritan sympathy with their position against the Anglicans. His work *Reduction of Episcopacy* was written as a conciliatory attempt to prevent the outbreak of the civil war when tensions increased in both England and Ireland. It proposed scheme by which the Anglican and Presbyterian traditions could be united into an established church throughout the British Isles. Only after his death, however, was it published.

His works were eventually collected by the Irish scholars C. E. Elrington and James H. Todd (between 1847 and 1864). The most influential of these was his *Annales Veteris et Novi Testamenti,* published in two volumes in Dublin between 1650 and 1654.

His lengthy studies gave rise to this famous chronology of the Bible, which placed the creation of the world in 4004 B.C. by calculating the lives of the patriarchs as given in the texts. The chronology he proposed was shortly afterward inserted into the margins of the authorized King James Bible, though by what authority is not known. Later it was even included in some editions of the Catholic Douay Bible, an indication of how wide its acceptance was.

As A. D. White comments in the *History of the Warfare of Science With Theology in Christendom,* it was "soon practically regarded as equally inspired with the sacred text itself." (In a less famous work published in 1642, Dr. John Lightfoot of Cambridge suggested that "man was created by the Trinity on October 23, 4004 B.C. at nine o'clock in the evening.") This chronology was widely accepted and could be found in many influential books, such as Joseph Haydn's *Dictionary of Dates,* well into the nineteenth century. Though historical and geological research during the nineteenth century completely undermined his chronology, it is still widely accepted by many Protestants.

Ussher died at Lady Peterborough's house at Reigate in Surrey, and was buried in Westminster Abbey by order of Oliver Cromwell. His personal library, amounting to some ten thousand volumes, among which were many manuscripts in Gaelic and Oriental languages, was purchased by the state and eventually donated to Trinity College in Dublin. But his real memorial may be in the millions who still follow his chronology and accept his date for the creation of the world unhesitatingly.

65

Patrick Sarsfield

c. 1655–1693

Patrick Sarsfield, earl of Lucan, is one of Ireland's legendary military heroes, whose name was constantly evoked by patriots of the nineteenth and twentieth centuries. He was brave and dashing at a time when war seemed a calling still fit for gentlemen.

He was born, it is thought, about 1655, at Lucan, where his family had an ancient castle (now replaced by a mansion built in 1772). He was the second son of Sir Patrick Sarsfield, by Anne, daughter of Rory O'Moore, the leader of the Catholic confederacy in 1641. The estate had been confiscated under Cromwell, but was restored to the Sarsfields in the 1670s.

His early life is obscure, but he followed a military career from an early age, being educated at a French military academy. In 1675, following the death of his elder brother, he unexpectedly inherited an estate valued at £2,000. In 1678 he was a captain in Monmouth's regiment in France. He returned to England with the regiment and remained there till 1685.

This was the period, between 1678 and 1681, of the political turmoil that arose from the false allegations of Titus Oates that Catholic conspirators were plotting to overthrow the Protestant regime in England. It led to some twenty-five executions and continued intolerance and distrust by many of Catholics, especially Irish Catholics. It was difficult being a Catholic officer in the army, especially because one depended on royal patronage. The accession of the throne of the

Catholic king James II improved matters. Sarsfield was commissioned a captain of dragoons in June 1685, and later a lieutenant in the Horse Guards. At the battle of Sedgemoor, in July of that year, he was wounded while fighting for the king against Monmouth.

After this he returned to Ireland, where he served the Catholic viceroy Lord Tyrconnell in reforming the army in Ireland. He was granted land in Kildare to add to his own estate, and married Honora de Burgh, the daughter of the earl of Clanrickard.

Promoted to colonel in 1686, he became a strong supporter of the cause of the ousted James II. In 1688 he was given command of a force of dragoons, which fought William III in England. Later he joined James in France, returning to Ireland with him in 1689. It was James who raised him to the title of Lord Lucan in February 1691, and promoted him to the rank of lieutenant colonel.

Sarsfield drove the Williamites under Lord Kingston out of Sligo, gaining control of Connaught, and he fought in every important engagement of the Williamite wars. In a more minor role he served in the king's own bodyguard at the battle of the Boyne in 1690. As deputy to General Boisselleau in Limerick, he forced the English to raise the siege of the city—his greatest triumph—by destroying the supply train of their army. With the help of a Catholic bandit named "Galloping" Hogan, he ambushed and blew up the train in August 1690 at Ballyneety. The siege was raised in September. He opposed the aging viceroy Richard Talbot, Earl of Tyrconnell, who wished to end the war, and secured the line of the Shannon against the Williamites.

The Irish army, which was poorly paid, was largely Irish and Gaelic speaking. The Williamite army was largely made up of foreign professional soldiers from Holland, Germany, Denmark, Scotland, and France, along with Irish Protestants and French Huguenots commanded by a Dutchman, Baron van Ginkel.

The French general St. Ruth arrived in May to take overall command. Through vanity he lost the vital crossing of the Shannon at Athlone, and decided to make his stand at Aughrim on July 12, 1691. Sarsfield protested. He did not wish to hazard all on one throw of the dice. He was sent to the rear of the army and given no hint of St. Ruth's plans. In fact, St. Ruth refused to share his plans or intentions with any of his officers, so confusion reigned when a cannonball struck his head. The Irish army, which had held the high ground until then, broke up.

"Chance, skill, and treachery all hit the mark," the Irish poet Richard Murphy said. "The soldiers panicked, thinking God had struck." Colonel Luttrell betrayed the Jacobites to the Williamites and all was lost. The Battle of Aughrim was a bloody disaster in which some nine thousand soldiers died. The bodies covered four miles of ground, like a flock of sheep. It was the last decisive battle in Irish history.

After this catastrophe for the Irish, Sarsfield miraculously led the defeated army back to Limerick, which was finally forced to surrender in 1691. The Treaty of Limerick was signed in September, Limerick was given up on October 3, and Sarsfield went into exile in France with most of the Jacobite army, some twelve thousand soldiers.

James II had already fled after the Boyne. Afterward, Sarsfield reportedly told the English, "Change kings and we will fight it over with you again." But he was never to have that chance. This was "the Flight of the Wild Geese," what the poet W. B. YEATS [8] saw, with the Flight of the Earls, as the two great disasters of the modern Irish nation. With the ascendancy of William III, the Protestant conquest of Ireland was now complete. The terms of the Treaty of Limerick relating to civilians were soon broken.

The historian Conor Cruise O'Brien has written, "The tragedy could not have been averted, or even notably softened, by the wisdom or humanity of any ruler. The people of Ireland had been caught and crushed in the play of international and ideological forces. . . . English and Irish, pressed into closer contact by these forces, discovered how diversely history had formed them. . . . The weaker party was doomed to be oppressed, and the weaker party was the native population of the smaller and more remote island."

James gave Sarsfield the overall command of the Irish Brigade, which had been granted to him by France for an intended invasion of England in 1692. But this scheme was abandoned. Sarsfield continued to serve under the French king, fought at Steinkirk in 1692, and as a *maréchal-de-camp* was mortally wounded at Neerwinden in the French victory over William of Orange, the Battle of Landen, on August 19, 1693. He died a few days later in the village of Huy, in Liege province, in what is now Belgium. On seeing his bleeding wounds, he is said to have exclaimed, "Oh, that this was for Ireland."

Patrick Sarsfield was almost the last of a great Irish family. He left a son, on whose death in 1719 the title became extinct. The estate at

Lucan then passed to a niece, who married a Vesey, and from them it passed by marriage to the Colthurst family. They were Protestants.

It was tragic and pointless end to a man who had been "the darling of the army" in Ireland. An officer had exclaimed, "The king is nothing to me. I obey Sarsfield." It was this almost mythical figure that entered the imagination of later generations of soldiers and poets. His exploits were the stuff on which the military enthusiasm of young Irish people of previous generations were fed. He remains the last cavalier of the Jacobite cause in Ireland.

66

William Thompson

1775–1833

An Irish precursor of Karl Marx may seem an historical anomaly, but William Thompson, a wealthy landowner and apostle of social justice, was just such an anomaly. According to Sidney and Beatrice Webb, the British socialists, Marx was "Thompson's disciple." At one time, before the fall of communism, a bust of William Thompson was among the items displayed at the International Communist Museum in Prague.

Perhaps the first Irish economist, William Thompson was born in Cork in 1775. His father was Alderman John Thompson, a prosperous Protestant merchant who had been mayor of the city and high sheriff of the county. In those days all such posts were not open to Catholics. When his father died in 1814, William inherited not only the lucrative family business in Cork itself, but also 1,500 acres at Cloonkeen near Rosscarbery, overlooking Glandore harbor.

He was now a man of property himself. However, the social conditions of his own tenants, and the population of Ireland as a whole, led him into a course of wide reading in political economy. He was not much interested in increasing his wealth. He lived in a large town house with a fine library, and was a prominent member of many of Cork's literary and scientific groups. But his ideas were not those of his own class.

Thompson was atheist. From his travels in Europe, he had returned filled with enthusiasm for the French Revolution. He walked around his lands at Glandore with the tricolor tied to his walking stick. In elections in 1812 and 1826 he supported Catholic interests, to the disdain of his relatives.

On inheriting the estate he gave his tenants long leases and began to work for the improvement of the land and his tenants' lives. He neither smoked nor drank, and by the end of his life had become a vegetarian. "I am not what is usually called a laborer," he remarked. "Under equitable social arrangements, possessed of health and strength, I ought to blush in making this declaration."

After studying the writings of Jeremy Bentham, he became an enthusiast for utilitarianism and socialism. He became an intimate friend of Bentham. He also supported the cooperative communities which the Scottish pioneer Robert Owen had established at New Lanark.

Thompson made his own mark as a writer, making important contributions to early socialist thought, anticipating the theory of surplus value which Marx was to later expound at length in *Das Kapital.*

"It is this exposition of the social right of the worker to the full product of his labor," writes the Irish economist Dr. Patrick Lynch, "that makes Thompson the founder of 'scientific' socialism and the most important forerunner of Karl Marx." Marx, of course, was far wider ranging in his study of economics than Thompson, and there is only one specific reference to Thompson in *Das Kapital.* But his ideas are there.

Thompson was also a pioneer in the advocacy of equal rights for women. His most important book was *An Inquiry Into the Principles of the Distribution of Wealth Most Conductive to Human Happiness: Applied to the Newly-Proposed System of Voluntary Equality of Wealth,* published in 1824. He considered unearned income from rents and stocks, as well as private property, as leading inexorably to social injustice. He saw the just distribution of wealth as the key to political economy and the advance of social progress.

His friend Robert Owen had based his appeal for social justice on the rich. Thompson realized that if the working class was to move forward, it must rely on its own efforts. Again, in his assessment of the influence of the economic environment on the shaping of political attitudes, he was certainly a most important pioneer in socialist thought. But he did not believe in state intervention; what he had seen of it in Ireland had been corrupt. He envisioned the state withering away to be replaced by a cooperative commonwealth.

A visit of Robert Owen to Dublin had inspired one cooperative experiment on an estate in Clare, which lasted until 1833. In 1830 Thompson himself published a work on establishing such communities, and pushed ahead with plans to transform his own estate at Glandore.

He drafted a constitution for it, giving women equal rights and allowing for the exclusion of the idle and vicious.

In these projects he had the assistance of Anna Wheeler, the daughter of an Anglican archbishop and the granddaughter of Henry Grattan. With her help he had written his *Appeal of One-Half of the Human Race, Women, Against the Pretensions of the Other Half, Men, to Retain Them in Political, and Thence in Civil and Domestic Slavery.*

He died at Cloonkeen, Rosscarbery, in West Cork on March 28, 1833. Though Thompson was without religion, a nephew who assumed he was his heir had him buried at Drumbeg. But Thompson had left his body for dissection, stipulating that the skeleton was to be preserved in a museum on the grounds of the first cooperative community to be established in the British Isles along his lines.

What became of his remains is now a mystery, though the doctor who exhumed the body said that the bones had been sent to Anna Wheeler "as a memento of love." When the will was read, the nephew was astonished to find that he and the family had been left nothing. William Thompson had left his estate to the benefit of the poor, to be run along the lines of New Lanark and according to the principles of Robert Owen. But after a quarter of a century of legal litigation, this will was set aside. Naturally, the lawyers profited the most.

The memory of William Thompson the man has faded. As Dr. Patrick Lynch pointed out, "His place in international socialist thought, and in the social democratic tradition in Ireland, deserves to be put into the proper setting and perspective. Irish people, at least, should recall the Cork landlord, who, like the United Irishmen, supported the people of no property; and who, in addition, furnished an important footnote, at least, to the history of economic thought wherever and by whom it is written."

HORACE PLUNKETT
(Hays Collection)

JOHN SCOTUS ERIUGENA
(Hays Collection)

BERNARDO O'HIGGINS
(Hays Collection)

Sarsfield

Carshires

William's Seige Train at 1690 Killenamona near Limerick

PATRICK SARSFIELD
(Hays Collection)

PETER LALOR
(Hays Collection)

JAMES GANDON
(Hays Collection)

WILLIAM PARSONS,
Lord Rosse's telescope *(Hays Collection)*

JAMES ARMOUR
(Brown Brothers)

EDMUND BURKE
(Mary Evans Picture Library)

WILLIAM JAMES PIRRIE
(Mary Evans Picture Library)

TURLOUGH CAROLAN
(Hays Collection)

CHARLES GAVAN DUFFY
(Hays Collection)

ARCHBISHOP JOHN JOSEPH HUGHES
(Culver Pictures)

WILLIAM R. GRACE
(The Granger Collection)

THOMAS FRANCIS MEAGHER
(Culver Pictures)

F. SCOTT FITZGERALD
(Hays Collection)

MARIA EDGEWORTH
(Hays Collection)

JOHN BARRY
(Hays Collection)

JOHN FORD
(Culver Pictures)

OSCAR WILDE
(Hays Collection)

GERRY ADAMS
(© Reuters NewMedia Inc./CORBIS)

67

Michael O'Clery

c. 1590–1643

If there is one work in Gaelic which has proved to be more influential than any other, there would be general agreement that it must be *The Annals of the Four Masters,* which the lay Franciscan brother Michael O'Clery and his three colleagues were responsible for. It is the essential work of reference to which everyone interested in the history of Ireland has to have recourse.

Michael O'Clery (in Gaelic Mícheál O Clérigh) was born in Donegal in Ulster about 1590, though the earlier date of 1575 has also been suggested. He was born the son of a local Gaelic chief at Kilbarron Castle, near Ballyshannon, and was baptized Tadhg, or Timothy. The O'Clerys had inherited the office of historian of Tir Chonaill, and Michael O'Clery was imbued with the love of history and poetry from an early age.

He was educated at various schools in Ireland before he went abroad to study in Europe, going into the Spanish Netherlands before 1621. He became a Franciscan brother, taking the name in religion of Michael in or about 1622 at Louvain, where Franciscans from Ireland had established a college in 1607.

Many writers and scholars of importance had been attached to this college, and it was a recognized center of learning in things Irish. It was intended to create religious literature in Gaelic that would be sent among the Irish in Ireland. A printing press, set up in 1611, produced many books over the next sixty years.

When O'Clery arrived there was already in hand a plan by Fr. Hugh Ward, Fr. Patrick Fleming, and others to collect and publish the lives of the Irish saints. O'Clery already had a reputation as a historian, and in 1626 he was sent back to Ireland by the head of the college to collect materials for this work. He was to stay in Ireland for the next eleven years.

While he was collecting and copying manuscript materials, such as the Book of Lismore, which he studied in 1629, O'Clery also assembled works of his own—calendars of saints' feasts, and genealogies of the families of kings and saints, which he finished at Athlone in November 1630. He completed his copy of the *Books of Invasions* at Lisgoole, Fermanagh, in December 1631. He also edited earlier works.

It was in collaboration with three other scholars that he compiled his greatest work, *The Annals of the Four Masters* (in Gaelic, *Annála Ríoghacta Eireann,* "Annals of the Kings of Ireland"), between 1632 and 1636. His helpers were Farfasa O'Mulcrony, Peregrine O'Clery, and Peregrine O'Duignan.

These annals had been collected from various earlier ones and edited into coherence. They cover the history of Ireland from the remotest days of its legendary past reckoned from the day of creation up to 1616 A.D. Though the early entries are sparse—bare notes of lootings, burnings, murders, battles, and the deaths and reigns of kings—as time advances toward the compilers' own day the entries fill out to provide an almost continuous narrative.

The book was complied in a little house on the banks of the River Drowse where it flowed from Lough Melvin into Donegal Bay. It was begun by the four of them on January 22, 1632, and finished on August 10, 1636. The work was given its more familiar name—*The Annals of the Four Masters*—by Fr. John Colgan as a tribute to the compiler and his friends. It was dedicated to their patron, Fergal O'Gara, lord of Moy Gara, the prince of Coolavin. In his preface to Fergal, O'Clery explains his purpose: "I thought that I could get the assistance of the chroniclers for whom I had most esteem, in writing a book of annals in which these matters might be put on record, for that should the writing of them be neglected at present, they would not again be found to be put on record even to the end of the world. All the best and most copious books of annals that I could find throughout all Ireland were collected by me—though it was difficult for me to collect them—into one place to write this book."

O'Clery was right about the dangers. Hardly any of the original materials he saw have survived to this day, many perishing in the turmoil of the Cromwellian and Williamite wars.

The great Dr. Douglas Hyde, later the first president of Ireland, observed of the annals: "It is not too much to say that there is not an event in the whole of Irish history from the birth of Christ down to the beginning of the seventeenth century that the first enquiry of the student about it must not be: 'What do the Four Masters say about this?' "

In 1637 O'Clery returned to Louvain, where he set about compiling a glossary of obscure words, a work which was printed in 1644, the year after his death. His collections were later used by Fr. John Colgan in his *Acts of the Irish Saints*, and in his triple work on the three patrons of Ireland—Patrick, Bridget, and Columba. The original plan to publish the lives of the Irish saints as a whole came to nothing with the death of Colgan's successor. In due course most of the material made its way into print during the nineteenth century, with the revival of interest in the Irish past. The annals themselves were translated and annotated by John O'Donovan, and it is his much praised edition which is usually read today.

O'Clery's own manuscripts are preserved in the Burgundian Library in Brussels. He died as he had lived, a poor scholar in the service of his country's past.

68

Ernest Walton

1903–1995

Science has not always been seen as an area in which the Irish have been seen to be preeminent, but with Ernest Walton, one of Ireland's Nobel Prize winners, the idea is invalid. Walton was at the leading edge of research into atomic energy, which has proved to be both the most contentious and most dangerous area of science in the twentieth century.

When the first atomic bomb was exploded at Alamogordo, New Mexico, on July 16, 1945, it was the end result of what Walton had begun, and the beginning of a new era of danger, and of awesome responsibility for the United States. Such are the profound changes that a small-scale scientific inquiry can precipitate.

With his colleague John D. Cockcroft, he achieved the first artificial disintegration of the atomic nucleus, or in simple language, they "split the atom" and opened the way for the atomic and hydrogen bombs.

Ernest Walton was born in Dungarvan, County Waterford, in October 1903. His father was a Methodist minister, while his mother came from a Protestant family long established in Armagh.

He was sent to the Methodist College in Belfast, where it quickly became clear that he had a talent for mathematics and science. He went on to study at Trinity College in Dublin, where he took a bachelor's degree in 1926, a master's of science in 1928, and a master's degree in 1934.

In 1927 he went on to Cambridge, where he joined the Cavendish Laboratory, then led by Ernest Rutherford. Though the Irish student was given little working space, he found congenial company in T. E. Allibone and John D. Cockcroft. At Rutherford's suggestion, he first began work on an experiment to increase the velocity of electrons by spinning them in a circular electric field produced by a changing magnetic field. The apparatus Walton built did not accelerate electrons sufficiently to disintegrate nuclei, but it did pave the way for a successful particle accelerator.

The problems they faced were illuminated by the arrival of the Russian (later American) physicist George Gamow. He had been working with Niels Bohr in Denmark, where he had worked on a wave mechanical theory of penetration of the particles. Gamow theorized that charged particles of rather lower energy than had been previously assumed could split nuclei, greatly simplifying the acceleration problem. His ideas opened the way for Walton and Cockcroft, and Rutherford gave them both permission, money, and space to continue. With a budget of £1,000 they created the first accelerator for atomic particles. Today the machine itself can be seen in the South Kensington Science Museum. It now looks like an amateur relic of the past, which it is, but its importance was immense.

It was on April 13, 1932, that Walton and Cockcroft found that their efforts had been successful. Walton's first observation of the telltale scintillations that marked the breakup of the nuclei were quickly confirmed by the pair.

Their achievement was historic for several reasons. It was the first time that scientists had produced a change in the atomic nucleus in a controlled situation. In the process they had found a new, and seemingly boundless, source of energy. They had confirmed Gamow's particle theory, and also Einstein's theory that energy and mass are interchangeable.

Their discovery was announced in a letter to the science journal *Nature,* and described at a meeting of the Royal Society in London on June 15, 1932. The news created a sensation worldwide. Their work inspired many other scientists with results that transformed scientific knowledge and the social life of the late twentieth century.

In 1932 Walton received his Ph.D., and in 1934 he returned to his alma mater, Trinity College in Dublin. In Dublin he was seen as a quite unflamboyant personality. He was not given to small talk, a very Ulster-like characteristic. He had married Winifred Wilson, who had also been a student at the Methodist College, and they had two sons and two daughters.

Walton was content to establish his department in Dublin University, and in 1946 was appointed Erasmus Smith professor of natural and experimental philosophy. Eventually, in 1951, Walton was awarded the Nobel Prize for physics along with Cockcroft. This was recognition of the highest order, but his wife told a neighbor that for his family, the prize meant they could now buy a car.

Though his friend John Cockcroft had followed a more high-profile career, Ernest Walton was content to concentrate his attention on more local developments in his native country. In 1952 he became chairman of the School of Cosmic Physics at the Dublin Institute of Advanced Studies (which had been established by EAMON DE VALERA [2] to provide a base for the German scientist Erwin Schroedinger, exiled by the Nazis). In 1960 he was elected a senior fellow of Trinity College, where the physics laboratory now bears his name. He died on June 25, 1995, having lived to see both the triumph, and as many would think, the failure of the atomic age.

69

Phil Lynott
1951–1986

Whatever may be his final reputation as a musician, rock star Phil Lynott will gain a place in history as the first preeminent black Irishman.

His mother was a Dublin girl who had gone to England to work as a nurse in the Midlands. Black men, either American or West Indian, were then a novelty rather than a distinct class in Britain. The father of her child was in fact a Brazilian, but as much a descendant of a freed slave as any other black in the Americas.

Philip Lynott was born on August 20, 1951. At the home where his mother gave birth to him, efforts were made by the nuns to have him given up for adoption: a young girl like her would not want to be saddled with a baby, especially a black baby. However, his mother was stubborn and strong willed, and kept him. But it was a difficult choice, and eventually little Phil was sent home to his grandmother and was raised as an Irish Catholic on a Dublin council estate along with his cousins.

One of the earliest photographs of the rock musician is one taken of him in a demure suit on the day he made his first communion, the essential rite of passage in Irish culture. Though a black child naturally stood out in the Dublin crowd, Phil Lynott grew up happily enough, well supported by his family, and encountered very little in Dublin by way of racial prejudice.

From very early on, his mother noticed that he had a stage presence, and as he grew up in the developing era of rock and roll, he fell into playing music almost inevitably. Music was as important to Phil and his friends as the air they breathed.

In 1969, along with Eric Bell from Belfast, and Brian Downey from Dublin, he formed a band called Thin Lizzy. Initially they made a name for themselves as something new at music venues in Dublin, before they were signed by Decca. They made two albums, which went almost nowhere commercially, never getting into the charts.

But everything changed for the band when they made a rocked-up version of an Irish traditional song called "Whiskey in the Jar." It was a case of Irish folk meets rock and roll, and was a wonderous and instant success. It reached the Top Ten chart in Britain, and popularized the band's curious combination of folk and hard-rock guitar.

But as is the way with rock bands, changes caught up with Thin Lizzy. Gary Moore replaced Eric Bell on guitar, and two other session men were hired. Two other guitarists were then recruited, a Scot, Brian Robertson, and Scott Gorham, an American.

The band was now fixed, and began the main phase of its musical development. There were a series of concerts during 1974 which developed their reputation. In 1976 they released an album called *Jailbreak*, which mounted the charts. A single called "The Boys Are Back in Town" went into the Top Ten in Britain and the Top Twenty in America, and was voted single of the year by the *New Musical Express* in London.

In 1980 Phil Lynott married Caroline Crowther, the daughter of popular British television personality Leslie Crowther. This was not a marriage made in heaven so far as Crowther was concerned. Lynott reunited with the band after some solo work. The hectic details of the changes of the band did not prevent its further progress.

Since he moved out of his family home, Lynott had been living the customary life of the modern rock musician, which meant sex, alcohol, and especially, drugs. Eventually it all caught up with him. He had split up Thin Lizzy in the summer of 1984, and at the end of that year an album called *Life-Live* was issued. But Lynott was on borrowed time. After a drug overdose toward the end of 1985, his body systems collapsed. His mother finally realized it was the end when a priest was called. On January 4, 1986, Phil Lynott died in an English medical center from pneumonia and heart failure, compounded with almost total liver dysfunction. His death at thirty-four was a great shock to his fans. His remains were brought back to Ireland for burial near his mother's home on the north side of Dublin.

In May 1986 Thin Lizzy was reformed, with BOB GELDOF [63] replacing Lynott for the charity concert in Ireland called Self-Aid, an offshoot of Band Aid, aimed at raising funds for young people.

Along with Geldof and U2 [36], Phil Lynott had been among the best known of Irish musicians and most influential in modern Ireland. His extraordinary presence and power made a deep impression on a generation. Only in England and elsewhere did he feel any resentment or prejudice against him because he was black. At home in Ireland the Irish-Brazilian was treated as part of the scene.

His memory has been kept alive by a series of books, one by his mother, and by reissues of his and Thin Lizzy's material. "Whiskey in the Jar," with its mixture of Irish folk and imported rock, was truly representative of Irish culture as it has evolved since 1945. But in time Phil Lynott may well come to have a greater significance for cultural historians as the first window into the multiracial Ireland of the future.

70

Peter Lalor

1823–1889

The role of the Irish in the drama of creating the very idea of Australia is summed up in the career of Peter Lalor, and by the events at the Eureka Stockade in the goldfields of the 1880s.

Born at Tinnakill, County Laois, on February 5, 1823, he was the younger brother of the Irish political leader James Fintan Lalor (himself a man of continuing importance in the Irish republican tradition), the child of a wealthy farmer and member of Parliament. His father had radical views and had resisted the imposition of tithes and was an advocate of the repeal of the Act of Union. The family remained in good circumstances until the famine. Later in life, Lalor's father claimed, "I have been for upwards of forty years struggling without ceasing in the cause of the people." Some of this passion was passed on to his sons.

Peter Lalor was educated at Carlow College and Trinity College in Dublin, and became a civil engineer. As a youth he did not share his family's political activities, and had no desire to mix himself up in them.

Like so many of his countrymen, the discovery of gold at Golden Point, Victoria, in October 1851, tempted him to emigrate to Australia with his brother Richard. They arrived in Melbourne in October 1852. At first he found work as an engineer on the construction of the Melbourne-Geelong Railway. He and his brother also had an interest in a provisions store in Melbourne.

Richard returned to Ireland, where he was later a Parnellite MP. In 1854 Peter moved to Ballarat (seventy-six miles west-northwest of

Melbourne), where he held rich gold claims. He intended to continue the provisions supply business in the fields.

He was involved in a protest by the miners, though not as a leading figure. "The people," he said, recalling the language of Irish politics, "were dissatisfied with the laws, because they excluded them from possession of the land, from being represented in the Legislative Council, and imposed on them an odious poll tax." The protest was one familiar to colonial America: no taxation without representation.

A miners' strike broke out when they refused to continue paying a license fee to the crown. This had its origins in the imprisonment of three miners after Bentley's Hotel was burned (the hotel's proprietor was believed to have murdered a miner, but had at first been cleared by the authorities). The Ballarat Reform League then developed a program of reforms. A mass meeting was held on November 29, 1854, to hear what the governor had to say, but his concessions were not enough. The twelve thousand miners, over whose head flew a Southern Cross flag, were for resistance.

The next day soldiers and police were sent to the goldfields, where they arrested some miners and withdrew with their prisoners. Other miners crowded onto the scene and occupied Bakery Hill, where they raised their flag. Lalor was the only one of the committee now present, and he called on the miners to arm and resist, swearing by the Southern Cross to defend their rights and liberties.

The next day the miners marched from Bakery Hill to the Eureka Stockade. Lalor was elected commander, and a stockade was erected. This followed the pattern planned by the Young Irish rebels that Lalor's brother Fintan had led. Peter Lalor, however, had no military background, and an American was appointed to deal with military matters.

The stockade was not intended as a complete defense. The miners returned to their tents for the night, leaving only 120 men, mostly Irish, in the stockade. Early on the morning of December 3, police and soldiers attacked. In the fighting at the stockade over twenty miners were shot dead, twelve wounded, and some 125 arrested.

Lalor, who had been leading the striking miners, lost his arm but escaped in the confusion. In due course the goldfields were granted representation, and Lalor was elected to the assembly as the member from Ballarat in November 1855. In the next half century the mines there produced £70 million, making them of crucial importance to the Australian economy as a whole.

Lalor defended the interests of the miners but did not follow their views on all matters. He was essentially conservative in his outlook. He was not, he explained, actually a democrat if that meant "Chartism, communism, or republicanism," but "if democracy means opposition to a tyrannical press, a tyrannical people, or a tyrannical government, then I have ever been, I am still, and will ever remain, a democrat."

His political career belongs to the history of Australia, but his views, which were liberal but not fully democratic, were influenced by the ideas of Young Ireland and the Americans who had flooded into Australia from California. In subsequent years Peter Lalor held several posts, such as postmaster general and commissioner of customs. He was speaker of the House from 1880 to 1888. He had to resign because of ill health, but was voted a grant of £4,000 for his patriotic services. He died at Melbourne on February 10, 1889.

The Eureka Stockade has entered into the mythology of Australia. It was acclaimed by no less a person than Karl Marx as a truly revolutionary episode, but the later career of Peter Lalor and modern historians suggest otherwise. The myth remains, enshrined in histories, novels, and films. And that myth, of a people's uprising, still influences the populist politics of Australia. Lalor brought to the new politics of Australia something of the passion that had informed his brother's efforts for land reform in Ireland. Ever since, in the politics of Australia the Irish element has been just as important as it has been in America.

71

James Gandon
1743–1823

Although widely accepted as the greatest Irish architect, a man who put his mark on the city of Dublin's public buildings in no uncertain manner, James Gandon was not Irish by birth.

His father was a French Protestant with mystical leanings who nearly ruined himself with experiments in alchemy. Young James was made of more practical stuff and from an early age he educated himself in the classics, drawing, and math. At fifteen he became an assistant in the office of an architect, Sir William Chambers, and later became his apprentice. A few years later, about 1765, he struck out on his own. In 1767 he published with John Woolfe a continuation of Colin Campbell's *Vitruvius Britannicus,* which was completed in 1771. He won his first gold medal for architecture at the Royal Academy in London in 1769. He continued to exhibit his drawings there between 1774 and 1780.

In 1769 he won second prize in a competition for a design for the Dublin Royal Exchange. Years later, having turned down an offer to go to Russia, he settled instead in Dublin, in 1781, to work on the new Customs House.

There was a great deal of local opposition from the merchant classes to the cost of the new building, over which there were riots. There was even armed opposition from residents near the old customs house further up the river. However, it was brought to a triumphant conclusion in 1791. By then Gandon had been asked to design an extension to the Houses of Parliament and the new Four Courts, and plan the King's Inns, the main base of Irish lawyers.

He resigned in protest over interference in 1808 and retired from practice to a house in Lucan, outside of Dublin. He was an original member of the Royal Irish Academy when it was established in 1785. It was thought that when George IV, the first king of England to come to Ireland in peace, visited in 1821 that Gandon would be knighted. But the visit passed without the old man receiving this indication of royal esteem. However, with the esteem of his friends, Gandon had no need of royal favors.

For many years Gandon had suffered from gout. He died at home on December 23, 1823. Three days later he was buried as he had wished, in the same vault as his friend, "the bibulous and altogether delightful antiquary" Capt. Francis Grose, in a private chapel in Drumcondra graveyard.

Gandon's work in Dublin represents the culmination of the eighteenth-century confidence that had elevated the ambitions of Grattan's parliament. But that was to end with the Act of Union and a more uncertain future. In 1942, to mark the two-hundredth anniversary of Gandon's birth, the Royal Institute of Architects in Ireland erected a plaque to his memory in the Drumcondra church.

In 1846 Gandon's biographer commented that Gandon was a man "whose urbanity of heart and blandness of manner converted acquaintances into friends, rendering a long-protracted life one continued exercise of benevolence and affection." Gandon had made and kept a host of friends, but as Maurice Craig, the premier historian of Dublin's architecture, observed, "even these private virtues are as nothing beside his services to architecture and to Dublin." Gandon was the man who did the most to create the stately appearance of the city, an appearance which has ruled and influenced the lives of Dubliners ever since. The dignity of Dublin as the capital of Ireland is largely his creation.

72

William Parsons, Lord Rosse
1800–1867

William Parsons, third earl of Rosse, is among the giants of nineteenth-century science and one of the most remarkable Irishmen of his day. Born in York on June 17, 1800, into a leading Irish family, he was a son of Laurence Parsons, the second earl of Rosse. He was educated at Trinity College, where he became a student in 1818. In 1821 he went on to Magdalen College in Oxford. That year he was also elected to Parliament as the member from King's County (now Offaly). He held the seat until 1834, but resigned in order to pursue his scientific interests. After he inherited his title he was a representative Irish peer at Westminster from 1845.

He was already deeply interested in astronomy and had made experiments with telescopes at his father's estate at Parsonstown (now Birr). The key element in a reflective telescope, such as Parsons had in mind, was its mirror.

William Herschel had already been working with reflecting telescopes, but he had never published any information about how he cast and polished his specula. Parsons had to make his own experiments. He described his work in 1828 in the *Edinburgh Journal of Science*. His speculum metal combined copper and tin in proportions to make a brilliant alloy. Because this metal was very brittle, his first mirrors were made up of a number of thin plates of the metal soldered on to a strong,

light framework of brass with the same expansion rate. He needed sixteen plates for a three-foot mirror.

In 1839 the three-foot mirror was finished and mounted, but it
presented difficulties due to its expansion, so Parsons decided to cast a
solid three-foot mirror. He achieved this, overcoming yet more technical difficulties in 1840. In 1842 he began work on an even larger six-foot
mirror, which was finished in 1845.

This was to be mounted in an instrument which came to be called
the Leviathan, and was the largest telescope of the nineteenth century.
It was fifty-four feet long and the tube was so wide that a man could
walk upright through it.

The mirror of Leviathan was seventy-two inches wide. The instrument took seventeen years to bring to completion. Using local crafts-
men—the sons of tenants on his estate whom he trained as technicians
and chemists—he had first to build a steam engine to drive the tools
needed to polish the mirror. The final mirror, mounted in the fifty-
eight-foot wooden tube, weighed four tons. He set a ball and socket
into the solid rock, and on this base laid out a platform of oak trunks
over which were laid twenty-seven cast iron plates. On this machinery
the telescope could swing from left to right by a chain drive. It was protected from the winds by two walls. It looked for all the world like part
of the Gothic castle in which the earl himself lived, surrounded by
drawbridges, ladders, and the moving tower in the center of it all.

Strange as it appeared, this was not amateurish work. The sheen
which Parsons and his team achieved was created by polishing off a
layer 1/10,000 of a millimeter thick from the prepolished mirror, evenly
from the center to the edge. This remarkable feat of precision made
the mirror almost free of distortion, and was rightly considered an
optical marvel.

The Leviathan established Birr as a leading astronomical site for
decades, for this was the largest telescope in existence until 1878. Rosse
and fellow astronomers invited to use the telescope made many extraordinary discoveries. Lord Rosse (the title to which Parsons succeeded
in 1841) brought to light the spiral form of nebulae, those strange
cloudlike formations in the distant reaches of the universe. The telescope was powerful enough to reveal many previously unknown features of these mysterious objects. It was seen that the annular and
planetary nebulae were very similar, and the remarkable spiral nebulae
were also studied. A special study was undertaken of the nebulae of

Orion, and the large drawings which resulted from the observations gave a remarkably clear idea of these objects.

Though it was eventually stripped down, the telescope itself survives, and its speculum is kept in London at the Kensington Science Museum. Rosse's wife was a noted photographic pioneer; his son, the fourth earl (1840–1929) was also a noted astronomer, while his third son, Charles Parsons (born in 1854), was the inventor of the steam turbine engine in 1884, which revolutionized shipping and was later applied to airplane jet engines. Rosse was president of the Royal Society from 1849 to 1854, and became chancellor of Dublin University in 1862.

Though wealthy and indulgent of his scientific interests, Lord Rosse was also a good landlord, especially so during the grim famine years at Parsonstown. He died at Monkstown on the seacoast south of Dublin on October 31, 1867.

His great telescope continued to probe the deepest mysteries of the universe from the small town in the Irish midlands. The discovery of the size and nature of the universe has been one of man's great intellectual adventures, probing as it does into the very first seconds following the Big Bang. Lord Rosse made his country a part of this great adventure.

73

James Armour

1841–1928

One of the most remarkable of Ulster's Presbyterians, "Armour of Ballymoney" still remains a potent example of what human generosity can achieve in any community divided against itself. Though Armour lived most of his life in a small country town, the Ulster writer Robert Lynd observed, "his qualities of brain and heart made him one of the most eminent and ultimately beloved Ulstermen of his day." James Armour's life carries a moral for all the world.

He saw all too clearly that the rival factions in Ireland were contending for and against a concept of empire that had ended at Yorktown. He was a liberal and a democrat, and believed that no danger came to anyone, his opinions or religion, from the extension of liberal policies and democratic values.

James Brown Armour was born at Lisboy, near Ballymoney, in County Antrim, the most Protestant part of Ulster, on January 20, 1841. He was educated locally at the Genaby School and the Ballymoney Model School. Later he attended the Royal Belfast Academical Institution, the leading Presbyterian school in Belfast.

He then studied classics at the University College in Belfast, and the Queen's College in Cork. This experience of living in the deep Catholic south of Ireland affected his outlook in many ways. He taught school to support himself during his studies, though his ambition was to become a barrister. However, he gave way to the wishes of his family to become the Presbyterian minister in Ballymoney in 1869.

Ballymoney is a small linen and agricultural center between Coleraine and Ballymena. A few miles away was the family home of William McKinley, the twenty-fifth president of the United States. Lying in the heart of an area of good agricultural land, Ballymoney was very typical of the planter town, created and settled by Scottish families who came over during the seventeenth-century Plantation of Ulster. Here they developed a prosperous linen industry and gave the little place its graceful airs with wide streets, fine Georgian terraces, and a final touch, the Masonic Hall, in 1852. Ballymoney was all very typical of loyal Ulster.

Unlike the McKinleys, Armour stayed in Ulster. In March 1883 he married a widow who had two sons by her first husband. Just as he had taught school to support his own studies, so he returned to teaching to support his new family. In 1883 he became an assistant at Magee College in Derry, where he remained for twenty-three years.

Like many Presbyterians Armour was a man who valued not only private judgment, but forthright speech. His spoke out from his pulpit and elsewhere on all the issues of the day. From 1885 onward these revolved largely around the issues of Ulster's future, raised by the Orange Order.

These were largely issues of identity. The Ulster people tended to favor union with England, while in the south the Irish party was moving toward home rule. In March 1893 the general assembly of the Presbyterian church in Ireland, whose members lived largely in the four counties of eastern Ulster, met in special session to debate the entire matter of home rule, and to condemn the Home Rule Bill.

Armour, however, moved an amendment to the resolution in favor of self-government in Ireland, allied with protection for all the rights and interests of the Presbyterian church. This speech, as he might have expected, was hissed and booed. He lost his amendment, and the original resolution was passed by a huge majority. But it never worried a Presbyterian conscience to be in the minority. At home in Ballymoney his congregation remained loyal to their minister. However, his fellow churchmen and other unionist Ulstermen shunned him for a while.

Armour campaigned for his views, collecting the signatures of 3,535 Presbyterians on a petition supporting the Home Rule Bill, to be sent as a memorial address to Gladstone, the British prime minister. He had always supported the tenants' right movement and condemned landlordism. In a debate with Dr. Anthony Traill of Trinity College he argued in favor of the nationalists against the ascendancy (the largely Protestant landed class) in Ireland, which Traill represented.

One of the great interests of many Catholics had long been the hope of establishing a Catholic university—Trinity and the Queen's College being regarded as Protestant institutions. A campaign was under way to dissolve the Royal University in Ireland and replace it with a truly national university into which the other colleges could be assumed. At the assembly in 1900 a report was presented condemning the proposed establishment of the Catholic university. Armour opposed its adoption.

With a relative now the under-secretary in Dublin Castle, Armour had a conduit to those in power, which he used well after the Liberal party victory of 1906. Two years later he was told he had a critical heart condition, forcing him to leave public life. At this time, many tributes were paid to him by all shades of opinion.

But Armour of Ballymoney was not quite done with affairs of state, heart or no heart. In 1912 the general assembly had decided that politics should not be allowed to bring divisions among Presbyterians. This was the period of the unionist revolt.

The following year a Laymen's Memorial (a motion by church members) from the floor against Home Rule was introduced to the assembly, and Armour moved an amendment to reaffirm the previous year's decision. In the heated atmosphere of the day this aroused great anger from his opponents. Only forty-three members voted with Armour, against some 921 for the resolution. He described the agitation being led by Edward Carson and James Craig, which had led to the setting up of the Ulster Volunteers to defend the Union, as "a wicked bluff." The partition of Ireland which they proposed would be ruinous for Ulster.

At the time of the Easter Rising he rightly pointed out that the insurgents had only been following the lead of the Ulster Volunteers. As Prof. Eóin MacNeill pointed out, Ulster had begun the rise of armed political parties in Ireland by smuggling in guns from Germany. The summer of 1914 had very nearly brought about a mutiny in the British army.

Armour warned the assembly of the dangers of denouncing minority views: "If you deny the right of private judgment and of free speech, how much do you have of Protestantism worth keeping?" he asked. "Nothing at all."

Armour supported the war effort and helped to recruit for the imperial army; he also acted as an honorary chaplain to the viceroy. To Armour, unionism meant the unity of all Ireland. At the general assembly he again spoke out against the Government of Ireland Bill, which brought Northern Ireland into existence. He said this would only promote racial and religious division in the province, and ruin the moral and economic prospects of the whole island. But, yet again, he was voted down.

His son later wrote, "One characteristic seems to have struck every observer, his fearless courage, his indomitable spirit, and the tenacity with which he held his ground against all-comers. An American admirer once wrote that he was fifty years before his time, an inconvenient gift in a province and indeed in a country, where past traditions are strong."

After fifty-six years, Armour finally retired from his ministry at Ballymoney, in September 1925. He died on January 25, 1928. To many of his countrymen, to whom the very notion of Presbyterianism means the union with Britain, Armour of Ballymoney is a beacon of another passage through the stormy waters of Irish history.

74

Charles Bianconi

1786–1875

With remarkable energy, this Italian emigrant to Ireland transformed the communications system of the country, helping to change what might have remained a poor country into a developing one.

Joachim Carlo Giuseppe Bianconi was born at Tregolo, in the duchy of Milan (now Lombardy), on September 24, 1786. Leaving school, where he had been an indifferent student, he set out from home to make his fortune. He arrived in Ireland at the end of 1802 as an apprentice to an Italian print seller, bringing the benefit of "art pictures" to the Irish. A pretty boy who appealed to ladies, he became his employer's traveling salesman. He soon went into business on his own, setting up his own shop in the country town of Carrick-on-Suir, and later in Clonmel. This business thrived and he made many friends, including DANIEL O'CONNELL [20].

The end of the Napoleonic wars in 1815—Waterloo had been fought on June 18—brought ex-military horses onto the market at cheap prices, as well as the end of the carriage tax. Having accumulated a little capital, Bianconi bought a horse and a jaunting car, and on July 6, 1815, he began a car service between Clonmel and Cahir in the south of Ireland.

The idea prospered, and his cars, popularly called the "Bians," were a common feature of the Irish roads. By 1823 his services ran over some 1,800 miles of road from twenty-three centers. By 1845 this network had grown to 3,800 miles and 120 centers. In 1857 he told the meeting of the British Association for the Advancement of Science in

Dublin that he still ran some nine hundred horses and sixty-seven cars over 4,244 miles a day. In 1864, income from passengers and parcels amounted to £40,000.

He charged passengers one-and-a-half pence per mile. This made his service cheap enough to be of very real benefit in rural areas, where those of small means could travel about. In 1843 Bianconi himself explained that "the farmer who formerly drove and spent three days in making his market, can now do so in one for a few shillings; thereby saving two clear days and the expense of his horses."

The improvement of roads followed. A report of 1838 noted that "even small portions of those roads were scarcely out of the engineers' hands before they were covered with the carts of farmers, eager to take advantage of the improvement." People moved their cottages nearer the new roads, and new villages and towns grew up at their junctions, especially in the west of Ireland. Charles Bianconi had become one of the agents of the social and economic transformation of Ireland.

The improvement in service brought with it an increase in tourist traffic, and the beginnings of the tourist industry, which is now of such importance to Ireland. The advent of the tourists brought about an improvement in the hotels and inns, and an overall improvement of life for the local people as well.

Bianconi, who was elected mayor of Clonmel in 1844, was a sincere Catholic, a fervent supporter of Daniel O'Connell, and a promoter himself of Catholic emancipation (which came in 1829). He generously donated to many Catholic charities, including the foundation of the Catholic University of Ireland, for which he purchased what is now Newman House.

Bianconi became a naturalized British citizen in 1831. In his annual report for 1857, the postmaster general said that "no living man has ever done more for the benefit of the sister kingdom." In the development of his extensive transport system, Bianconi displayed extraordinary energy as well as ingenuity. While he promoted the social connections of Ireland, he also increased its economic resources by promoting increased trade. His cars were the first stage in the development of increased speed in communication and transport, marked by the introduction of the railways and the electric telegraph in the 1830s, and by the use of telephones after 1875. The nature and quality of life in Ireland was changed by these means. In 1815 parts of the country might as well have been in the seventeenth century; by the time of Bianconi's death communication with America was instantaneous.

The heyday of the cars was soon over. The railways, promoted initially by WILLIAM DARGAN [75], had arrived. Bianconi saw where the future lay and bought shares in the new companies, and used his cars to provide local feeder services to their stations. Bianconi retired in 1865, selling off his business to his agents in the county towns across the country.

He lived out the rest of his life at Longfield, his house near Clonmel, in Tipperary, and died there on September 22, 1875. His daughter had married Daniel O'Connell's son Morgan John O'Connell, and in 1885 she published a biography of her father.

Later still, the cars became a part of fond memories of many nineteenth-century childhoods. The painter JACK YEATS [26] had fond recollections of them, for as a child he had traveled to and from Rosses Point in Sligo on one. The first play he ever saw was the wild melodrama *The Shaughrun* (1874), by the Irish-American Dion Boucicault. In his painting *In Memory of Boucicault and Bianconi,* he has the hero and villain of the play at a local beauty spot striking poses in front of a long car. What Bianconi had started as a business enterprise had entered the mythology of Irish art.

75

William Dargan
1799–1867

On the lawn outside the National Gallery of Ireland in Dublin there stands a slightly larger-than-life statue. On the plinth is carved a single word: Dargan. This is a memorial not only to the originator of the National Gallery itself, but also to the creator of the first railway in Ireland. Dargan (like Bianconi earlier) transformed the nature of life in Ireland for everyone, both economically and culturally.

William Dargan was born in County Carlow on February 28, 1799, the year after the great rebellion, which had deeply shocked the whole island. His father was a farmer, but William was sent out of Ireland to be educated in England. He began his working life with an apprenticeship in a surveyor's office.

One of the first important jobs in which he was involved was aiding Thomas Telford, the great civil engineer, in laying the new road to Holyhead, the little port in north Wales from which the Irish ferries were to depart. When this was completed Dargan came back to Ireland and worked on several other developments. But the advent of the railways gave him his first real opening as a businessman.

He found backers for his own scheme, a railway to run from Dublin to Kingstown, as it was then called, where the boats from Britain docked. The construction was authorized in 1831 by Parliament. The first train ran out of Dublin, on December 17, 1834, and caused great excitement.

Dargan now turned north to develop the Ulster railway, which opened on August 12, 1839. This was planned to link up with the Ulster Canal (also his work) so that a new transport route was available across the province. He created the line to Carrickfergus and Ballymena, and a line along the coast to Bangor.

This was the heyday of the railway boom. Tracks were being laid down everywhere, and Dargan was one of the main contractors for the jobs. He grew wealthy, but railways were not the last of his innovations.

Inspired by the great exhibition at the Crystal Palace, which the prince consort had promoted in London in 1851, he suggested that Dublin should also have a great exhibition. A committee was gathered, and he agreed to underwrite the scheme. A part of this exhibition was to be a display of fine art drawn from collections all over the British Isles, and from several European nations.

This exhibition opened on May 12, 1853 on what was then called the Duke's Lawn, the open area on Merrion Square behind the Duke of Leinster's townhouse. The exhibition premises were huge, and it proved to be very popular when it was opened to huge crowds in May; it was visited by the queen in August. However, Dargan lost money on it. By now he was living in a large country house, Mount Anville, just outside Dublin, where Queen Victoria visited him and his family. Dargan, however, refused a title.

The pictures gathered for the exhibition inspired the idea of a National Gallery, which opened after many vicissitudes in 1864. Though Dargan had inspired the idea, many other people were involved, including civil servants of the treasury. As a result, the negotiations over the scheme, the planning and erection of a building to stand on the exhibition site, and the gathering of pictures for a collection became a complicated saga in its own right. Dargan's portrait was painted by the gallery's first director, George Mulvany. A plaque on the east wall of the gallery recalls that it was erected "by the contributions of the fellow-countrymen of William Dargan, Esquire, aided by the Imperial government in commemoration of his munificent liberality in founding and sustaining the Dublin Industrial Exhibition of 1853." The last touch put to the building before it opened, in December 1863, was the hoisting into place of Farrell's statue of Dargan, more than a decade after his exhibition had opened.

In the meantime, Dargan had been involved in many other schemes, one of which was a flax mill in Chapelizod on the Liffey. However, not all of these ventures were successful. In 1854 he opened the New Line to Bray and Wicklow, which was to lead to the development of Bray as a resort and even a commuter town. By now he was chairman of the Dublin-Kingstown Railway, which at the beginning of the railway age had an important effect on Ireland. Though it brought about many economic improvements, it also hastened the departure of emigrants to England and beyond.

Dargan had always tried to keep the reins of his businesses in his own hands. In 1866 he suffered a riding accident and was laid up, and matters began to go awry. As a writer of the time remarked: "His affairs became disordered and his health and spirit were undermined." Mount Anville had to be sold to an order of nuns who used it as an exclusive girls' school. He died in his town house on February 2, 1867.

Dargan had played a part in many things: bringing the railways to rural and seacoast areas, promoting the development of resorts such as Bray, and the development of large-scale industries. It was all very much in the nineteenth-century style of the pioneering man of business.

Yet it may well be that the National Gallery was among his most important inspirations. Generations of Dubliners have certainly thanked him for it. It was a haven of peace and enlightenment for GEORGE BERNARD SHAW [49] when he was a young man in the 1870s, when the gallery was almost the only beacon of culture and civilization in the city of Dublin.

76

Sir William Rowan Hamilton

1805–1865

As a mathematician, Rowan Hamilton is to be ranked with Descartes and Fermat, though to many the crown of his life's work (as he saw it) seems strange and obscure.

He was born in Dublin at midnight between August 3 and 4, 1805. Though there was always some dispute about his origins, he always claimed to be Irish, and hoped his life's work in mathematics would reflect on the national credit of Ireland.

His father was a successful attorney, an exuberant and eloquent man, but one also given to overindulgence in drink. Hamilton inherited some of his characteristics, but his brains came from his mother, who died when he was only twelve.

By then he had been sent away to live with his uncle, a clergyman in Trim who was a formidable scholar. He imparted his love of languages to his nephew; Hamilton read Hebrew by the age of seven, and Latin, Greek, and four European languages by the age of twelve. By then he had also acquired a smattering of Syriac, Persian, Arabic, Sanskrit, Hindi, and Malay—an extraordinary accomplishment even for a genius. These language studies were posited on his father's notion that he might work for the East India Company. In retrospect, all this seems to have been an extraordinary waste.

However, even as a boy his mathematical talents became apparent. When he was ten his computational skills were tested in a contest with Zerah Colburn, the now forgotten American child prodigy nicknamed "Calculating Boy," and did not come off too badly. He read Euclid, doubtless in the original Greek, and soon moved on to Newton's *Arithmetica Universalis* and then the *Principia*. By 1822, it was clear that he could understand much of this, and he continued to pursue these studies, becoming largely self-taught as a mathematician.

At the age of seventeen, while reading the *Mécanique Céleste* of Laplace, he discovered an error. This introduced him to Dr. Brinkley, the astronomer royal for Ireland, whom he astonished with a paper on the osculation of certain curves of double curvature. Clearly, this widely read young man was a mathematical genius of the first order. He also caught the attention of Sir John Herschel and Professor George Airy, the leading British astronomers of the day.

In 1823 he entered Trinity College in Dublin. "This young man," his friend Dr. Brinkley remarked after Hamilton had presented his paper on light rays to the Royal Irish Academy, "I do not say *will* be, but *is*, the first mathematician of his age." To some it seemed that a second Newton had arrived. He proved that certain rays of light emerge from a crystal, not as single or double rays, but as conical pencils. This led to his convincing proof of the "undulatory theory of light."

In 1827, while he was still an undergraduate, he was appointed Andrews professor of astronomy in the university of Dublin. He ended his undergraduate career by being elected astronomer royal at the age of twenty-two without even applying for the position. Many distinguished astronomers were passed over, but it gave him a post in which he could develop not only his astronomy, which had interested him since the age of fourteen, but have the time to do other work as well.

This involved the elaboration of some "curious discoveries" he had made at the age of seventeen, which he eventually published as *A Theory of Systems of Rays*. The techniques he introduced were to prove of fundamental importance to the development of theoretical physics in the twentieth century. His methods were just what was needed for the theory of wave mechanics associated today with quantum theory and the theory of atomic structure. He presented an abstract of his work to the Royal Irish Academy in April 1827.

He had well-developed literary tastes, and was a friend of Wordsworth and Southey. His own poems, which one critic said, "retain a straightforward clarity, strength, and dignity" were collected by his biographer, Robert Perceval Graves. Wordsworth himself thought that Hamilton was one of the most remarkable men he had ever met, next only to Coleridge, his fellow poet.

Hamilton had had two unhappy love affairs before he married an invalided lady. It was a bad match which brought him little comfort. After ten years he realized that he was slipping into alcoholism and gave up the conviviality that had been a feature of his younger years. He was never quite free of this threat.

While he and his wife were out walking one day (October 16, 1843), he was suddenly struck by the notion of quaternions, his great discovery. This was a new method of dealing with the science of space mathematically. It was a new system of algebra and geometry that expressed relations of space in regard to direction as well as quantity, and was based on the application of a new interpretation of what had been hitherto considered "impossible quantities." Having no paper on hand, Hamilton scratched the math involved onto the stonework of a bridge over the Royal Canal at Ballyboggan, near Cabra. A contemporary, Professor Peter Tait, later claimed that Hamilton's method was one "which can only be compared with the *Principia* of Newton and the *Mécanique Céleste* of Laplace."

The last two decades of Hamilton's life were devoted to the elaboration of quaternions and their application to many fields; *Elements of Quaternions* was published after his death. He left behind manuscript books and a huge collection of papers, which were found to be in an extraordinary muddle, largely due to his domestic difficulties. Hidden deep in the piles of papers, dinner plates were found with still uneaten chops on them.

The now reclusive Hamilton died in Dublin of gout on September 2, 1865. He had been described as the greatest man of science that Ireland has produced. Among the many honors that came to him (including a knighthood in 1835), none pleased him more than a last tribute that came to him as he lay dying: he had been elected the first foreign member of the National Academy of Sciences of the United States.

77

Edmund Burke
1729–1797

Outside Trinity College in central Dublin stand two statues, one of the poet Goldsmith, the other of Edmund Burke. For the nineteenth century, they represented the two aspects of Anglo-Irish culture which the college was most proud of. Though Goldsmith is still much admired, it is Burke as a political writer and statesman who has come to be seen as the more influential. He remains the greatest philosopher and expounder of the antirevolutionary philosophy that Ireland has produced.

Like that of his country, Burke's was a divided, perhaps even confused, identity. His father came from a Catholic family, but being an attorney, he had conformed to the Church of Ireland for professional reasons. His mother was a Catholic from County Cork. Burke himself seems to have been born not at his father's house in Dublin, but at his uncle's house in rural Cork. As a small child he was sent to live among his Cork relatives, where he would have absorbed the Catholic culture. His education proper began at Ballitore, in Kildare. From there he entered Trinity College, which he seems to have found intellectually stimulating, and where he distinguished himself. He was to be a lawyer and was sent by his father to study at the Middle Temple in London. In London he married a Catholic, Mary Nugent (who remained a Catholic all her life). Burke's view of Christianity was an inclusive one, covering both the Catholicism of his mother and the nominal Anglicanism of his father. In later life he was secretive about his background and his relations, as the nature of his upbringing might not have appealed to many in London political circles.

Burke did not care for the law; his father did not care that his son wished to be a writer. Breaking with his father, Burke entered on the lower rungs of a political career. In 1756 he made his name with a satire on Bolingbroke called *A Vindication of Natural Society*, but the irony was easily misunderstood. Far more successful was his essay *The Sublime and the Beautiful*. His literary career continued, and among his books was one dealing with the settlement of America, a continent always of interest to him. He began the *Annual Register*, a record of political, social, and criminal events which still continues, and from the beginning proved a success and an essential source for later historians.

When William Hamilton was made Irish chief secretary, Burke served as Hamilton's secretary in Dublin. His views on the social situation of his native country were reinforced by this stay. As John Morley, himself immersed in Irish affairs, later wrote: "He always took the interest of an ardent patriot in his unfortunate country; and made more than one weighty sacrifice on behalf of the principles which he deemed to be bound up with her welfare."

Though he was entitled to a small pension for his services, Burke quarreled with Hamilton and gave it up. England was now passing into a period of political change under George III, who wished to break with the settlement of 1688 and rule with more authority rather than the permission of a set of great families. In 1765 Lord Rockingham became prime minister in a reversal of fortune for the king, and appointed Burke his secretary. This remained a lifelong friendship. But Rockingham fell from power, largely because he was not supported by William Pitt. This ended any possibility of a wise policy toward the American colonies. Burke had by then been elected a member of Parliament. From the day of his election until 1790 he was to be one of the essential guides of a revival of the Whig party, from which, in due course, would spring the great Liberal party of the nineteenth century. In opposition, Burke showed by his writings and speeches that he had a wide-ranging and firm grasp of the details and prospects of political life that was unrivaled.

Oddly enough for a man who had been a penniless scribbler a few years before, Burke was now able to buy an estate costing £22,000, which brought him £500 a year in rents. His finances were another mysterious aspect of his life. He spent more than he made—far more—for he was a friendly man who kept up with his friends and others of interest in London.

Burke was more than a politician; he was an eminent man of letters. Until very recently, his description of Marie Antoinette was among those pieces of famous prose which every schoolchild in Ireland studied.

The main themes of his political life, aside from his sympathy for Ireland, were the fate of the American colonies, the beginnings of the British imperial adventure in India, and the French Revolution. These events inspired Burke's most eloquent pieces. His desire for a policy of reconciliation in Ireland led to the loss of his seat. But he was soon reelected from another borough and held several offices in government. However, these were small matters compared with the saga of the impeachment of Warren Hastings for his highhanded and cruel actions against the natives in India, which Burke championed in Parliament beginning in 1781.

In 1790 he published *Reflections on the Revolution in France,* which appeared in eleven editions at the time, and drew fierce responses from the romantic admirers of the bloody events in Paris; one of these being Tom Paine's *Rights of Man.* Though it gained Burke a universal reputation, it also led to a break with the leader of his party, Charles James Fox, a more radical man than Burke, in May 1791.

When the long trial of Warren Hastings concluded with his acquittal in April 1795, Burke gave up his seat in Parliament. Though his writings and speeches on the whole defended the value of tradition and good order, he was not a great admirer of the landed oligarchs of the Whig party. He was a representative of "the new man," the sort of person who rose through the ranks of British society and would become a great feature of the nineteenth century.

Burke died at his house in Beaconsfield on July 9, 1797. He remains an outstanding figure, a proponent of a view of society which has many admirers. Like many other Irishmen later, he had made a career for himself in British public life. "There have been," his admirer John Morley concluded, "many subtler, more original, and more systematic thinkers about the condition of the social union. But no one that ever lived used the general ideas of the thinker more successfully to judge the particular problems of statesmen. No one has ever come so close to the details of practical politics, and at the same time remembered that these can only be understood and only dealt with by the aid of the broad conceptions of political philosophy. And what is more than all for the perpetuity of fame, he was one of the great masters of the high and difficult art of elaborate composition."

It has been the lament of many Irish people since that these amazing talents could not have served his native country more directly than they did. But Burke was caught by the political circumstances of his day, and like all leaders of men, had to make what he could of them.

78

Ernest Shackleton
1874–1922

There have been notable Irish explorers who have made their contribution to the slow unveiling and discovery of the world. Such figures as Sir Richard Burton, Admiral McClintock, and Surgeon Major T. H. Parke are well known. But none achieved more, and more bravely, than Ernest Henry Shackleton, the polar explorer.

He was born on February 14, 1874, at Kilkea in County Kildare in the east of Ireland. His family were of Anglo-Irish stock, and he was educated at Dulwich College (also the alma mater of P. G. Wodehouse and Raymond Chandler). He entered the British merchant marine because it was a career likely to offer adventure.

On the first of Capt. Robert Falcon Scott's expeditions to the Antarctic, from 1901 to 1904, he acted as a lieutenant. Their ship *Discovery* had been specially built for the purpose of ice exploration. It was the plan that the ship would remain for a winter in the ice of McMurdo Sound after a preliminary cruise along the coast of what Scott called King Edward Land. It took a little time to develop the right techniques for sledging on the ice, but then the expedition began a series of shore journeys. The principal one was made by Scott, Shackleton, and Dr. Edward Wilson over the ice toward the south. Though they lost many dogs, they reached 82 degrees, 17 minutes south. But on the return leg, Shackleton's health gave way and he had to be sent home on the relief ship. He missed out on the excitement of the second year.

On his arrival in London, Shackleton began planning another expedition of his own, which started in 1908 from a port in New

Zealand in a small whaler called *Nimrod,* reaching a position ninety-seven miles from the South Pole. This expedition made use of Mongolian ponies rather than dogs. Its greatest achievement was a journey made by Shackleton himself with three companions up the Beardmore Glacier, opening a route to the polar plateau and the goal of the South Pole itself. In all the annals of polar exploration, this ranks as one of the greatest journeys by sledge ever made without the aid of supporting parties. (These days, so-called explorers have everything, including journalists, flown in by air.) They narrowly escaped death from the cold and exhaustion, much the same causes that led to the disaster that overwhelmed Captain Scott and his party on their return from the pole in 1912. But Shackleton managed to preserve his party and return to the ship, all without losing a single man. On his return to the United Kingdom he was knighted in 1909. He described the adventures of the expedition in a book, *Heart of the Antarctic* (1909).

Two years later, on August 1, 1914, unperturbed by the death of Scott, he left England on the *Endurance,* for the Imperial Trans-Antarctic Expedition, which he had carefully planned. It was intended to cross the continent from the Weddell Sea to the Ross by way of the South Pole. The *Endurance* reached the Weddell in December 1914, soon after the First World War had begun. It moved slowly south, but though they made some significant discoveries, they could find nowhere to land, and drifted north again with the ice. On October 27, 1915, the ship was crushed to destruction in the ice and had to be abandoned. The party of twenty-eight camped on an ice floe. They drifted north on this for 164 days, until it broke up. The survivors took to their small boats, and six days later landed on Elephant Island, where they recamped on a small patch beneath the great cliffs of ice.

Shackleton and five of the men now set off on an even more hazardous effort. By small boat they succeeded in reaching South Georgia, 759 miles away. He then tried to return to the men on Elephant Island but failed. Then, with the help of a Chilean trawler, he managed to rescue all of the men on August 30, 1916.

Though the men under Shackleton survived, some of the party in the Ross Sea perished when they were also carried away by the ice. Despite that, this epic boat journey, which had tested Shackleton's skills as a leader, is the most famous episode in the history of exploration. His courage and sense of command seems to some to be superior to the often foolish attitudes of Scott and his party, who killed themselves by hauling their sledges to the pole and back, by hand. Shackleton's last book, *South,* published in 1919, describes the hazards of this trip. The journey has been described in more detail by one of the party, Cmdr. F. A. Worsley, and is a classic of its kind.

Shackleton had to wait until 1921 to mount another expedition. In September 1922 he set out a third time, on the *Quest.* But this was to be his last expedition. On January 5, 1922, he died on South Georgia of angina following influenza. His companions buried him on the island, and the expedition continued its work under the command of Frank Wild.

Frank Worsley said of the funeral: "When looking at Shackleton's grave and the cairn which we, his comrades, erected to his memory on a windswept hill of South Georgia, I meditated on his great deeds. It seemed to me that among all his achievements and triumphs, great as they were, his one failure was the most glorious. By self-sacrifice and throwing his own life into the balance he saved every one of his men— not a life was lost—although at times it had looked unlikely that one could be saved."

79

William James Pirrie

1847–1924

For a long time, Ireland was seen only as an agricultural country. When heavy industry did begin to develop it was around Belfast, across the North Channel from Clydeside. This was in the heartlands of Presbyterian Ireland, and naturally an association was seen between its firm Scotch principles and the fecklessness endemic in other, more Catholic parts of the country. This concentration of industry was to play a part in the eventual partition of the island in 1922.

A key figure in the industrial development of Ireland, and of the shipping business worldwide, was William James Pirrie. He was, in fact, born in Quebec in May 1847. His parents, however, were Irish. James Alexander Pirrie came from Little Clandeboye, Down, his wife was from Antrim. The boy was brought up back in Ireland at Conlig, near Belfast, where he went to school at the Royal Belfast Academical Institution.

When he left school at sixteen he entered the shipbuilding firm of Harland and Wolff as a pupil. His native talent was soon manifest, and he was rapidly promoted, becoming a partner in 1874. He was then only twenty-seven. The rest of his life was spent at Harland and Wolff, which he saw grow into one of the most important shipbuilding companies in the world. When it was converted into a limited liability company he became chairman of the board.

Pirrie began his career at an opportune time. The transition from wooden to steel-built ships was under way, and he followed, indeed promoted, many of the most important developments in the industry over the next few decades. The shipping business was the making of Belfast. In 1800 it was little more than a market town—the population was only 20,000. The Queen's Island shipyard was opened in 1851, and by 1880 the population had grown to 230,000. By 1901 the population was 348,965. Whereas the population of Ireland as a whole was shrinking due to emigration, Belfast was happily expanding, with most of its citizens depending on the shipyard. And by then, though much could be made of the city's radical past, it had become the center of Protestant resistance to home rule.

Though there had been giant ships before (Brunel's *Great Eastern*, for instance), Pirrie could be said to be the creator of the large modern ship. As the decades advanced, the ships which the firm built grew larger and larger. The *Oceanic,* the *Celtic,* the *Cedric,* and the *Baltic* were famous in their day. This line of ships culminated in the *Olympic* (1911), the *Titanic* (1912), and the *Britannic* (1914). But these ships were unfortunate, the *Titanic* sinking on its maiden voyage in spectacular and famous circumstances; the *Britannic* being sunk in the First World War while being used as a hospital ship. That, too was a mysterious event. The superstitious spoke of a curse on the shipyard because of its intolerance to Catholic workers.

Most of the advances made both with regard to the design of the ships and their engineering arose from suggestions made by Pirrie himself in these first decades of expansion. As the ships grew in length and width he was conscious of the need to ensure strength in the frames through new methods of construction.

The Pirrie ships were the first to place the passengers' accommodations amidships, and to create many of the arrangements and amenities now familiar in oceangoing liners. There were also great changes on the engineering side. New kinds of balance and expansion engines reduced vibration and improved efficiency.

One important development was the change from coal-fired ships, which meant the establishment of a worldwide bunker system that used oil fuel, and later diesel engines. This development was to have important consequences for the development of the oil industry, as marine shipping became a major consumer of fuel.

The firm had connections with many important shipping companies, and was sole builder for the White Star Line in England and the Bibby Line in the United States. It also built ships for the Peninsula and Orient line for use on routes to India and Australia, and for the

Royal Mail Steam Packet Company, among others. As the ships and their capacity grew, the firm also emphasized the need for harbor facilities to develop in tandem.

In 1902, Pirrie was one of the movers behind the creation of the Mercantile Marine Company, which brought many smaller interests on the North Atlantic routes into a more efficient conglomerate, or cartel. Pirrie grew Harland and Wolff into a business filling 230 acres on the Belfast and Clyde shorelines, employing some fifty thousand men. The First World War affected the yard dramatically. Liners were converted to war use, and gunboats and warships were built quickly. A new airplane department was added as the fighter plane became the new instrument of war.

In March 1918, Pirrie was made controller general of merchant shipping, in reaction to the effects of the German U-boat campaign against shipping on the Atlantic. This he tackled with typical energy.

Pirrie had been given a peerage in the House of Lords in 1906, and when the king visited Belfast to open the first sitting of the new parliament of Northern Ireland he was made a viscount. He died at sea on June 6, 1924, while on a trip to see ports in Latin America, and to urge the governments there to think of expanding their facilities to meet the rising trade in the postwar years.

By 1922, 180 people had been killed in East Belfast and throughout the shipyards in the sectarian struggles that arose over the partition of Ireland. Again, in 1935 and in the 1960s troubles stalked the derricks. (This was the background to Ulster dramatist Sam Thompson's famous play *Over the Bridge*.) The yards that Pirrie created became the core of the community strife in Northern Ireland. But in serving the worldwide needs of shipping, he had also created the employment much needed by the Belfast community. That the benefits would be shared by all was a problem beyond him to solve; that it was beyond the communities, too, is the tragedy of Ireland. Yet, in August 1969, some eight thousand workers who remained in the Pirrie yards voted at a mass meeting to maintain "peace and goodwill in the yard, and throughout the province." It may yet come.

80

Fr. Theobald Mathew

1790–1856

When the United States embraced Prohibition in the 1920s, it was the culmination of a temperance movement that had begun a very long time before. Among the first movers of the crusade against drink was an Irish priest known to all as the Apostle of Temperance.

Theobald Mathew, known to his family as Tobias, was born at Thomastown Castle, outside Cashel, in County Tipperary, on October 10, 1790. His father, James Mathew, was a distinguished Catholic, and Theobald was the fourth of twelve children by his mother, Anne Whyte. His charm and kindness stood out from childhood: "Darlin' master Toby, a born saint," exclaimed his mother, who was hopeful that he would fulfill her dream of having a priest in the family.

At the age of twelve, Mathew was sent to St. Candice's Academy in Kilkenny, where he stayed for seven years. In Kilkenny he came under the influence of two Capuchins, a Franciscan order, and in 1807 he entered Maynooth College to study for the priesthood, but left. The following year he was accepted into the Capuchins. He was ordained on Easter Sunday, 1814, and spent a year in Kilkenny before being sent to join the Capuchin friars in Cork. There he soon distinguished himself with his gentlemanly ways. Based in the Little Friary, he set about creating a school, industrial classes, and benefit societies. He created a cemetery for Cork's Catholics by buying up the botanic gardens in 1830. In 1822 his superiors recognized his talents and appointed him provincial of the Capuchins. He held this post for twenty-nine years, eventually resigning because of ill health.

In 1832, Cork was visited by a plague of cholera, which carried off many thousands. In Ireland, the temperance movement had been begun among the Quakers, but in 1838 Fr. Mathew became head of the Cork Total Abstinence Society after much urging from many prominent people in Cork, including William Martin, a Cork friend. The first meeting was held on April 10, 1838, and Fr. Mathew was the first to record his own pledge of total abstinence. He proved to be a wonderfully charismatic leader. Very soon he had persuaded many thousands to "take the pledge" not to drink again.

The political situation was, as so often in Ireland, disturbed by troubles of one kind or another. Fr. Mathew kept the movement a nonpartisan one and retained and expanded his support among Protestants in Munster.

He had a extraordinary presence, and many simple folk credited him with healing powers, although he was always anxious to deny them. As a preacher, Fr. Mathew drew thousands all across Ireland to him. He was in Limerick in 1839, and in Dublin in 1840. By 1843 he could write to a friend, "I have now, with the Divine Assistance, hoisted the banner of Temperance in almost every parish in Ireland."

The English novelist William Thackeray, no lover of either the Irish or the Catholic church, met him during a visit to Cork in 1842. "Avoiding all political questions, no man seems more eager than he for all the practical improvements of this country. Leases and rents, farming improvements, reading societies, music societies—he was full of these, and his schemes of temperance above all." Thackery's own countrymen would share in his crusade. During the years 1842 and 1843 Fr. Mathew traveled in Scotland and England, preaching temperance and signing up thousands more to the pledge. It is said some two hundred thousand people were enrolled.

The grim shadow of the famine passed over Ireland, beginning in 1845. Fr. Mathew had been among the first to alert the government as to what was happening, as want and distress grew in Cork and other areas of Munster. In the cities he was deeply involved in famine relief; he even stopped the work on the Capuchin church and gave the money for food. Ireland was left stunned by the disaster, and the temperance movement lost ground. In 1847 Fr. Mathew was the choice of the local clergy for bishop of Cork, but he was passed over by Rome.

In the spring of 1848 his untiring work finally caught up with him; he suffered a stroke. Despite his evident ill health, he went to America in 1849 and visited twenty-five states, pledging hundreds of thousands of people. These numbers seem extraordinary, but it is claimed that he enrolled up to seven million people in the United States at a time when the population of Ireland was 6,552,367 (1851 census).

Temperance was not unknown in the United States. In 1836, "cold water societies" had been introduced by the Rev. Thomas Hunt, who provided pledge cards to children to take home for others to sign. The first Prohibition law was passed in Tennessee in 1838. By the early 1840s, Temperance societies were much in vogue, supported by both Protestant clergymen and mill owners, who thought sober workers would be better for business. A temperance novel by Lucius Sargent, *My Mother's Gold Ring* (1834), sold 113,000 copies. By 1872 a Prohibition party was able to hold its first convention to nominate a candidate for the presidency. With all this enthusiasm in America, it is not surprising that on his travels Fr. Mathew managed to sign up many pledges.

In December 1851 he returned to Cork, his health broken. He was saddened that many of those millions who were said to have taken the pledge had gone back to drinking once his presence had passed. He felt his mission had failed, but his name and reputation would enable many others to carry on his work in later years, not only in Ireland but elsewhere in the world. As the American experiment showed, there is no easy answer to the problem of drink, to which has now been added the even worse scourge of drug addiction. But the success of Fr. Mathew, as limited as it was, shows what can be done about social problems through energy, persistence, and personal charm. Fr. Mathew died in Queenstown (now Cobh), just outside Cork, on December 8, 1856, and his simple grave soon became a place of pilgrimage.

81

Turlough Carolan

1670–1738

Traditional Irish music, as performed by the Chieftains or the River-dance Company, has swept the world in recent decades. But these high-profile performers owe much more than they may realize to the lonely talent of the last of the old Irish harpers, Turlough Carolan, "the last of the Irish bards."

Also known as O'Carolan and the descendant of an ancient family, he was born about 1670 at Nobber, in County Meath. Sometime about 1684 the family moved to Ballyfarnon, in Roscommon. There they were patronized by the MacDermott family, who owned the local iron foundry. Turlough was reared and educated with the children of the house. At the age of fourteen he lost his sight due to smallpox. Mrs. MacDermott then took charge of his future. She apprenticed him to a harper, and he was trained to play by ear. In 1691, when he came of age, she provided him with a horse, a man to hold it, a small sum of money, and off he went on his travels about Ireland as a harper. It was his custom to call on persons of rank and high station in big houses and play for them for either money or his supper. His talents were equally popular among the poor of the cottages. Carolan was not just a harper; he was also a composer, and would dedicate the tunes he composed on the road to the person who gave him food and lodging at the end of the day. Though he found his way into most counties of Ireland, most of his time was passed in northern Connaught or southern Ulster. He was welcomed not only by the old Gaelic families, but also by the newer, largely Protestant, gentry.

The historian Charles O'Conor of Belanagare said that Carolan was moral and religious, but convivial and "seldom surprised by intoxication." He also wrote poems, addressed in a personal way to the ladies of the houses where he lodged. Some two hundred of these are known.

Carolan married Mary Maguire from Fermanagh, and they had seven children before she passed away in 1733. He himself became ill at Tempo in Fermanagh in 1738, and returned to the only place he could then call home, the house of the MacDermotts at Alderford, in Roscommon. He died there on March 25. In one of the Stowe manuscripts, Charles O'Conor recorded: "Saturday the XXV day of March, 1738, Toirrdealbach O Cerbhallain died today, in the sixty-eighth year of his age. The mercy of God may his soul find, for he was a moral and a pious man." Carolan was buried at Kilronan, at Lough Meelagh, and it was said that his well-attended wake lasted four days.

Donald O'Sullivan, who gathered all that could be learned of Carolan fifty years ago, collected some two hundred tunes which had survived. Some had been reprinted in his lifetime, others after his death by his son. These surprisingly are lost. Some fifty of his tunes were collected by Edward Bunting, the pioneer collector of Irish music. Carolan worked in the very ancient tradition of Gaelic music, but he was also open to other European influences, notably the Italian music then fashionable in Dublin. His harp is preserved in Clonalis, the home of the O'Conor Dons, in Roscommon. James Kandiman collected some twenty of his poems, and Dr. Douglas Hyde another twelve. An edition of some of his songs was published in Dublin by John and William Neale about 1720. This is the earliest surviving example of printed music in Ireland. Thomas Moore, in the settings of his poems, utilized some of Carolan's airs, as in "O Banquet Not" and "The Young May Moon." Others were introduced into the ballad operas popular in the eighteenth century.

It is to Carolan, in one way or another, that the tradition of Irish music returns. Much of what is played today is in fact eighteenth-century dance music, but his original compositions from the early seventeenth century are redolent of the thousands of years of Irish culture which lie behind them. The harpers that followed him were not composers but merely players, who dwindled in number. The harp itself, which had been well adapted to earlier forms of music, could not play the music of the eighteenth century well, so it was displaced by the harpsichord, the violin, and then the piano.

To preserve some of this heritage, harp festivals were held at Granard, in Longford, in 1781 to 1785, and in Belfast in 1792. This last was organized by Edward Bunting, and it is to his notations of the tunes as eventually published some years later, that we owe much of what it known about this ancient music of Ireland. The use of Carolan's music by Moore kept later generations in touch with Ireland's music. Now, three hundred years after his birth, today's audience is able to recover the true corpus of Carolan's music.

82

Charles Gavan Duffy

1816–1903

As an Irish revolutionary and Australian statesman, Charles Gavan Duffy had a remarkable career indeed, for in both roles he was a man of importance and influence.

The son of a shopkeeper in Monaghan, he was born on April 12, 1816. His total formal education was a few months at a local school; otherwise he taught himself. He read widely and voraciously, as perhaps only the genuine self-taught can. Almost inevitably, he grew up to become a journalist, contributing from an early age to the *Northern Herald.* In 1836 he moved to Dublin, where he joined the staff of the *Morning Register.* In 1839 he moved to Belfast to work as the editor of a new Catholic paper, *The Vindicator,* and remained in Belfast till 1842. He found the time to study law and was called to the Irish bar, but he did not practice.

Returning to Dublin in the summer of 1842, he came in contact with two young barristers, THOMAS DAVIS [23] and John Blake Dillon, with whom in October he founded the *Nation,* perhaps the most influential newspaper ever published in Ireland. It supported DANIEL O'CONNELL [20] and the Repeal Association, and its efforts helped to fill the association's meetings. O'Connell was duly grateful. When the government prosecuted O'Connell in 1844, Gavan Duffy was tried with him and afterward joined him in Kilmainham Gaol. Both were released later that year by order of the House of Lords.

All across Europe this was an era of reviving nationalism, as a younger generation rejected the cautious precedents of those who had survived the Napoleonic wars. In 1834 an international association of republican societies had been formed, which included Young Germany, Young Italy, Young Poland, and Young France. In Britain, however, Young England was a reactionary group of young Tory aristocrats who sought a return to medieval ideals. And so, in Ireland, a Young Ireland party was formed in imitation of the Continental movements.

Among his most valued contributors, Gavan Duffy included the leading figures of Young Ireland. The stated ambition of the paper was "to create and foster public opinion in Ireland and to make it racy of the soil." As most of the writers were staunchly middle class, they did not mean anything crudely vulgar by this, rather, that all that they wrote would have a national reference. The paper was widely read and deeply influential. From its pages were gathered the songs and ballads that made up *The Spirit of the Nation,* which became a bestseller and was read everywhere, or rather sung everywhere, for it contained the patriotic ballads that passed almost at once into popular currency, and are today part of the folk tradition of Ireland.

Impatient young men that they were, the Young Irelanders soon broke with the aging O'Connell. The repeal movement had been a failure, and the famine had devastated the country. The outbreak of rebellion across Europe in 1848, first in Paris, in February, and then in the German states and elsewhere, inspired Young Ireland also to rise in arms. But in July 1848 Gavan Duffy was arrested and his paper suppressed. This did not prevent a brief flurry of insurrection by William Smith O'Brien and others in Tipperary, but it was quickly put down and the leaders were imprisoned.

Though some of the Young Irelanders were deported, Gavan Duffy survived four trials unconvicted and was released in 1849. He revived the *Nation* and became involved in the land reform movement along purely constitutional lines with Frederick Lucas and others. They founded the Tenant League in 1850, and at the general election of 1852 forty MPs (including Gavan Duffy from New Ross) were elected to Parliament, pledged to its aims and independent opposition. This was the beginning of a true Irish party. But its aims were betrayed when two leading members accepted offices from the government. Lucas died, the reform measures failed in the House of Lords, and Gavan Duffy was in despair.

Gavan Duffy left Ireland in ill health. In 1855, he emigrated to Australia where he began a law practice. He felt he had had enough of public life, but he could not resist politics. He was elected to the colonial assembly in Victoria and became minister of public works, minister of public lands, and prime minister of Victoria in 1871. A knighthood followed in 1873.

He championed the laborers and farmers, many of them Irish, against the capitalists and squatters (in Australia, farmers with large spreads of land). By the time he retired he had gained a reputation as one of the most distinguished Australian public figures.

Gavan Duffy left Australia in 1880 and went to live in the south of France. There he wrote a biography of his friend Thomas Davis, two histories of the Young Ireland movement, and his autobiography. This last was called appropriately *My Life in Two Hemispheres*. After he died, in Nice, on February 9, 1903, his remains were brought back to Ireland and were interred in Glasnevin, with the other heroes of Ireland. His son, George, was a lawyer who acted for SIR ROGER CASEMENT [94], while his daughter, Louise, was a republican and educator. To have radically influenced the public life of two countries, in two different parts of the world, is an achievement that ranks Gavan Duffy high in the pantheon of the great Irish.

83

Archbishop
John Joseph Hughes

1797–1864

As the first Catholic archbishop of New York, John Joseph Hughes had a profound influence over the development of American social and political life. He arrived in New York as archbishop the year after a financial panic, when nativists, those opposed to the immigrants arriving from Ireland, Poland, and Norway, complained that they contributed to low wages, the decline of the apprenticeship system, and a depressed state of the labor market generally. Hughes saw the city through the years of the Irish famine, when hundreds of thousands arrived. He was a crucial figure at a crucial moment in history.

Hughes was an immigrant himself, having been born in Tyrone, one of the counties of Northern Ireland, in June 1797—the year before the outbreak of the great rebellion by the United Irishmen from which springs the revolutionary tradition of modern Ireland.

He was the third of seven children born to Patrick Hughes and his wife, Margaret McKenna. The Hughes family was uninvolved in the disturbances. John was educated at the local schools, and soon decided on a vocation. In 1816, Patrick Hughes and his eldest son left Ireland for the United States. John was sent for the following year, and when these three were settled the rest of the family came, in 1818.

They settled in Chambersburg, Pennsylvania, where the young John worked in the stone quarries, as a road mender, and as a gardener.

He tried several times for admission to Mount St. Mary's Seminary at Emmitsburg, Maryland, but was told there was no room. He went to work as a gardener until a vacancy occurred, in 1820. He was ordained a priest for the diocese of Philadelphia in 1826.

When Hughes came to Philadelphia, the Catholic cathedral there was embroiled in a controversy between the archbishop and his lay trustees, which left Hughes unpaid at times. When a new church without lay trustees was opened, Hughes ruled it with a firm hand that was to serve him throughout his career. Though active in pastoral work, he gained controversy through his political activities. He was a redoubtable preacher of Catholic emancipation and a supporter of DANIEL O'CON-NELL [20]. He did not believe in suffering silently the anti-Catholic sentiments then rife in Philadelphia and throughout America. He founded the *Catholic Herald* and also a society to publish tracts. In 1830, under the name Cranmer, he published a series of supposed anti-Catholic letters in a Protestant paper, which he then exposed as a hoax. He did not see Catholicism as an obstacle to civil and religious liberty. His talents as a controversialist were soon recognized, and after delays of several kinds he was consecrated as coadjutor of New York in 1838. He became administrator in 1842 and archbishop in 1850.

When he arrived, the church was poorly equipped to serve the needs of a population which was rapidly expanding. In October 1839 he went to Europe, and also Dublin, to raise funds for his diocese in the cities he visited. After a controversy in New York, there were two major results: the total secularization of the U.S. public school system, and the creation of the parochial schools as they are known today. He led his people during the anti-Catholic riots of 1844 and became well known all over the United States, though he was often attacked in the press.

Hughes was also involved in national and international affairs. He was opposed to the abolitionist movement on the odd grounds that freedom would injure the slaves. He disapproved of Irish antislavery attitudes as an interference in America's internal affairs. He was well known in government circles and undertook a mission to Europe in 1861 to 1862 for President Abraham Lincoln to gain papal support for the North. His last public appearance, in July 1863, was to help the governor of the state put down the antidraft riots among the Irish in New York.

Though often autocratic and intolerant of disagreement, Hughes was a born leader and fighter for his own people. He was determined to prove that Catholics, especially Irish Catholics, were not second-class American citizens. The place of both the Irish and the Catholic church in modern America owes much to the determined leadership of John Hughes. He died in New York City on January 3, 1864, from Bright's disease after a lingering illness.

84

William R. Grace

1832–1904

The Irish in America were not among the most notable or creative of businessmen, but there were exceptions, one whom was the greatest shipping magnate of all time, William Russell Grace.

Grace was born at Queenstown, to the east of Cork, on May 10, 1832. He was the son of James Grace and his wife Ellen (formerly Ellen Russell). Cork was then the leading seaport in Ireland, with a brisk export and import trade as well as a large naval base.

The sea, perhaps inevitably, attracted Grace, and as a boy he ran away as a scullery hand on a clipper ship bound for the United States. Arriving in the new country, he spent two years as a clerk in a New York business house. Through his father in Ireland, he acquired a part interest in a ship's chandlery in Liverpool before he was twenty-one.

But at heart Grace was an adventurer. Again through his father's influence, he went to Callao, Peru, as a clerk in the shipping office of Bryce and Co. There he was joined by his brother Michael, and together they reformed the business as Grace Brothers and Co. Very quickly it had agents in Boston, Baltimore, and Liverpool, and was dominant in the South American trade. The two brothers were soon men of wealth.

In 1860, soon after his marriage to Lillius Gilchrist of Thomaston, Maine, illness forced William to leave Peru, and five years later he arrived in New York to settle, establishing the firm of W. R. Grace and Co. It was through this firm that he began to expand into other concerns which would include the Grace Steamship Co., a merchant marine fleet that carried most of the trade between the United States and South America. It had interests in Peruvian textiles, Brazilian rubber, Chilean nitrates, and many other commodities. The whole business was served by Grace banking houses.

In South America he had other interests, especially in Peru. He was an adviser to the Peruvian government and held most of the supply contracts for the Peruvian railway system; he also equipped the Peruvian army and navy.

Latin America was an unsettled place. At the end of the War of the Pacific between Chile and Peru (1879–1883) Peru had lost the nitrate-rich province of Tarapaca by the terms of the Treaty of Ancon, in 1883. Peru also was left with a huge national debt, and was unable to meet its international obligations to foreign debtors, especially British and American bondholders. In 1890 Grace finalized the Grace-Donoughmore coarrangement through which he took over the management of Peru's national debt, which involved the cancellation of two issues of government bonds worth $250 million in exchange for rich railroad, real estate, and mining concessions. This arrangement was ratified by the Peruvian Congress on October 25, 1889.

Many of the bondholders were British capitalists in the City of London. The Peruvian Corporation Ltd. was set up to manage the concessions under the nominal directorship of the Anglo-Irish peer Lord Donoughmore and a board of the bond holders, but in reality Grace managed it. He virtually "owned" Peru. This extraordinary adventure earned him the opprobrious nickname the Pirate of Peru.

The company secured ownership rights for its members in the two state railways of Peru for sixty-six years. They had all the production of Peruvian guano output up to three million tons (except for that taken from the Chincha Islands). The Peruvian government also promised to pay the company £80,000 a year for thirty years. And it finally got the ownership of the silver mines at Cerro de Pasco.

In all of this there were some advantages for the people of Peru. The company promised to complete the unfinished railways and repair those already in existence. The terms of the original agreement were revised in April 1907 (after Grace's death), by which the corporation's lease was extended for seventeen years and the government agreed to continue the annual payments for thirty years, although it was to receive half of the national receipts in exchange. It was perhaps one of the most extraordinary settlements in history. Yet the management of

Peru's finances, much as it might have been resented by some nationalists, was a form of enlightened imperialism which served to advance the wealth of William R. Grace and the welfare of the Peruvian nation at the same time.

Grace was also involved in affairs closer to home. He won praise for the relief he provided to Ireland in 1879, when the crops failed and there was widespread distress, which the duchess of Marlborough, the wife of the viceroy, attempted to relieve through an international appeal in the *Times* of London in December. In 1880 Grace was elected mayor of New York with the help of the Irish vote—the first Catholic to hold that office in a major U.S. city.

"Boss" Tweed had died in April 1878 in the Ludlow St. jail, he and his cronies having stolen up to $200 million from the city funds. Grace was one of a group of New York businessmen who had come in behind the new leader of Tammany Hall, "Honest John" Kelly, and rather than waste time on the Republican party, had come to terms with the ruling Democratic party. Grace proved to be both affable and efficient. He began a drive against police corruption and organized vice. His administration, which he reformed, prevailed on several of the streetcar companies to pay their back taxes, while Grace also managed to lower the tax rate for the city. In 1884 he was elected to a second term.

He then returned to his business interests. In 1891 he established the New York and Pacific Steamship Co., later the Grace Steamship Co., and finally, in 1895, he drew all his interests together into William R. Grace and Co. In 1897 he set up the Grace Institute for training women in domestic science, secretarial, and other vocational skills. This was a new idea—for the new woman was already making herself felt in the businessplaces of America. He died in New York City on March 21, 1904, but his business interests long survived him.

85

Joe McGrath

1887–1966

The founder of the Irish Hospitals Sweepstakes was one of the most remarkable Irish businessmen of his generation, a man who never said no to a challenge.

Joseph McGrath was born in Dublin, and showed his talent by joining a firm of accountants, Messers. Craig Gardner. He also joined the Irish Republican Brotherhood and fought on Marrowbone Lane during the Easter week rebellion. He was arrested and jailed in Wormwoodscrubs and Brixton jails. In the general election of 1919 he was returned on the Sinn Fein ticket for the St. James division of Dublin. In early 1920 he and Robert Barton were among the prominent members of Sinn Fein arrested by the authorities, but by August 1921 he and Barton were acting as messengers between EAMON DE VALERA [2] and Lloyd George, after the truce between the two sides, and again to the Anglo-Irish conference at Gairloch in September with Harry Boland. He supported the treaty, and in January 1922 was named Minister for Labor in the provisional government of the Irish Free State. During the civil war he was a member of what might be called the War Cabinet. In September 1922 his title was changed to Minister of Labor, Industry, Commerce, and Economic Affairs. In the first election of the Irish Free State he was elected from northwest Dublin, and was later elected TD from North Mayo.

Early in 1924, at the time of the army mutiny (when some conservative officers protested at government reductions in the army), he supported the officers, and later that year he and eight others of the national group resigned from the Dail, protesting what he described in the group's paper the *Nation* as "government by a clique and by officialdom of the old regime." He resigned his Dail seat in October 1924, and left politics.

One of the first great enterprises of the free state government was the Shannon Hydroelectric Scheme at Ardnacrusha. In 1925, Joe McGrath became labor adviser to Siemens-Schuckert, the German electrical firm contracted to build the giant installation.

This was only part of his business interests. In 1930 he and two others, Richard Duggan and Spencer Freeman, launched the Irish Hospitals Sweepstakes, after the Free State government had legalized charity sweepstakes. The Irish hospital system was in danger of collapsing through lack of funds. The first race on which they ran a sweep was the November Handicap of 1930. They sold an unbelievable £658,000 of tickets, about £22 million in today's funds. The hospitals got £132,000, or one-fourth of the total expenditure of all the hospitals in the Irish Free State. The promoters got £46,000. And so it went, earning McGrath and his friends millions.

Though illegal in many places, including the United States and Britain, the tickets were still sold. In the United States Joe McGrath was able to use the IRA to outlet the tickets. His contacts left Clan na Gael and went into business, their "physical skills" as revolutionaries deterring the Mafia from moving in on the act.

Though it was suspended during the war, the sweepstakes resumed in 1947 and went on till recently, when the need for it was no longer apparent. Its overall value to the Irish economy was astonishing. Tony Farmar wrote, "For the sweep as a whole, the net income to Ireland in 1932, after deducting the overseas prizes, was £3.5 million— somewhat more than the government's receipts from income tax."

Its huge success, with tickets being sold worldwide, made Joe McGrath and his family exceptionally wealthy. This provided him with the capital to enter into other areas of business, such as the long established Dublin Glass Bottle Co. In 1951 he became involved with efforts in Waterford to revive the glassmaking industry. This was the beginning of Waterford Crystal, a firm which he built up over the next fifteen years into one of the most famous brand names in the world, worth another fortune in exports to the Irish economy.

In his leisure time he was an avid racing fan, and became a well-known owner and breeder of racehorses. In time his horses won all the classic Irish races. Arctic Prince won the Epsom Derby in England in 1951.

McGrath was a member of the Irish Racing Board from 1945 until his death, its chairman from 1956 to 1962, and president of the Bloodstock Breeding Association of Ireland in 1953. He died at his Cabinteely home, outside Dublin, in March 1966.

In a land starved for capital, Joe McGrath was perhaps its first capitalist, a figure rare in Ireland at any time in the past. He touched Irish life at so many points that it must have been hard for many to get a clear view of his achievements. But the creator of the Irish Hospitals Sweepstakes and Waterford Crystal belongs in a special gallery of achievement.

86

Thomas Francis Meagher

1823–1867

To his contemporaries, Thomas Francis Meagher was simply known as Meagher of the Sword. It was a tribute to his dramatic rhetoric, but though he had lived as a soldier for much of his life, he left his country several important inheritances, including the national flag of present-day Ireland.

Thomas Francis Meagher was born in Waterford on August 3, 1823, where his father was a prosperous merchant. The family fortune had been made a generation before in the Newfoundland trade, which was an important part of the economy of the thriving seaport. In 1829 his father, Thomas Meagher, became an MP and mayor of Waterford.

Thomas Francis was educated at Clongowes Wood College, a select college run by the Jesuits. From there he was sent to a sister school, Stonyhurst, in England, which provided elements of a university education. At these schools Meagher was noted for his rhetorical and literary skills, both from reading the speeches of DANIEL O'CONNELL [20] and debating with other students.

At first he became involved in Daniel O'Connell's Repeal Association, having been dismayed at the incompetence of the authorities in the face of the famine. But this was a constitutional movement which did not appeal to his more ardent nature. In 1845 he joined the more revolutionary Young Ireland movement, and in 1847 was one of the founders of the Irish Confederation.

In February 1848 revolution broke out in France. Meagher went with William Smith O'Brien to Paris to support the revolutionaries as part of an Irish delegation to Lamartine to congratulate the people of France on the establishment of a republic. He returned to Dublin with a French gift to the Irish nation—a new tricolor in imitation of the French flag. It was green, white, and orange. He explained that it was to represent the union of the two traditions in Ireland in peace. This became the accepted flag of the republican movement, and is now the official flag of the Irish state.

His highly dramatic and inflammatory speech led to his arrest and prosecution, but the jury disagreed. In July 1848, the Irish Confederation established a "War Directory," of which Meagher was a member. He and Smith O'Brien traveled throughout southern Ireland urging revolution among the people. But the Young Ireland uprising in July 1848, Ireland's response to the European year of insurrection, was a comic failure and again led to his arrest. He was tried for high treason and in October was sentenced to hang.

His death sentence was commuted. Instead, in July 1849 he was deported to Van Dieman's Land (now the Australian state of Tasmania) with Smith O'Brien and Terence Bellew MacManus. In 1852 he made a dramatic escape from the penal colony, and when he reached New York in May he received a tremendous welcome from his countrymen.

Meagher then took up the law and was admitted to the New York bar in 1855. His talents soon brought him into prominence among the leaders of the Irish community. He founded and edited the *Irish News*, first issued on June 1, 1856, and was much in demand as an author and lecturer. For *Harper's* magazine he made two exploring trips through Central America, which provided new material for his lectures.

When the Civil War broke out, Meagher raised, in New York, a company of Zouaves, of which he was the captain. (The Zouaves had a distinctive uniform with baggy trousers, derived from those worn by native troops of the French army in Algeria after 1830, which had been suggested by Lincoln's friend, Elmer E. Ellsworth, for wear by the company of volunteer fireman from New York City.) They went to the front line with the 69th New York Volunteers and took part in first battle of Bull Run, in July 1861. Returning to New York, he organized an Irish Brigade for the Army of the Potomac. On February 3, 1862, he was promoted to brigadier general and appointed its commander. He led his brigade through the Peninsular Campaign to the Battle of

Chancellorsville, and it proved itself at the battle of Fair Oak in June 1862, and in the Seven Days, at Antietam, and Chancellorsville. At Fredericksburg, on December 13, 1862, the brigade was cut to pieces and Meagher was wounded in the field. In May 1863 he resigned, complaining that he had not been allowed to withdraw his soldiers to recover their morale.

However, he was recommissioned in December 1863, and was given command of the military district of Etowah, with his headquarters in Chattanooga, Tennessee. Here he saw incidents of brutality by the Union Army against the Southern civilian population that reminded him of the worst excesses of British rule in Ireland. After a very short time he resigned, and was then assigned to Sherman's army in Savannah, Georgia, from which he was discharged when the war ended.

Meagher supported President Andrew Johnson's Reconstruction policies. The president then appointed him territorial secretary of Montana, in July, 1865, and he was named acting governor in September 1866. He had many problems in the gold-mining camps and plains settlements. His support of Johnson and the Catholic religion did not make him a welcome figure to the powerful local vigilantes who actually ruled the territory. His efforts to root them out were a failure.

While on a scouting trip against hostile Indians near Fort Benton, on the night of July 1, 1867, he fell from the steamer on which he was traveling and drowned in the Missouri River. His body was never recovered. Unfriendly critics said he was drunk.

It was the English novelist William Thackeray who gave Meagher his nom de guerre Meagher of the Sword, as a consequence of a typically fiery speech the young man gave extolling the virtues of the sword at a meeting of the Repeal Association in Dublin, in July 1846:

> The soldier is proof against an argument—but he is not proof against a bullet. The man that will listen to reason— let him be reasoned with, but it is the weaponed arm of the patriot that alone can prevail against the battalioned despotism.
>
> Then, my Lord, I do not condemn the use of arms as immoral, nor do I conceive it to be profane to say that the King of Heaven bestows His benediction upon those who unsheath the sword in the hour of a nation's peril.
>
> Abhor the sword? No, my Lord, for in the passes of the Tyrol, it cut to pieces the banner of the Bavarian.

Abhor the sword? No, my Lord, for at its blow, a great
nation started from the waters of the Atlantic, and the crippled colony sprang into the attitude of a proud republic—
prosperous, limitless, and invincible.

Daniel O'Connell prevented him from saying more, and the Young
Irelanders walked away from O'Connell. This appeal to the sword, to
physical force, thrilled his audience and countless later admirers.
Meagher stands squarely in the center of the Irish revolutionary tradition to this day, but as O'Connell realized, and as Meagher himself came
to see in Tennessee and Montana, the sword may do in wartime, but the
affairs of any community cannot be ruled by it on all occasions. To pros-
per, the republic he was so proud to serve needed peace. As a rhetori-
cian Meagher was outstanding, but as the old Irish saying has it, "Fine
words butter no parsnips."

87

Richard Martin

1754–1834

Known to his Georgian contemporaries as Humanity Dick, Richard Martin was a pioneer in the ethical treatment of animals. But he had other claims to fame as well.

He was the eldest son of Robert Martin, one of a family settled in Galway since the thirteenth century, and his first wife, Bridget Barnewall, a daughter of Lord Trimlestown. He was born in Dublin in February 1754, but he is associated with the rugged shore of the west of Ireland.

He was the first of his family who was brought up a Protestant from childhood, for many Catholics became at least outwardly Protestant in order to hold on to their lands in the eighteenth century. After attending Harrow School, he abandoned his studies at Cambridge to enter Parliament in 1776. He was called to the Irish bar in 1781. Although he joined the Connaught circuit, he was merely attempting to gain the qualification needed to act as a magistrate. He acted in one case only, a famous action between two brothers named Fitzgerald, which caused a social stir at the time. He was high sheriff of Galway in 1782, and continued his public life as colonel in the Irish Volunteers, and of the local Galway Yeomanry, as befitted his social position.

His home was at the castle of Ballinahinch on an estate that covered two hundred thousand acres, all he could see for thirty miles, deep in the wilds of Connemara. He was called the King of Connemara, but in the days of rapacious landlords he had a good reputation among his tenants. This huge estate made him one of the largest landlords in the

west, and it was he who built much of the present family house standing in a magnificent location overlooking the Owenmore River. It is featured in William Thackeray's travel book *An Irish Sketch Book* and in
MARIA EDGEWORTH'S [91] letters. Martin was thought to have been the
model for Godfrey O'Malley, the uncle of the hero in Charles Lever's
novel *Charles O'Malley*, and the novel *The Martins of Cro Martin*, also
by Charles Lever, is based on his family history.

Martin married twice. By his first wife he had two sons and a
daughter. His second wife was the mother of three daughters and a son.

He was a member of the Irish Parliament, representing several
seats until it was abolished by the Act of Union, a measure he supported. In 1801 he was reelected from Galway, and he remained a
member of Parliament until 1826, when his election by eighty-four
votes was challenged and he was unseated.

He was a friend of the Prince Regent, but fell out with him for a
time when the prince became George IV, as Martin supported the
rejected Queen Caroline. Martin supported Catholic emancipation
(granted in 1829), but, anxious for his seat, he made it known that he
would not vote to suppress the Catholic Association, the power base of
DANIEL O'CONNELL [20], and the Catholic church. But it was not his
role in Irish politics that made him famous, rather his love of animals
and his readiness as a duelist. His fights with "Fighting" Fitzgerald and
Eustace Stowell were relayed in his own words in Sir Jonah Barring-
ton's *Personal Sketches of His Times*.

He worked to abolish the death penalty for forgery, and introduced a bill to allow those charged with serious offenses the benefit of
legal counsel. He twice refused a peerage.

In spite of opposition from the political establishment, he managed
to get through Parliament an act "to prevent the cruel and improper
treatment of cattle." This was the first act in the world to prevent cruelty
to animals and was the beginning of a long campaign in Victorian and
modern times against cruel practices on the farm, in racing, and nowa-
days in scientific research. He was one of those who founded the Royal
Society for the Prevention of Cruelty to Animals, in 1824.

After losing his seat he retired to Boulogne in the north of France,
a haunt of British and Irish debtors, where he died on January 6, 1834,
at the age of seventy-nine.

His heir, Thomas Martin, died from a fever he contracted while
visiting his tenants in Clifden Workhouse during the famine year of

1847. His daughter, Mary Letitia Martin, was the author of a novel, *Julia Howard,* about the west of Ireland, but she was ruined by the famine, during which she had worked to relieve the suffering and died ten days after she and her husband reached New York in 1850.

The huge estate had been mortgaged to an insurance company, which foreclosed on it and sold it off for very little in the Encumbered Estates Court. In 1926 it was bought by the famous cricketer Prince Ranjitsinhji, the Jam Sahib of Nawanagar, and today it is a country house hotel of great elegance, where the memory of Richard Martin is honored.

These days it is fashionable to deride "Victorian values," but it is often forgotten that those values are the source of much of the legislation that exists regarding the proper treatment of animals, factory workers, the mentally ill, and so on. In this respect the modern world has little claim to the same moral values. Today Richard Martin's name and his love of animals and of his Connemara wilderness is honored all over the world by the innumerable groups and societies devoted to animal welfare, as well as important issues of ecology. An enlightened landlord and a progressive legislator in his own day, Martin remains a moral example through his campaigns for the kinder treatment of animals.

88

James T. Farrell

1904–1979

Though he seemed to have passed out of literary fashion for a while, when he died in 1979, James T. Farrell had, almost alone among his literary contemporaries, encompassed so much of a certain kind of Irish and Irish-American experience in such novels as his *Studs Lonigan* trilogy that there is little doubt that he will be seen as a classic American author. Admirers such as Norman Mailer have already begun to bring him back to that eminent and proper position.

James Thomas Farrell was born on Chicago's South Side in 1904, and died in his Manhattan apartment in 1979. It was a long and often difficult journey from poverty to fame and then to neglect.

He went to school among his Irish compatriots on the South Side of the city, where he attended St. Cyril High School, run by the Carmelite fathers, and from which he graduated in June 1923. He attended evening classes at De Paul University, and then went to the University of Chicago for three years.

He had numerous odd jobs: as a shoe wrapper in a Chicago chain store, a clerk in an express office, a filling station attendant, a clerk for a cigar company on upper Broadway in New York City, a salesman on Long Island, and an undertaker's assistant. He began writing as a campus reporter for the *Chicago Herald Examiner.*

This was a hard grind, but with the publication of *Young Lonigan* in 1932 he made a name for himself as an exponent of the realistic or naturalistic style of novel. As might be expected, this led to harsh reviews and often worse. In 1937 his book *A World I Never Made* was prosecuted for obscenity—three years after the ban of JAMES JOYCE'S [25] *Ulysses* was lifted. However, there were also rewards, such as a Guggenheim Fellowship in 1936. *The Young Manhood of Studs Lonigan* (1934) and *Judgment Day* (1935) completed a trilogy which won the Book-of-the-Month prize in 1937. It has been described as being, among other things, "a devastating indictment of American Catholicism's shortcomings," but all critics agree that it is his greatest achievement.

Farrell belongs, with John Steinbeck, John Dos Passos, Jack Conroy, John O'Hara, Norman Mailer, and James Jones, to a stream of realistic writers who have been ousted by the preference of academic critics for modernist writers influenced by Joyce. He also belongs to the era of the Great Depression, and it may be that the more prosperous America of today would rather forget the poverty of its past.

Farrell's political views were always radical, a protest against "conditions which brutalize human beings and produce spiritual and material poverty." But he was often at odds with orthodox members of the Communist party—an American of independent mind like Farrell was simply not cut out to toe any party line. He went on writing to the end of his life, but aside from the Lonigan trilogy, his other forty-nine books received far less attention in later years.

At the end of the 1930s he could write: "My fiction is written in the naturalistic or realistic tradition. What I have already written is part of a plan of books on which I am engaged for over ten years. When and if this plan is completed, it will consist of twenty-five or more works, including novels, novelettes, short stories, sketches and plays . . . The purpose of these works is, generally stated, to recreate a sense of American life as I have seen it, as I have imagined it, and as I have reflected upon and evaluated it. I am concerned in my fiction with the patterns of American destinies, and with presenting the manner in which they unfold in our time. My approach to my material can be suggested by a motto of Spinoza which I have quoted on more than one occasion: 'Not to weep or laugh, but to understand.' "

The model for this enterprise was Emile Zola's vast nineteenth-century series about the life of one extended French family over several generations. But Zola hoped he was writing a "scientific" account of destiny, in which the lives of his characters were predetermined. But Farrell, due to his Catholic background, had little time for such predestination. Typically Irish, he retains for his characters some possibility of acting freely, and of changing their lives through their own determination. If he is sometimes sentimental, then so is Hemingway. This sense for human feelings is perhaps also a part of his Irish heritage.

James T. Farrell died on August 22, 1979, of a heart attack in his Manhattan apartment in New York City. He was the last, and perhaps one the greatest exponents of the novel in the American naturalistic tradition. Rough and raw, he had done enough in a lifetime to ensure himself lasting fame, and influence over the future of American fiction when literary fashion changes.

89

F. Scott Fitzgerald

1896–1940

The name of Scott Fitzgerald is forever associated with the Jazz Age, but this has perhaps done him a disservice. He represents a particular kind of Irish-American experience, one in total contrast to that of JAMES T. FARRELL [88] and JOHN O'HARA [99]. He reminds us, if we needed reminding, of the huge variation in the experiences of Irish Americans. Some of them had not only lace curtains on the windows, they had polished silver on the sideboard.

After his death, his daughter Scottie investigated the complicated family background of her father and the families with which he was connected. Fitzgerald had cherished the thought that he had rich Southern connections, but far more important were his Irish ones. His grandfather, Philip McQuillan, had been born in Fermanagh in Northern Ireland, though little is known of his paternal grandfather, Michael Fitzgerald. Fitzgerald, however, married Cecilia Scott, who had Southern connections to Francis Scott Key, the author of the American national anthem.

Francis Scott Key Fitzgerald was born in St. Paul, Minnesota, on September 24, 1896. He was baptized a Catholic and reared in a Catholic household—formative experiences (as we know from James Joyce and other writers) involving guilt and rebellion, which can never be forgotten, even when the religious basis of one's childhood is rejected in later life. His early years were spent in St. Paul, but then the family moved to Buffalo, New York.

The last two years of his preschool education were passed in the Newman School in Hackensack, New Jersey. In the fall of 1913 he entered Princeton University, but with the advent of the First World War, he left college without a degree, having obtained an army commission as a second lieutenant. But during the war, which for Americans only began in 1917, he saw no military action.

In March 1920 his first novel, *This Side of Paradise,* was published, and the following month, on April 3, he married Zelda Sayre in the rectory of St. Patrick's Cathedral in New York City. Such a private ceremony, in the priests' house rather than in the church, was the usual thing for a Catholic marrying a Protestant, but this seems to have been his last formal connection with the Catholic Church of his youth and ancestors. However, he never really escaped from the moral atmosphere of his early years and its strict rules. His later life never seemed quite to live up to the standards he set himself, and it was this tension that forms much of his writing.

It was as a short-story writer, especially of a popular literary yet commercial story, that Fitzgerald made his name. In the days of the prosperous magazines, a living could be made from writing for them. His first novel captured something of the hectic college life he had left behind, but always hankered after. This was followed by *The Beautiful and the Damned* in 1922, but it was *The Great Gatsby,* published in 1925, which established him as a major literary figure, and it is generally agreed to be not only his masterpiece, but a novel of special significance to the American experience.

After this, Fitzgerald began to suffer literary and personal difficulties. He and his wife moved to Paris, met Ernest Hemingway, JAMES JOYCE [25] and other writers of the period. He and Zelda lived in the south of France and began a life of traveling. Then, in the spring of 1930, Zelda's mental health collapsed, and she was placed in a sanitarium. "I left my capacity for hoping on the little roads that led to Zelda's sanitarium," Fitzgerald recorded in one of his notebooks. Even a late relationship with the columnist Sheilah Graham did little to assuage his loss.

His next book, *Tender Is the Night,* did not appear until 1934, and from then on his career disintegrated. The critics were, on the whole, kind to the book, which sold moderately well, but it was no great seller, and it left the author with unpaid debts and a feeling that there was some fault in the novel which he could still put right.

His novel *The Last Tycoon* was left unfinished at his death and had to be arranged for publication by his friend, the critic Edmund Wilson. This book, which had cost him much turmoil, was moving in a new direction. However, Fitzgerald was unable to follow it—his talent was dying.

He went out to that graveyard of talents, Hollywood, in 1937 to work on movies for money. Here he met Sheilah Graham, a young journalist whom he spent a measure of time introducing to the intellectual history he himself had so enjoyed. But little else seemed to go right. His difficulties and debts mounted. In his notebook he says: "Then I was drunk for many years, and then I died." And he did, on December 21, 1940. His was a career of promise which was never quite realized, but his works have influenced our ideas about the 1920s, and America as a whole, in an important way.

90

Mother Mary Aikenhead

1787–1858

No account of the great and influential Irish would be complete if it did not include an Irish nun somewhere on its list. There are many misconceptions about the life of a nun, but as the life of Mary Aikenhead, the founder in 1815 of the now worldwide order of the Irish Sisters of Charity, amply demonstrates, a religious life did not prevent a woman from having a full career or exercising immense influence on the world beyond the convent walls.

Mary Aikenhead was born in Cork on January 19, 1787. She was the daughter of a Church of Ireland physician, David Aikenhead, and his wife Mary Stackpole, who was a Catholic. Mary was initially brought up in the Anglican tradition, but her father became a Catholic shortly before his death, and she, too, was received into the Catholic church on June 2, 1802.

She had an early ambition to serve the poor, and looked to find some order that was actively engaged in community charitable work. When she became a nun, she was selected (somewhat against her will, it is said) by Dr. Daniel Murray to form just such a religious community, which they did with the permission of the Roman authorities.

Mary Aikenhead and one of her colleagues then spent three years at the Micklegate Bar Convent in York for the novitiate. She took the name Sister Mary Augustine, though according to the custom that prevailed in the British Isles, she was always known as Mrs. Aikenhead.

(This custom dated back to penal times, when communities of nuns claimed merely to be living in common.)

The Religious Sisters of Charity, as the order was called, were inspired by the original French sisters founded by St. Vincent de Paul in Paris. Their rule was modeled on that of the Jesuits. The first vows were taken on September 1, 1815, and Mary Aikenhead was appointed superior general. They began their work when the two nuns returned to an orphanage on North William Street in Dublin, which was to be their new home. They took the usual vows of poverty, chastity, and obedience, to which was added a fourth vow—to serve the poor.

They cared for the orphans, established a day school, and went out into the community to visit families in their homes. Their numbers rose, and more institutions were added to the original. They taught in the parish school, in free schools, and opened a Magdalen refuge for girls who were expecting babies outside marriage.

Sixteen years of unrelenting work took their toll, and in 1831 Mary Aikenhead's health gave way, leaving her an invalid for the rest of her life. But her mental energy remained. This is perhaps the real significance of religious orders for women, that they provided what was in effect a professional role for them in areas of management and social action which would otherwise have been closed to them in those days. Moreover, they attained what the women's movement of today espouses: a sense of community, sisterhood, and shared purpose far removed from the narrow confines of the domestic scene.

In 1832 Ireland was visited by cholera, during which time Mary Aikenhead directed her sisters' heroic labors. In 1834 the congregation received its papal approval. It was also the year when she opened St. Vincent's Hospital in Dublin, which was the first Irish Catholic hospital. Removed to a new site at Elm Park, it still exists. She pioneered the staffing and managing of hospitals by religious women trained in modern nursing. In time, convalescent homes, homes for the blind, deaf, and crippled, old peoples' homes, mothers' clinics, hostels, and recreation centers were set up, all in addition to the original schools.

The Irish nuns spread to England and Scotland. In 1838 the Irish Sisters of Charity became the first nuns to go to work in Australia, with which Ireland had many connections. (In Australia they are now called the Daughters of Mary Aikenhead.) Later still, they went to the United States, where they are well established in Los Angeles, and to Zambia and Nigeria.

In the middle of the nineteenth century, when much was made of the efforts of Florence Nightingale during the Crimean War, said by many to be the first modern war, the Irish Sisters of Charity also worked in the Scutari hospitals, but with far less personalized fanfare than the British "Lady With the Lamp."

During the last twenty-seven years of her life, Mary Aikenhead had to direct these worldwide operations from her bed, for she had been crippled by an incurable spinal condition. She died in Dublin on July 22, 1858. Aside from her great skills as an organizer, many had been impressed with her deep spiritual qualities and her sense of mission as a gift from God. In 1921 the cause for her beatification was issued in Rome. This matter, always a long affair with the Catholic church, makes progress. Her name may yet be added to a small roster of modern Irish saints.

In Ireland, it used to be said that if one wanted the country to be properly run, it should be given to the charge of a reverend mother and a Christian Brother. At a time when management skills in many areas of public life and social action were lacking, Mary Aikenhead proved the truth behind the old joke.

91

Maria Edgeworth
1767–1849

Though her name may not be familiar to all, except, perhaps, students in Ireland who have to read her novel *Castle Rackrent* as part of their literature courses, Maria Edgeworth has an important place in the history of not only Irish but European and American literature. Sir Walter Scott admitted that it was from her earthy tales of Irish life that he derived the notion of writing his own series of romantic novels of Scottish history. His novels, in turn, inspired James Fenimore Cooper, Alessandro Manzoni, Ivan Turgenev, and many others who attempted to combine scenes of domestic life within a setting of national destiny. Out of the novel so many Irish schoolchildren groan over arose a whole aspect of the romantic movement in literature.

This was something of an achievement for a lady, and she was a lady, who lived much of her life in a mansion house on her father's estate isolated in the bogs of western Ireland. Her father, Richard Lovell Edgeworth, was an important figure, not only in the life of his daughter, but in intellectual society in general. He was a much married man, with a passion for invention and education. Together with his daughter he wrote *Practical Education,* a book of great importance in the development of modern education, for they based their whole system, derived from Rousseau to some extent, on the reasoning and conversations of children, largely his own. Like the best of modern education it was child-centered.

Maria's life was not lived in the shadow of her father; indeed, if anyone hears of him it is through his connection with her. Maria

Edgeworth was the second child and eldest daughter of Richard and his first wife. She was born in her grandparents' house at Black Bourton, in Oxfordshire, on New Year's Day 1767. They were the type of family that traveled much in England and France, but after 1782 much of their time was spent in Ireland at Edgeworthstown. Her letters are a rich source, not only of her own life, but of the hectic times they lived through. She had met rather grand families as neighbors, such as the family of Lord Longford and others. She also got to know the ordinary people around town and on her father's estate.

Though she wrote a great deal under her father's influence, her novels were her own. Her first one, *Castle Rackrent*, appeared anonymously in 1800, the year of the Act of Union. It tells the story of a tumbled and decayed great house in rural Ireland and the decline of the family over several generations through the eyes of Thady, a loyal family retainer, whose praise of their lifestyle reads as an ironic commentary on the whole state of Ireland that had just led to the uprising of 1798. Maria Edgeworth wrote many other tales and stories, often of fashionable life, of which *The Absentee* is among the most important, dealing again with Irish affairs.

In 1802 the family went to Europe, and she refused an offer of marriage from a Swedish count. Though she seemed unperturbed, her stepmother thought she regretted the decision. At home again, her work was done (like Jane Austen's) in the middle of family life crowding around her in the drawing room. In 1813 the family was in London, where they were much sought after, and she met Sir Walter Scott. When *Waverley*, the first of Walter Scott's novels which was published anonymously, appeared, she knew from the style it was by him. She visited his home at Abbotsford, Scotland, in 1823, and Scott himself was at Edgeworthstown in 1825.

During the famine years, Maria Edgeworth did all that she could for the stricken peasants of her district. She died on May 22, 1849, and is buried in the family vault in the parish graveyard.

Her *Castle Rackrent* is undoubtedly the first realistic Irish novel. It influenced the works of George Moore, JAMES JOYCE [25], and others. She invented the regional novel, and though to some metropolitan tastes that may seem a small claim to fame, it is on her regional novels that the literature of many countries, including western America, rests.

92

John Barry

1745–1803

The creator of the American navy and its traditions, John Barry, was born in Ireland at Tacumshane, County Wexford, in 1745, the year of the last Jacobite uprising against the Hanoverians. In the British Isles this was the last military gesture of the old Catholic order, to which his family belonged. He was brought up with a strong religious sense, which he retained to the end of his life.

Barry went to sea as a boy, at fourteen it is said, eventually becoming a shipmaster in the port of Philadelphia, which had many Irish connections even at that time. He was engaged in the trade to and from Latin America and the ports of the West Indies up until 1774.

In 1775 he sailed to British ports on the *Black Prince*, the largest, finest, and fastest of the American merchant marine fleet. He was one of those involved in signing the nonimportation act, which was one of the colonies' first moves toward breaking the link with Britain.

When the American Revolution broke out, John Barry was one of the very first captains to be commissioned by the Continental Congress. Seeing the trend of events at home, he hurriedly left Liverpool on the *Black Prince* to return to Philadelphia. He arrived there on October 13, the very day that the Continental Congress resolved to outfit two armed cruisers, one with fourteen guns, the other with ten.

Though he was then in the full flow of his own trading prosperity, he threw in his hand with the patriotic colonial movement and enlisted in the Continental navy. From that day to his death his name stood at the head of the Navy List, in which the seniority of naval officers is recorded; he had no other commander over him and reported directly to Congress, the president, or the government committees.

In command of the brig *Lexington* (with fourteen guns), named for one of the first battles of the Revolutionary War, he captured the British sloop *Edward* off Chesapeake Bay on April 7, 1776. This action was historic, as it was the first capture of a foreign vessel by a commissioned American warship in which the enemy was forced to lower its flag to the United States. In fact, his vessel was the first to carry the Continental flag to victory at sea. Later the same year, Barry led a raid of four ships on a British contingent on the Delaware River below Philadelphia, seizing important supplies.

At sea he captured three more ships before returning to Philadelphia to superintend the construction of warships on the Delaware River. He was given command of a ship, but it later had to be destroyed—despite his protests—to prevent it from falling into the hands of the enemy.

With four small boats he rowed down to Philadelphia and with his twenty-seven men captured a British ship which held 136 officers, men, and marines. It was an extraordinary feat of arms that unsettled the British, and it is thought that it hastened their withdrawal from the city. Then he came to the aid of Gen. George Washington, helping him and his despairing army cross the Delaware River. For a while he served in the U.S. Army, commanding a volunteer artillery company at the Battle of Trenton on December 26, 1776.

He took over the naval command at Philadelphia, and from 1780 to the end of the war commanded the frigate *Alliance,* engaging in several sea battles. He carried the Marquis de Lafayette to France. On another voyage he captured two English sloops. He was badly wounded in this engagement.

On another cruise he captured nine prizes, that is, enemy ships which would later be sold to reward his own men. His engagement with the British man-of-war *Sybil,* on March 10, 1783, was the last sea battle of the American War of Independence. (A log of the *Alliance,* kept by John Kessler, gives a vivid impression of the days at sea between 1781 and 1783.)

With the peacetime reorganization of the navy, Barry was made senior captain, and offered his services to Washington to fight the Barbary pirates. From then until his early death he supervised the creation and progress of the U.S. Navy. In 1794 he was given the command of the new frigate *United States,* and was named a commodore on the Navy List.

During the sea war with revolutionary France, Barry's command covered all the U.S. ships in the West Indies. This undeclared war arose from the United States' failure to fulfill the treaty obligations it had entered into with France during the Revolution. Under his command, the *United States* carried the commissioners who negotiated the end of the war to France. On February 22, 1797, the last birthday he spent in government, Washington personally conveyed to him a naval commission, *Number One,* making him commander in chief of the naval forces of the United States.

Though a strong man for discipline, Barry was much admired by his sailors and officers, and never had any trouble in making up a crew. He was affable and humorous, and like many of his countrymen from Ireland he had a quick temper, but any excess violence he at once apologized for. On his ships he saw to it that religious duties were strictly observed (even though he was a Catholic and his men mostly Protestants).

For many years he had suffered from asthma, which finally killed him soon after he retired. When John Barry died, at his home in Philadelphia on September 13, 1803, his name headed the serving list of U.S. Navy officers. He was buried in St. Mary's Catholic churchyard in Philadelphia, where his grave was almost lost sight of, though his reputation never faded. There is now a statue of him in front of Independence Hall in Philadelphia.

"Commander Barry," Joseph Dennie wrote as early as 1813, "may justly be considered the Father of our navy. His eminent services during our struggle for independence, the fidelity and ability with which he discharged the duties of importance which he filled, give him lasting claim upon the gratitude of this country."

For his countrymen he was an example of distinction in an area largely thought to be dominated by British talents. Another statue of him now dominates the wooden quays along the harbor in Wexford, one of the few memorials to sailors in Ireland. For Irish nationalists, his courage was an example of just what the Irish race could achieve in war. To Americans, he left a gallant naval tradition which has lasted to this day.

93

John Ford
1895–1973

Some of John Ford's films are among the most famous ever made. Through them he created not only a lasting vision of America, but also an idea of Ireland which was accepted by many Irish Americans as a reality. In truth, both were deeply personal to the man himself.

Ford was born Sean Aloysius O'Feeney to Irish immigrants at Cape Elizabeth, Maine. His family connections were with the west of Ireland, and he was a distant cousin of the celebrated Irish author Liam O'Flaherty, author of *The Informer.* He was educated at Portland High School, but lasted only three weeks or so at the University of Maine. Instead, he went to California to join his brother Francis, who was working in Hollywood for Universal Studios. For four years he worked as a bit player, stuntman, and special-effects man at Universal, appearing in D. W. Griffith's *Birth of a Nation.* In 1916 he changed his name to Jack Ford, and the following year he became a director. He married Mary McBryde Smith in 1920 (they had one son and one daughter), and in 1923 he moved on to Fox Films, where he began his longtime association with the screenwriter Dudley Nichols.

In later years, Ford claimed he made westerns, but they represented only a small part of his output. He won an Oscar for his version of *The Informer* in 1935, but equally important were *Stagecoach, Young Mr. Lincoln, The Grapes of Wrath, My Darling Clementine, She Wore a Yellow Ribbon, The Searchers,* and *The Man Who Shot Liberty Valance.*

Ford had a long struggle to get *The Informer* made, because the studio bosses were not enthusiastic about a novel of revolutionary vengeance set in Dublin during the troubles. Ford astutely changed the setting of the film from the grim days of the Irish civil war of 1922-1923 back a few years to the war of independence in 1920, making the police British rather than Irish. The informer betrays his old comrade to get money to go to America, but he is tracked down by the "organization" and killed.

Indeed, it was grim stuff, but it represented a view of Ireland that was realistic and moving. Ford had already made some Irish-related films (*The Shamrock Handicap, Mother Machree, Riley the Cop*), but his interest as a filmmaker was in creating an idea of America rather than Irish America.

In 1952 he finished a project that had been in the making since before the war: *The Quiet Man,* starring John Wayne as an American boxer who has vowed never to fight again and Maureen O'Hara as the girl he wants to marry. It enjoyed a huge success, and was of some importance in the emergence of a national film industry in Ireland. In later years it also brought visitors by the hundreds of thousands to the beautiful country around Cong in Galway where it was filmed. But in its details it presented an idealized Ireland, free of clashes of culture or politics (as when the villagers cheer lustily for the Protestant bishop to ensure that the local rector can stay).

In 1965, Ford returned to Ireland and the earlier revolutionary years to make *Young Cassidy* (1965), based on the rich autobiographies of the playwright SEAN O'CASEY [55], which recounted the years of grim poverty he endured before he achieved fame and success.

John Ford claimed to be apolitical, and that he loved only America. He was a longtime member of the U.S. naval reserve, fought with the marines in the South Pacific (being wounded at Midway), and was given the rank of rear admiral by President Nixon on retiring.

The film critic John Baxter places John Ford very exactly: "He was an immigrant, a Catholic Republican; he speaks for the generations that created the modern United States between the Civil and the Great Wars [1865–1917]. Like Walt Whitman, Ford chronicled the society of that half century, expansionist by design, mystical and religious by conviction, hierarchical by agreement, an association of equals within a structure of command, practical, patriotic and devout." In his films, Ford mythologized the armed forces and the church as paradigms of structural integrity. "All may speak in Ford films, but when divine order is invoked, the faithful fall silent, to fight and die as decreed by a general, president, or some other member of the God-anointed elite."

All of this comes directly from John Ford's Irish background, but these were values which were not confined to his community, but were shared by a significant number of other Americans, to make his vision of America, what it had been and what it was, their vision too. He carried with him a sense of history, both Irish and American, that informed that vision.

At the end of his film *The Last Hurrah*, based on the kind of Boston politics from which the Kennedys emerged, Mayor Frank Skeffington, an old-time Irish ward boss at heart, loses rather than compromises with the modern world. John Ford had a great respect for tradition, the traditions of love, family, and community. His people say little; their actions speak for them. In true Irish fashion, the dances and fights and feasts that are such a feature of his films, and reach their apex in *The Quiet Man*, reinforce a sense of community. His people sing, eat, and get drunk as acts of communion.

For his own generation and later ones, John Ford created an image of America. For many Europeans, his America is the *real* America, but in his Irish films, too, he has created an ideal of a land that still captures the hearts and imaginations of many millions. It is an epic achievement of which Sean O'Feeney would have been proud.

94

Sir Roger Casement

1864–1916

A figure of controversy in his own lifetime, Sir Roger Casement is even more controversial today. Before his execution 1916 the controversy surrounded both his work as a diplomat and his activities as an Irish republican. Now the focus is on the nature of his sexuality, and the authenticity of his notorious *Black Diaries*. But the continuing influence and future reputation of Casement will depend on a reappraisal of him as a most unusual person—a gay Irish patriot. Already acclaimed as a hero of the Easter Rising, in this role we are only beginning to understand him.

Though he was born in Sandycove, outside Dublin (on September 1, 1864), Roger Casement was an Ulsterman, reared in the north, and educated at Ballymena Academy. Going to sea, he went to Africa with the merchant marine in 1884. There he eventually joined the British Colonial Service in 1892.

He was posted to far parts of Africa in the consular service. In 1904 he made an official report to the British Parliament on the inhuman treatment of black workers in the remoter parts of the Congo Free State (now Congo), then a personal domain of King Leopold of Belgium. This report caused an international scandal, and led to the Belgian government taking over the administration of the colony from the king.

Casement was then posted to South America, where he conducted a similar inquiry into the treatment of West Indian workers of the wild rubber workings on the upper reaches of the Putumayo River, on the border of Ecuador and Peru. Here rubber bosses ran the whole district with no regard to proper law and order. Though he was empowered only to look into how the West Indian blacks were being treated, Casement was equally concerned about the treatment of the Amerindians, who were little more than the brutalized slaves of the rubber companies. His report caused another international outcry when it was released in 1912. For these services Casement was knighted by the king. He retired from the colonial service in 1912.

By now his interests were engaged with Ireland and its affairs. He joined the Irish National Volunteers when they were set up in 1913, and was involved in the importation of guns from Germany in 1914. Thinking that the war would be like the Franco-Prussian War of 1871, he saw England's disadvantage and Ireland's opportunity. He traveled to Berlin by way of Norway, to plead the case of Irish revolutionaries for military aid.

He toured the prisoner of war camps to persuade Irish soldiers captured by the Germans to join a putative Irish brigade in the service of the German Empire. (Many of these would have been poor Dubliners who may have heard of the banner Connolly had strung across the front of Liberty Hall: "We serve neither king nor kaiser, but Ireland.") He found few to follow him.

In April 1916 the German government at last dispatched a cargo boat, the *Aud*, to Ireland with a cargo of guns and ammunition. Casement followed in a submarine. He landed at night on Banna Strand, outside Tralee, and hid in an ancient fort, where he was arrested the next morning by the local police. Meanwhile, the *Aud* failed to make contact with the local republicans, whom Casement intended to alert. It was sighted by the British navy and had to be blown up by her crew to avoid capture.

Within hours of his arrest, Casement was sent to London for interrogation. Police raided his flat in London and seized his papers. Left among these, they alleged, were a series of diaries which revealed that Casement had for many years been an active homosexual. Sexual relations between men was then a serious offense, but the charges laid against him were far more serious. Under a medieval act he was charged with the treasonable offense of aiding and giving comfort to the king's enemies.

He was duly convicted. A campaign for his reprieve from a death sentence was begun and was backed by many influential people in England, Ireland, and the United States. His supporters included Sir Arthur Conan Doyle and GEORGE BERNARD SHAW [49]. To counter this campaign, the British authorities called in the American ambassador and some British notables, and showed them either pages removed from the diaries or typed-up extracts—accounts differ as to the actual appearance of the documents. No one seems to have been shown the actual diaries themselves, and this later aroused the serious suspicion of fraud.

Sir Arthur Conan Doyle said that as a doctor he was unsurprised by such things, and that treason was a more serious matter in any case, but he based his view of the affair on his opinion that Casement, whom he had known well at the time of the Congo revelations, was now quite insane. Others, however, were shocked, and silenced.

Casement was hanged in Pentonville Gaol on August 3, 1916; his body was buried within the jail. In 1965, the year before the fiftieth anniversary of the Easter Rising, his remains were brought back to Ireland and were reinterred with state honors among other Irish patriots in Glasnevin Cemetery, in March 1965.

For most Irish people, Casement's fame rested on his role as one of the republican patriots of 1916, but the scandal of the diaries remained. Many Irish writers, including W. B. YEATS [8], were convinced that the diaries produced in 1916 had been forged by the British Secret Service to discredit Casement with the Irish-American community; they simply could not countenance the possibility that the documents might be genuine.

In the 1920s a set of the typed copies of the diaries had been passed to a British journalist, Peter Singleton-Gates, but he was prevented by the invocation of secrecy laws from publishing them. At the time, this may have been as much to spare the Irish Free State government embarrassment as to hide the guilt of the British authorities. However, he retained the copies. In 1959 he eventually issued them through a Paris publisher (better known for the first edition of *Lolita*) under the rather lurid title of *The Black Diaries of Sir Roger Casement*. Further controversy followed, which eventually ended with the disputed documents being placed in the British Public Record Office. Though they could be read, they could only be given limited technical examination.

More recently, new editions of the diaries relating to the investigation of the Putumayo incident have been published, again causing controversy. There seems little doubt that the diaries are genuine. What should now concern the admirers of Casement is the totality of his public life rather than the details of his sex life. Though he died for Ireland, his real life had been devoted to the welfare of Africans and Indians, in an effort to prevent them from being mercilessly exploited. On the basis of the diaries, his love for them seems to have arisen initially from sexual admiration. There would be nothing wrong with this, but it is the heroism of his campaign rather than the nature of his private life that should concern the future.

In his lifetime, Casement exerted great influence in ameliorating conditions in wretched parts of the world—one of them the very "heart of darkness" which Conrad wrote of. He will remain a hero to those who work to free the world of slavery and exploitation.

95

Ned Kelly

1855–1880

To his contemporaries, the bushranger Edward Kelly was a criminal. To modern Australians Ned Kelly is a national hero. Such are the strange contrasts in the evolution of Irish feelings about Australia, and Australian feelings about the Irish.

Ned Kelly was born in June of 1855 in Beveridge in the state of Victoria. His father had been transported from Tipperary in Ireland as a convict. His mother, also from Tipperary, was a Cody, a remote cousin of America's own Buffalo Bill. As boys, Ned and his brothers were themselves always in trouble because of charges of horse stealing. Ned served three years in jail for this.

In April 1878 the police attempted to arrest his brother Daniel on a horse-stealing charge. The whole Kelly clan resisted, and Ned wounded one of the policemen. Mrs. Kelly and some of the family were detained, but Ned and Daniel escaped into the bush. There they were joined by two other Irish bandits, Joe Byrne and Steve Hart.

For the next two years, the "Kelly Gang" haunted the states of Victoria and New South Wales. Rewards were offered for their capture, but to no avail. They held up towns, robbed two banks, and murdered three policemen and a civilian between October 1878 and June 1880. But the police eventually caught up with them.

On June 29, 1880, they were tracked to a wooden shanty at Glenrowan, near the town of Benalla. They were surrounded by the police, and the little house was riddled with bullets and then set on fire. Out of the flames and smoke emerged the almost phantom figure of Ned Kelly, clad in a suit of armor made from sheet iron. But this did not protect his lower limbs. He was shot and wounded in the leg, and was then captured when he fell over and could not rise. He was taken to Melbourne, where he was tried and convicted of murdering a policeman. The last of the bushrangers, he was hanged at Melbourne Old Gaol on November 11, 1880. And very properly too, said respectable Australia.

But Ned Kelly, his family, and the members of the Kelly Gang were Irish; they were not respectable Australians. When he was hanged, Ned's last words were, "Such is life," but life for the poor Irish in Australia was cruel and hard. The key feature of his life was not his bank robbing or horse stealing. It was a semiarticulate message to the world, which has come to be called the Jerilderie Letter, his testament in which he attempted to explain what he was about, but basically an incoherent plea for social justice. At the time (and later) there were rumors that he sought to create an outback republic, or a "United States of Australia," but what Ned Kelly's political ideas really were is still much discussed. Certainly an Irish hatred of all things English, imbibed from his parents, played a large part in them.

The life he spoke of was an almost aboriginal one, nasty, brutish, and short. Though he was branded a criminal, and still is by some who have adopted the police's view of his activities, to others he is something else: a bandit, or primitive rebel. He is part of the remembered history of the people rather than the official history of the state, the history of ballads rather than the history of police reports.

As concerns Ned Kelly, the Australians have "printed the legend." He has become a part of the mythology of a young nation, their counterpart of Robin Hood, William Tell, or Davy Crockett. This is due in part to the folklore of the early days, and in part to the extraordinary use to which Kelly's legend has been put by Australia's most important modern painter, Sir Sidney Nolan, himself of Irish extraction. In a series of pictures, done at different times of the painter's career, the image of Ned Kelly in a black suit of armor is posed against the searing browns, reds, and yellows of the Outback. This is an Australia of the imagination, the artist's Australia, where Ned Kelly has joined the immortals. He has become an essential part of the Australian identity, the part belonging to the independent man, his own boss, the free man.

As the historian Eric Hobsbawm explained: "The bandit myth is also comprehensible in highly urbanized countries which still possess a few empty spaces of 'outback' or 'west' to remind them of a sometimes imaginary heroic past, and to provide concrete *locus* for nostalgia, a symbol of ancient and lost virtue, a spiritual Indian territory for which, like Huckleberry Finn, man can imagine himself 'lighting out' when the constraints of civilization become too much for him."

He suggests that there is perhaps more than social documentation, or a longing for adventure to the literary or popular images of the bandit, with which Ned Kelly belongs: "There is what remains when we strip away the local and social framework of brigandage: a permanent emotion and a permanent role. There is freedom, heroism, and the dream of justice."

96

William Brown

1777–1857

Today, Argentina is one of the few Latin American countries with a large and active Irish community. Though there was a little emigration between the wars, most of these Southern Cross Irish are the descendants of emigrants who went to South America in the latter part of the nineteenth century. But even before that, some Irishmen had played their part in bringing Argentina into existence. One of these was William Brown.

Though the country had been settled by Spaniards, in May 1810 a provisional government came into existence as a reaction to the placing of Napoleon's brother on the throne in Madrid. Four years earlier, the colonists had already defended themselves against a British expedition, and felt they could become independent with little difficulty. The government thought, in European terms, of raising an army, but of course, as was soon pointed out to them, to protect the country they should have been raising a navy. This was the critical task that fell to the lot of an Irish sailor, William Brown, now known as the Father of the Argentine navy.

William Brown is thought to have been born in Foxford, in Mayo, on June 23, 1777, and to have been connected to the Brown family to which the marquis of Sligo belonged. In 1786 he emigrated with his family to America. His father died soon after they reached the New World, so he went to sea as a cabin boy on a merchant ship.

In 1796 he was impressed into the British navy and made his mark there. In a few years he was in command of an English merchant ship of his own. He was involved in the South American trade, and finally settled in Buenos Aires with his family in 1812.

His arrival coincided with the movement to liberate Latin America. Two years before, the viceroy had acceded to the wishes of the colonists to set up the council with the grand title of the Provisional Government of the Provinces of the Rio Plata. He then retreated across the river to Montevideo. The provisional government had already seen some of its ships defeated in 1811.

On March 1, 1814, Brown accepted a command in the new navy of the Argentine republic. He was given the peculiar rank of naval lieutenant colonel. He had support from some but not all of the revolutionaries; San Martin, for instance, who thought the army should be enlarged.

With the assistance of another Irish seaman, Captain Baxter, he gathered together a small squadron of two corvettes, three brigs, a brigantine, a schooner, and some even smaller ships. Three ships were ready by March, one of which was under the command of yet another Irishman, John Santiago King. Brown defeated the Spanish at the mouth of the Uruguay River, at Montevideo, May 16–17, 1814.

Admiral Brown, as he was now, served as delegate governor of Buenos Aires. In the grandiloquent style of the period he promised to respect and protect the rights of the people. Of his appointment, San Martin remarked: "I have not the honor of knowing him, but as a son of the country he will merit from her an everlasting recognition for the distinguished services he has given her."

However, Brown was not done with the sea. Under letters of mark from the new government which gave him the license to attack enemy ships without being charged with piracy, he sailed for several years as a privateer. He even entered the Pacific Ocean to harass the Spanish ships there.

He retired and settled quietly in Buenos Aires. Then, in December 1825, Brazil declared war on Argentina and blockaded the River Plate. Again, Brown took command of the situation. He routed the enemy squadron twice in 1826, but in April 1827 he was defeated by a superior force.

Peace between the two countries was negotiated, and he remained in the naval service until 1845. From 1842 to 1845 a civil war broke out, and he again commanded the government forces at sea. He then retired once more, this time to a small estate outside Buenos Aires. He took no further part in public life.

Brown had not forgotten the land of his fathers, however. In July 1847 he set sail to revisit Ireland. He hoped to contact relatives in Liverpool, but went at once to Ireland on his arrival in England. He found the country, and Mayo in particular, gripped by the horrors of the famine. In Foxford he met a brother who could not recognize him; however, he gave generously for the relief of his native place.

On his way home he encountered Giuseppe Garibaldi in Montevideo. In his memoirs, Garibaldi recalls that he thought Brown was one of the greatest admirals of his time, which was a very considerable tribute indeed from the liberator of Italy.

Brown died in Montevideo on May 3, 1857, and was given a state funeral. A decree by his successor as governor of Buenos Aires praised him as "the living monument of our naval glories." A more interesting tribute was paid to Brown some years later, by Velez Sarsfield (perhaps a connection of the great earl of Lucan). He said that he considered it the duty of an officer not to discuss the orders of government, "but to obey them within the limits imposed by military honor and the dignity of men." In past incidents, Brown could not be persuaded to cut the throats of prisoners, or be prevented from offering funeral honors to an exiled general. To be remembered as a man of honor two centuries after one's birth is an achievement.

97

Oscar Wilde

1854–1900

Wilde was the remarkable son of remarkable parents. His father was Sir William Wilde, surgeon and archaeologist, one of the most celebrated intellectual figures in nineteenth-century Ireland. Sir William was the author of two books which are still read about the River Boyne and Lough Corrib, in Mayo. Both of these mingle topography and archaeology in a most readable way. However, it was his work on the medical aspects of the Irish census of 1851, which dealt in large part with the effects of the famine on the population of the country, for which he was knighted. In 1851 he married Jane Elgee, who already had a reputation of her own as a patriotic poet under the pen name Speranza, and who had contributed fiery poetry and prose to the *Nation* when it was edited by CHARLES GAVAN DUFFY [82].

William was a tiny little man with factual tastes, Jane was large, flamboyant and fanciful—she claimed to be a descendant of Dante. Sir William suffered socially in the aftermath of a libel action in which it was alleged he had raped one of his patients, but he reestablished himself before he died, in 1876.

Their son, Oscar Fingal O'Flahertie Wills Wilde, was born on October 16, 1854, at 21 Westland Row, although a little later the family moved to a larger mansion at 1 Merrion Square. He was raised with an appreciation of what it meant to be in the public eye. He was educated at Portora Royal School, and at Trinity College in Dublin, where he first began to emerge as a personality under the friendship of a celebrated don of the day, John Mahaffy, the professor of Greek. He then went on to Oxford, where he became friends with the art critic John Ruskin. The combination of Greek culture and aesthetics affected his own development. He won a first-class degree and the Newdigate Prize for his poem, "Ravenna."

He moved to London at the age of twenty-five, and was, from then on, basically a Londoner. There his novel aesthetic views added to his college reputation, and he was the subject of genial satire by Gilbert and Sullivan in the character of the poet Bunthorne in their comic opera *Patience* (1881).

Following this reputation, he went on a money-making lecture tour of America, where he proved to be a big success, even with the hard-bitten gold diggers of Montana. However, his first play, *Vera,* produced in New York, was a failure.

Wilde married an Irishwoman, Constance Lloyd, by whom he had two sons, born in 1885 and 1886. But as his story "The Portrait of Mr. W. H." showed, he was beginning to explore other aspects of his sexuality. At this time he met Robert Ross and was initiated into homosexuality.

In 1891 he first met his nemesis in the form of Lord Alfred Douglas, the dandyish son of the notorious marquis of Queensbury, who was responsible for drawing up the rules of prizefighting. *The Picture of Dorian Grey,* with its hints at sinister dark sins, was a further step in a revolt against the morality of the day. His essays "The Decay of Lying" and "The Soul of Man Under Socialism" followed. But these paradoxical and political pieces were not a full demonstration of his evolving genius.

In 1892 the first play of his last period, *Lady Windermere's Fan,* was produced in London. He described this as "one of those modern drawing-room plays with pink lampshades." This was quickly followed by *A Woman of No Importance, An Ideal Husband,* and *The Importance of Being Earnest.* He was at the very height of success, with two plays running in London, when disaster fell upon him.

By this time he was leading a dangerous life with Lord Alfred, and involved with male prostitutes and other shadowy figures in the homosexual underworld of London. Lord Alfred and his father were feuding, and the marquis took exception to Wilde and began to hound him.

On February 28, 1895, the marquis left a card with the porter of Wilde's club addressed "Oscar Wilde posing as sodomite." The porter put it in an envelope and gave it to Wilde on his next visit. Lord Alfred urged him to sue the marquis for libel, which he did. At the trial all the details of his private life were exposed, and he lost the case. Rather than flee the country, as was the custom with exposed homosexuals in the polite society of Victorian London, he lingered, and was arrested at the Cadogan Hotel and put on trial for sexual offenses. The jury disagreed at the first trial, but at a second he was convicted and sentenced to two years with hard labor at Reading Gaol.

Wilde's prison experiences provided him with two important works: *De Profundis,* an attack on Lord Alfred Douglas, and a little later "The Ballad of Reading Gaol," by far his most successful poem, perhaps because it was his most objective.

Once released from prison, he went abroad. His wife Constance, who had separated from him on the advice of her relatives to protect her two boys, gave him an allowance. But this was stopped when he took up again with Lord Alfred. Some old friends of a more decent kind, such as Robert Ross, remained friends, but otherwise he was shunned as an outlaw, gaped at in cafes, and pointed out in public places. He became fat, unhealthy, and finally ill. He died on November 30, 1900, in the Hôtel d'Alsace in the Rue des Beaux Arts in Paris. He was received into the Catholic church shortly before he died. He is buried in Père Lachaise cemetery, where his grave, now surmounted by a monumental sculpture by Jacob Epstein, is a place of literary pilgrimage.

Wilde had been bankrupt, but Ross eventually recovered his copyright for the benefit of his sons. He deposited a copy of the full version of *De Profundis* in the British Library, protecting it from Lord Alfred, who had destroyed what he thought was the only copy. Wilde's son Cyril was killed in the First World War. Vyvyan lived on and wrote a memoir about his father, and his son, Merlin, is now the guardian of the Wilde estate.

When Wilde was tried, his nationality was not in question. At his trials it did not matter to the jury if he was Irish or British. More recently, Irish writers and academics have attempted to recapture him for Irish, rather than English, literature. His conversational style of story-telling has been related to the Gaelic style that so interested his parents. More importantly, he was, like Sheridan and Goldsmith before him, an outsider in the society he depicted in his plays. He was alert to the comic possibilities of the London drawing room in a way that the natives were not. Thus, the social satirist was given full play. Finally, his gift of language is thought to have its origins in the verbal skills native to Irish of all periods.

Whatever its background, *The Importance of Being Earnest* is a classic of the English-language theater, but it is not Wilde's literary qualities that maintain his notoriety. He is widely seen as a gay martyr in a repressive society, which is enough to keep large numbers of people interested in him and to keep his work alive. For the scandal-ridden son of scandal-ridden parents, it is a strange but perhaps appropriate apotheosis.

98

T. K. Whitaker

1916–

When the full history of Ireland in the second half of the twentieth century is written, the name of T. K. Whitaker will be given a special place of honor. Yet his entire life was passed as a public servant in the employment of the government.

Thomas Kenneth Whitaker was born in Rostrevor, Country Down on December 8, 1916, the son of Edward Whitaker and his wife Jane, soon after the Easter Rising. He was educated by the Christian Brothers in Drogheda. After school, he joined the Irish Civil Service, then almost the only route to success for the intelligent in Ireland. While in the civil service he took a bachelor's of science and a master's of science as an external student at London University. Eventually, he rose to become secretary of the Department of Finance, in 1956. Here he was given the lead in drawing up the plan for the economic development of Ireland, published by the government in 1958, to which the present prosperity of Ireland can be traced back.

Though Ireland was an open democracy, in 1922 it was not a rich country. Though there were large brewing and distilling interests, there was very little other industry because the country lacked capital. Under the governments of both WILLIAM COSGRAVE [56] and EAMON DE VALERA [2], much emphasis was placed on agricultural and rural development. Keeping people on the land was a major priority, but it became clear that many people were still emigrating or leaving the country to live in the city. To retain these young people and to provide new jobs in the cities, especially in Dublin, which was rapidly becoming the country's major population center, remedies had to be found, and they could not be obtained merely from private resources. So in Ireland a form of benign state intervention arose in which much capital investment came directly from the state. The blue book on economic development laid out the criteria through which the Irish economy would be planned. It allowed for the creation of the Industrial Development Authority, which funded the building of factories in specific locations and encouraged foreign and Irish manufacturers to make use of them. These were largely placed for social reasons, but Ireland had many attractions for foreign investors, which have become increasingly important since the computer revolution. Today there is a large, socially fluid, well-educated, English-speaking pool of labor which has proved to be both diligent and flexible.

In the 1990s, Ireland has come to be seen as the "Celtic Tiger." Indeed, its prosperity has carried it to twenty-first place among the industrial nations, and in many ways its development eclipses those of some Far East economies, since it is not founded on a disguised sweatshop economy. These astonishing triumphs in a country like Ireland, with a long-standing image of famine, poverty, and disorder, are a political and social triumph of the first order.

This success is due in large measure to the foresight, good sense, and perception of T. K. Whitaker, but it also emphasizes how lucky Ireland was to have civil servants like him. When Ireland gained its independence, it inherited a civil service system from the previous British administration. Some civil servants retired, but many stayed on; others were recruited. There were stiff exams to enter the service, and in the decades up to the 1960's the perception was that the best jobs were not in industry or business but in government service.

The cream of the country's talents entered the civil service, so much so that the number of poets, playwrights, and historians in the service was astounding. Like all civil services, it has its problems of delay and bungling, but it also has great reserves of intellectual power. And it was these that resulted in the Whitaker regime.

This notion of disinterested public service was of immense value to the country. When other countries in Africa and Asia gained their independence, it could be seen that without this kind of well-paid and highly motivated civil service, corruption and tyranny soon took over. Ireland developed as a democracy thanks to men of integrity like T. K. Whitaker.

Today, Ireland's capital base has expanded, and investment can be made with less government intervention. But the state socialism of the Whitaker era served Ireland well, and the influence of his ideas pervades the whole of Irish life to this day.

When Whitaker retired from the civil service it did not mean more time for his interests of fishing, golf, and music. He became a governor of the Central Bank of Ireland from 1969 to 1976. He was also a director of the brewer Arthur Guinness, of Bord na Gaeilge, and the Agency for Service Overseas (Ireland's Peace Corps). Among the final distinctions paid him was his election as chancellor of the National University of Ireland, a post which had once been filled by de Valera.

From 1977 to 1982 Whitaker was a member of the Irish Senate. Other honors include membership in the Council of State, chairman of the Constitution Review Board, and president of the Royal Irish Academy. He has also received many honorary degrees for his service to the community.

99

John O'Hara

1905–1970

Though in Ireland he would not be thought of as an Irish writer, John O'Hara was an important literary voice for an important part of the Irish community in America. O'Hara had been a friend of other writers, such as F. SCOTT FITZGERALD [89], but because he was a widely read author, his merits were underestimated by the academy. His great commercial success has prevented him getting the recognition he deserves as a chronicler of modern times.

John O'Hara was born in Pottsville, Pennsylvania, on January 31, 1905. He was the eldest child of Dr. Patrick Henry O'Hara, a well-thought-of medical man, and his wife Catherine (Delaney). Like his seven siblings, John was reared as a Catholic in an Irish family. He also received a largely Catholic education, being sent to Fordham Preparatory School, the Keystone State Normal School, and Niagara Preparatory School in New York State. He was expelled from all three schools, but managed to pass the exams for Yale. However, he never entered, as his father died in March 1925, and there was no money.

For the next decade he fell into a routine of odd jobs, from time to time living largely from hand to mouth. He was a ship's steward, an evaluating engineer, and a soda jerk. For a while, he was secretary to the journalist Heywood Broun, and his own journalistic career was a hectic one. He worked on two newspapers in his native state, then on three others in New York City. Other jobs included working as film critic for the *Morning Telegraph,* football editor of the *New Yonkers,* and even for a short time as managing editor of the *Pittsburgh Bulletin Index.*

Along the way he married Helen Petit, in 1931, but divorced her. His first novel, *Appointment at Samarra*, was written in a rented room in New York City. When he was down to his last three dollars, he made contact with three publishers, offering them the book's first twenty-five thousand words if they would be prepared to subsidize its completion. He was accepted by Harcourt, Brace, and when it was published in 1934 the book became a critical and commercial success.

A critic later observed that O'Hara had a positive hatred of the generation before his, and some of this began to emerge in 1935, in his collection of short stories *The Doctor's Son and Other Stories*. The same year saw the publication of *Butterfield 8*, his novel about a New York call girl. Though this, too, was a success (and was later filmed) many critics thought his short stories superior. Those collected as *Pal Joey* were the basis for a musical and a film with Frank Sinatra.

O'Hara said of himself: "Being a cheap, ordinary guy, I have an instinct for what an ordinary guy likes." Though O'Hara was a friend of F. Scott Fitzgerald and the influence of the older writer has been detected in his work, the realism of Hemingway may have had a greater effect. O'Hara was interested in people, often ordinary unintellectual people, and the details of social life in Pennsylvania and New York.

The critic Edmund Wilson called O'Hara "primarily a social commentator; and in this field of social habits and manners ... he has done work that is original and interesting ... He has explored for the first time from his peculiar semisnobbish point of view a great deal of interesting territory." Others were not so admiring, referring to the "voice of the hangover generation"—those who had come out of the Prohibition years into the bleaker 1930s—and characters "below moral condemnation."

The ambition of every American writer is to write the great American novel. After a silence of eleven years, O'Hara returned to the novel in 1949, publishing *A Rage to Live*. This became an immense commercial success, with seventy-five thousand copies printed even before publication.

The novel left the setting of the big city to return to O'Hara's homeland, a small Pennsylvania town. It dealt with an upper-class lady and her love affairs. This, he said, was "the big one," and readers found it a vivid and captivating read. But it failed to have the literary qualities he had hoped for. It seemed to some to lack purpose, depth, or social function (according to the *New York Times*), and to be lacking any final meaning (according to *Time*).

Critics seemed to have remained of the same mind for the rest of

O'Hara's career, during which he published regularly. Nevertheless, the distinction of *Appointment in Samarra,* with its sense that people have a fate which they cannot avoid no matter what they do, has been recognized. John O'Hara, a special kind of American writer, died at his Princeton home on April 11, 1970.

The key to O'Hara seems to be the desire to escape from an Irish Catholic background into some socially more acceptable way of life, but finding that human nature is flawed and ultimately a fairly degraded thing. A Catholic doctor like his father would have seen many unacceptable things but faced them with a feeling that there was some ultimate purpose. O'Hara could not feel this.

In the bleak vision of America he presents, he strikes at the commonly held view of America as the best of all places in the best of all possible worlds. This, too, seems to be a very Catholic form of despair, and in this sense what O'Hara derives from his origins and upbringing may possibly be of the greatest importance. His vision of America was one, as his sales reveal, with which many millions of Americans feel a great affinity.

As a writer of Irish-American origins, he may not have the literary distinction of a JAMES JOYCE [25], W. B. YEATS [8], EUGENE O'NEILL [45], or F. Scott Fitzgerald. But his cold moral view of the nature of America and the Americans has been deeply influential.

100

Gerry Adams

1948–

In May 1998 the people of Ireland, north and south, voted their over-whelming support for the Good Friday Agreement. After some thirty years of political turmoil and over two thousand deaths (the majority at the hands of terrorists), this new settlement in Ireland opened up the prospect of peace for the rising generation of young Irish people.

A key figure in this agreement was Gerry Adams, an unemployed barman from Belfast, who has been a leading figure in both the Irish Republican Army (an illegal organization in both north and south), and Sinn Fein, the party of minority republican opinion in the north.

Gerard Adams was born in Belfast on the Falls Road on October 6, 1948, the son of Gerard Adams and his wife Anne, formerly Hannaway. Neither Adams nor Hannaway are Gaelic names, but rather the names of English families long settled in Ireland. He was educated at St. Mary's Christian Brothers School in Belfast. He was in his early twenties when the troubles broke out in 1969, and he renewed his family's involvement with republican politics. In 1971 he married Colette McArdle, by whom he has one son.

In that same year he was interned for suspected terrorist activities, and it was while "behind the wire" that his political education began as well as his rise to power among the ranks of the IRA. He was released and again interned in 1973. Later he was imprisoned, though released in 1976.

He was elected to the Northern Ireland Assembly as a Sinn Fein deputy in 1982, and to the United Kingdom parliament as the Sinn Fein representative from West Belfast, but refused to take his seat. He lost this seat in 1992 to an SDLP candidate, but regained it in 1997. But, again, he did not take his seat in Westminster.

Among the leading Sinn Fein personalities, Gerry Adams has also made his mark as a writer. He is the author of *Falls Memories* (1982), an autobiography of his childhood experiences growing up in that republican quarter of Belfast. He has also written *Politics of Irish Freedom* and *Pathway to Peace* (both in 1988). *Cage Eleven* (1990) is another chapter of his autobiography. His short stories were collected in *The Street* (1992). Yet another chapter of his autobiography appeared as *Before the Dawn* in 1996.

Informed observers believe he has long been a member of the Army Council of the Provisionals. Though he has never admitted membership in the IRA, an offense in itself, one of his stories describes in vivid detail the shooting of a British soldier.

Over the long years of struggle he has moved, as MICHAEL COLLINS [3], EAMON DE VALERA [2] and others before him, from the simplicities of physical force to the intricacies of political persuasion. His experiences have led to this changed outlook. Though many of his political opponents, north and south, still distrust him, he has exerted a tremendous influence not only over political events in Ireland, but also, through his frequent visits to the United States, over how those events are seen by the Irish-American community and the government of the United States.

The deployment of Irish-American opinion has persuaded a series of American presidents to interest themselves in Irish affairs (against their will in some cases). But this involvement has revealed in some ways how far apart the Irish and the Irish-American communities have grown. Irish-Americans think about Ireland in terms of the past, and have little conception of how it has changed.

Ireland is now a prosperous, indeed, overprosperous country. Appeals based on historic poverty have now little attraction to modern Irish people. When the Good Friday Agreement comes into force it will leave Gerry Adams with the even greater task of leading his party in a new political situation. But this has been what Irish leaders have had to do in the past, what de Valera had to do in 1927. He is unlikely to make much headway against the established parties in the south unless Sinn Fein develops policies for a new Ireland in a new millennium.

This is a striking role for any man who values what he can do for his country, and who thinks, as all leaders do, of the verdict of history on their lives. Gerry Adams is a man of immense influence whose greatest opportunity may be before him, but only if he can evolve along with the changing conditions. In the summer of 1998, after an appalling bomb was planted in Omagh by a republican splinter group, Adams finally announced that the war was "over, done with, finished." The promise of peace would have to be maintained with all the influence of his moral authority.

By the middle of 1999, the refusal of the Irish Republican Army to disarm (and thereby dissolve as a military organization) left Adams and the leaders of Sinn Fein stranded. An impasse that called for real leadership on the part of Gerry Adams existed. Destiny called on him to follow the IRA into a historical *cul-de-sac*, or to follow the path that de Valera had the courage to take in 1926. Though the Northern Assembly has become a working and workable body, the gun has yet to be taken out of Irish politics. The contentious issue of the IRA giving up its weapons was given added urgency following the events of September 11, 2001. The IRA found that its American supporters, long so tolerant of terrorism in Ireland, had moved with the new current of feeling that political violence had no place in civilized society.

His future, like that of Northern Ireland, remains uncertain. Both will be followed with deep concern by Irish people everywhere, many of whom will hope that Gerry Adams will be able to find his way to a broader horizon, as have so many Irish patriots in the past. The world will watch with interest.

FURTHER READING

The literature on some of the people in this book is immense. The following sources provide up-to-date and authoritative viewpoints. Most are for a general readership, though in some cases older books, more academic books, or popular articles have had to be cited for lack of any other suitable sources. I have generally listed the first edition, but many of these books will have appeared in American or Australian editions, including paperbacks. In a few cases, very old books have had to be cited, as the individuals, while important, have not attracted the attention of recent biographers. Inevitably, many important books on Irish subjects appear in editions published only in Ireland. However, most of the books listed will be readily available through local library systems, or can be ordered over the Internet.

1. St. Patrick
Bieler, Ludwig. *The Life and Legends of St. Patrick.* Dublin, 1949.
Bury, J. B. *The Life of St. Patrick.* London and New York, 1905.
de Paor, Liam. *St. Patrick's World.* Washington D.C., 1993.
Dumville, David. *St. Patrick, 493–1993.* Woodbridge, 1993.

2. Eamon de Valera
Coogan, Tim Pat. *De Valera: Long Fellow, Long Shadow.* London, 1993.
Longford, Frank, and O'Neill, T. P. *De Valera: The Official Biography.*
   Dublin, 1970.

3. Michael Collins
Coogan, Tim Pat. *Michael Collins, A Biography.* London and New York,
   1990.
Forester, Margery. *Michael Collins, the Lost Leader.* London, 1989.

4. John Fitzgerald Kennedy
Kennedy, Rose Fitzgerald. *Times to Remember.* New York, 1974.
Mitchell, Arthur. *JFK and His Irish Heritage.* Dublin, 1993.

Schlesinger, Arthur M. Jr., *A Thousand Days.* New York, 1965.
Sorensen, Theodore. *The Kennedy Legacy.* New York, 1970.
White, Theodore H. *The Making of the President 1960.* 1961.

5. Charles Stewart Parnell
Kee, Robert. *The Laurel and the Ivy.* London, 1993.
Lyons, F. S. L. *Charles Stewart Parnell.* London, 1977.

6. Mary Robinson
O'Sullivan, Michael. *Mary Robinson: The Life and Times of an Irish Liberal.* Dublin, 1993.
Siggins, Lorna. *The Woman Who Took the Park: Mary Robinson, President of Ireland, 1990–1997.* Edinburgh, 1994.

7. Patrick Henry Pearse
Edwards, Ruth Dudley. *Patrick Pearse, The Triumph of Failure.* London, 1979.
le Roux, Louis. *Patrick H. Pearse.* Dublin, 1932.

8. William Butler Yeats
Foster, R. F. *W. B. Yeats: A Life.* Vol. 1, "The Apprentice Mage." London, 1997.
Jeffares, A. Norman. *W. B. Yeats, A New Biography.* London, 1989.

9. John Boyle O'Reilly
McManamin, F. G. *The American Years of John Boyle O'Reilly.* Washington, D. C., 1959.
Schofield, W. G. *Seek for a Hero: The Story of John Boyle O'Reilly.* New York, 1956.

10. Patrick Ford
Bagenal, P. H. *The American Irish.* Boston, 1882.
Rodechko, James P. *Patrick Ford and his Search for America: A Case Study of Irish-American Journalism, 1870–1913.* New York, 1976.

11. Wolfe Tone
Bartlett, Thomas. *Theobold Wolfe Tone.* Dublin, 1997.
Elliott, Marianne. *Wolfe Tone, Prophet of Irish Independence.* New Haven, 1989.

12. Mike Quill
Quill, Shirley. *Mike Quill—Himself: A Memoir.* Greenwich, Conn., 1985.
Whittemore, L. H. *The Man Who Ran the Subways.* New York, 1968.

13. George Boole
MacHale, Des. *George Boole, His Life and Work.* Dublin, 1985.
Smith, G. C., ed., *The Boole-De Morgan Correspondence, 1842–1864.* Oxford, 1982.

14. Seán Lemass
Horgan, John. *Sean Lemass: The Enigmatic Patriot.* Dublin, 1997.
O'Sullivan, Michael. *Sean Lemass.* Dublin, 1994.

15. James Craig, Lord Craigavon
Buckland, Patrick. *James Craig, Lord Craigavon.* Dublin, 1980.

16. James Connolly
Greaves, C. Desmond. *The Life and Times of James Connolly.* London, 1972.
Morgan, Austen. *James Connolly: A Political Biography.* New York, 1988.
Reeves, Carl, ed. *James Connolly and the United States.* Atlantic Highlands,
    N.J., 1978.

17. Brian Boru
Llywelyn, Morgan. *Brian Boru.* Dublin, 1970.
Newman, Roger C. *Brian Boru, King of Ireland.* Dublin, 1983.

18. Alfred Harmsworth, Lord Northcliffe
Bourne, Richard. *Lords of Fleet Street: The Harmsworth Dynasty.* London,
    1990.
Ferris, Paul. *The House of Northcliffe: The Harmsworths of Fleet Street.*
    London, 1971.

19. Edmund Rice
Keogh, Dáire. *Edmund Rice, 1762–1844.* Dublin, 1996.
Rushe, Desmond. *Edmund Rice: The Man and His Times.* Dublin, 1995.

20. Daniel O'Connell
Edwards, Robert Dudley. *Daniel O'Connell.* London, 1975.
MacDonagh, Oliver. *The Emancipist: Daniel O'Connell.* London, 1989.
Trench, Charles C. *The Great Dan.* London, 1984.

21. Arthur Guinness
Guinness, Michele. *The Guinness Legend.* London, 1989.
Mullally, Frederic. *The Silver Salver: The Story of the Guinness Family.*
    London, 1981.

22. Sybil Connolly
Connolly, Sybil. *In an Irish House.* New York, 1995.
O'Byrne, Robert. "Sybil Connolly, Designer, Dies Aged Seventy-Seven." *Irish
    Times,* May 8, 1998.
Williams, Gabrielle. "Fashion Queen." *Irish Tatler,* July 1998.

23. Thomas Davis
Molony, John N. *A Soul Came Into Ireland: Thomas Davis, 1814–1845.*
    Dublin, 1995.
Sullivan, Eileen A. *Thomas Davis.* Lewisburg, Penn., 1978.

24. Michael Davitt
Moody, T. W. *Davitt and the Irish Revolution, 1846–82.* Oxford, 1981.
Sheehy-Skeffington, Francis. *Michael Davitt: Revolutionary, Agitator, and Labour Leader.* London, 1908; new ed., London, 1967.

25. James Joyce
Costello, Peter. *James Joyce: The Years of Growth.* London, 1992.
Ellmann, Richard. *James Joyce,* 2nd ed. New York, 1982.

26. Jack B. Yeats
Arnold, Bruce. *Jack Yeats.* New Haven and London, 1998.
Pyle, Hilary. *Jack B. Yeats.* London, 1970.
Rosenthal, T. G. *The Art of Jack Yeats.* London, 1997.

27. Archbishop Thomas Croke
Tierney, Martin. *Croke of Cashel.* Dublin, 1975.
Walsh, P. J. *Life of William J. Walsh, Archbishop of Dublin.* Dublin, 1928.

28. Cyrus Hall McCormick
Casson, Herbert N. *Cyrus Hall McCormick: His Life and Work.* New York, 1909.
Hutchinson, W. T. *Cyrus Hall McCormick,* 2 Vols. New York, 1930–35.
McCormick, Cyrus, III. *The Century of the Reaper.* Chicago, 1931.

29. John L. Sullivan
Langley, Tom. *The Life of John L. Sullivan, the Boston Strongboy.* Leicester, Great Britain, 1973.
Sullivan, John L. *I Can Lick Any Sonofabitch in the House.* Edited by Gilbert Odd. London, 1976. This is a new edition of *Life and Reminiscences of a Nineteenth-Century Gladiator* (1892), ghosted for Sullivan.

30. Richard Croker
Lewis, Alfred Henry. *Richard Croker.* New York, 1901.

31. Joseph R. McCarthy
Buckley, W. F., Jr., and Bozell, L. B. *McCarthy and His Enemies: The Record and Its Meaning.* Chicago, 1954.
Goldman, E. F. *The Crucial Decade: America 1945–1955.* New York, 1956.
Latham, Earl. *The Communist Controversy From the New Deal to McCarthy.* Cambridge, Mass., 1966.

32. Robert Boyle
Hunter, Michael. *Robert Boyle by Himself and His Friends.* London, 1994.
Sargent, Rose-Mary. *The Diffident Naturalist.* Chicago, 1995.

33. Hugh O'Neill
Falls, Cyril. *Elizabeth's Irish Wars.* London, 1950.
O'Faolain, Sean. *The Great O'Neill.* London, 1942.

Walsh, Michelene. *An Exile of Ireland: Hugh O'Neill, Prince of Ulster.* Dublin, 1996.

34. Jonathan Swift
Ehrenpreis, Irvin. *Swift: The Man, His Works and the Age.* London, 1967.
Glendinning, Victoria. *Swift.* London, 1998.
Noakes, David. *Jonathan Swift: A Hypocrite Reversed.* Oxford, 1985.

35. George Berkeley
Hone, J. M. and Rossi, Mario. *Bishop Berkeley.* London, 1931.
Luce, A. A. *The Life of George Berkeley, Bishop of Cloyne.* London, 1949.
Warnock, J. G. *Berkeley.* Notre Dame, 1983.

36. U2
Bowler, Dave, and Day, Bryan. *U2: A Conspiracy of Hope.* London, 1993.
Dunphy, Eamonn. *Unforgettable Fire: The Story of U2.* London, 1987.

37. James Larkin
Fox, R. M. *Jim Larkin, Irish Labour Leader.* New York, 1957.
Larkin, Emmet. *James Larkin.* London, 1965.

38. John Toland
Evans, Robert R. *Pantheisticon: The Career of John Toland.* New York, 1991.
Sullivan, Robert E. *John Toland and the Deist Controversy.* Harvard, 1982.

39. Tony O'Reilly
Fallon, Ivan. *The Luck of O'Reilly: A Biography of Tony O'Reilly.* New York and London, 1994.

40. Terence Vincent Powderly
Browne, H. J. *The Catholic Church and the Knights of Labor.* New York, 1929.
Shannon, William V. *The American Irish.* New York: Macmillan Company; London, Collier-Macmillan, 1963.
Ware, N. J. *The Labor Movement in the United States, 1860–1895.* New York, 1929.

41. John Louis O'Sullivan
Obituary, *New York Tribune*, March 26, 1895.
Pratt, J. W. "John L. O'Sullivan and Manifest Destiny." *New York History,* July 1933.

42. James Cardinal Gibbons
Ellis, J. T. *The Life of James Cardinal Gibbons,* 2 Vols. Milwaukee, 1952.
Will, Allen S. *The Life of James Cardinal Gibbons.* Baltimore, 1911.

43. John Devoy
Ó Lúing, Sean. *John Devoy.* Dublin, 1961.
Ryan, Desmond. *The Phoenix Flame: A Study of Fenianism and John Devoy.* London, 1937.

44. Paul Cardinal Cullen

Bowen, Desmond. *Paul Cullen and the Shaping of Modern Ireland.* Dublin, 1983.

MacSuibne, Peadar. *The Good Cardinal Cullen.* Dublin, 1967.

45. Eugene O'Neill

Shaughnessy, Edward L. *Down the Nights and Down the Days: Eugene O'Neill's Catholic Sensibility.* Notre Dame, 1996.

Sheaffer, Louis. *O'Neill, Son and Artist.* Boston, 1973.

46. Grace O'Malley

Chambers, Anne. *Granuaile: The Life and Times of Grace O'Malley.* Dublin, 1988.

47. St. Columban

The Life and Writings of St. Columbanus. Philadelphia, 1914.

Macmanus, Francis. *Saint Columbanus.* London and Dublin, 1983.

48. Samuel Beckett

Bair, Deidre. *Samuel Beckett.* New York, 1980.

Cronin, Anthony. *Samuel Beckett: The Last Modernist.* London, 1996.

Knowlson, James. *Damned to Fame: The Life of Samuel Beckett.* London, 1996.

49. George Bernard Shaw

Holroyd, Michael. *Bernard Shaw.* London, 1997.

Ussher, Arland. *Three Great Irishmen: Shaw, Yeats, and Joyce.* London, 1953.

50. Finley Peter Dunne

Dunne, Finley Peter. *Mr. Dooley Remembers.* Edited by Philip Dunne. Boston, 1963.

Ellis, Elmer. *Mr. Dooley's America.* New York, 1941.

Mr. Dooley and the Chicago Irish: The Autobiography of a Nineteenth-Century Ethnic Group. Edited by Charles Fanning. Washington, D.C., 1987.

51. Archbishop Daniel Mannix

Brennan, Niall. *Dr. Mannix.* Melbourne, 1965.

Murphy, Frank. *Daniel Mannix.* Melbourne, 1948.

Santamaria, B. A. *Archbishop Mannix: His Contribution to the Art of Public Leadership in Australia.* Melbourne, 1978.

52. Maud Gonne MacBride and Constance Gore-Booth, the Countess Markievicz

Levenson, Samuel. *Maud Gonne.* London, 1972.

Norman, Diana. *Terrible Beauty: A Life of Constance Markievicz.* London, 1987.

Voris, Jacqueline van. *Constance de Markievicz.* Amherst, Mass., 1967.

53. John O'Donovan and Eugene O'Curry
Boyne, Patricia. *John O'Donovan.* Dublin, 1987.

Royal Irish Academy. *Centenary Exhibition: John O'Donovan and Eugene O'Curry.* Dublin, 1961.

Walsh, Rev. Paul. *Irish Men of Learning.* Dublin, 1947.

54. Horace Plunkett
Anderson, R. A. *With Horace Plunkett in Ireland.* London, 1935.

West, Trevor. *Horace Plunkett.* Washington, D.C., 1986.

55. Sean O'Casey
Krause, David. *Sean O'Casey.* London, 1960.

O'Connor, Gary. *Sean O'Casey, A Life.* London, 1988.

56. William Cosgrave
Collins, Stephen. *The Cosgrave Legacy.* Dublin, 1996.

57. John Hume
Drower, G. M. F. *John Hume Peacemaker.* London, 1995.

Routledge, Paul. *John Hume: The Biography.* London, 1997.

White, Barry. *John Hume, Statesman of the Troubles.* Belfast, 1984.

58. St. Columcille
Adamnan of Iona. *Life of Columba.* Edited and translated by A. O. Anderson and M. O. Anderson. New York, 1962.

Finlay, Ian. *Columba.* London, 1979.

59. John Scotus Eriugena
O'Meara, John. *Eriugena.* Dublin, 1979.

60. Fr. Charles Coughlin
Lee, A. M., and Lee, E. *The Fine Art of Propaganda.* New York, 1972.

Magil, A. B. *The Truth About Fr. Coughlin.* New York, 1935.

61. Ian Paisley
Bruce, Steve. *God Save Ulster: The Religion and Politics of Paisleyism.* Oxford, 1986.

Cooke, Dennis. *Persecuting Zeal.* Dingle, 1996.

Paisley, Rhonda. *Ian Paisley, My Father.* Basingstoke, 1988.

62. Bernard O'Higgins
Clissold, Stephen. *Bernard O'Higgins and the Independence of Chile.* London, 1968.

63. Bob Geldof
Geldof, Bob. *Is That It?* London, 1986.

64. Archbishop James Ussher
Anderson Carr, James. *The Life and Times of James Ussher.* London, 1895.
Barr, James. *Why the World Was Created in 4004 B.C.: Archbishop Ussher and Biblical Chronology.* Manchester, Great Britian, 1985.
Dowden, John. *Archbishop Ussher.* Dublin, 1902.
Wright, W. B. *The Ussher Memoirs.* London, 1889.

65. Patrick Sarsfield
Curtayne, Alice. *Patrick Sarsfield.* Dublin, 1934.
Todhunter, John. *Life of Patrick Sarsfield, Earl of Lucan.* Dublin and London, 1895.
Wauchope, Piers. *Patrick Sarsfield and the Williamite Wars.* Dublin, 1992.

66. William Thompson
Dooley, Dolores. *Equality in Community.* Cork, 1996.
Lynch, Patrick. "William Thompson and the Socialist Tradition." In *Leaders and Workers,* edited by J. W. Boyle. Cork, 1966.
Pankhurst, R. K. P. *William Thompson, Pioneer Socialist.* London, 1991.

67. Michael O'Clery
Jennings, Brendan. *Michael O'Clery, Chief of the Four Masters.* Dublin, 1936.

68. Ernest Walton
Andrade, E. N. da C. *Rutherford and the Nature of the Atom.* New York, 1964.
Crother, J. G. *The Cavendish Laboratory, 1874–1974.* London, 1974.
Wilson, David. *Rutherford: Simple Genius.* Boston, 1983.

69. Phil Lynott
McCleeve, Pamela. *Phil Lynott: Dancing in the Moonlight.* London, 1990.

70. Peter Lalor
Buckley, David. *James Fintan Lalor.* Cork, 1990.
Curry, H. C. *The Irish at Eureka.* 1954.
Eureka Stockade, film directed by Harry Watts, 103 minutes. Australia, 1949.
Turnbull, Clive. *Eureka: The Story of Peter Lalor.* Melbourne, 1949.
Turner, H. G. *Our Own Little Rebellion.* Melbourne, n.d., c. 1880.

71. James Gandon
Craig, Maurice, ed. *The Life of James Gandon.* London, 1969.
McParland, Edward. *James Gandon.* London, 1985.

72. William Parsons, Lord Rosse
Ball, Sir Robert. *Great Astronomers.* London, 1895.
Thiel, Rudolf. *And There Was Light: The Discovery of the Universe.* New York, 1967.

73. James Armour
Armour, W. S. *Armour of Ballymoney.* London, 1934.
McMinn, R. B., ed. *Against the Tide: The Papers of Rev. J. B. Armour.*
  Belfast, 1985.

74. Charles Bianconi
Bianconi, M. O'Connell, and Walton, S. J. *Bianconi: King of the Irish Roads.*
  Dublin, 1962.

75. William Dargan
de Courcy, Catherine. *The Foundation of the National Gallery of Ireland.*
  Dublin, 1985.
Share, Bernard. *Irish Lives.* Dublin, 1969.

76. Sir William Rowan Hamilton
Graves, R. P. *Life of Sir William Rowan Hamilton.* 3 vols. Dublin and
  London, 1883–89.
Sir William Rowan Hamilton: The Mathematical Papers. Cambridge,
  1936–37.

77. Edmund Burke
Ayling, Stanley. *Edmund Burke: His Life and Opinions.* London, 1988.
O'Brien, Conor Cruise. *The Great Melody.* London, 1992.

78. Ernest Shackleton
Huntford, Roland. *Shackleton.* London, 1985.
Lansing, Alfred. *Endurance: Shackleton's Great Voyage.* London, 1959.
Mill, H. R. *My Life of Sir Ernest Shackleton.* London, 1924.

79. William James Pirrie
Obituary notice, the *Times,* (London), June 9, 1924.
Transactions of the Institute of Naval Architects, vol. 66, 1924.

80. Fr. Theobald Mathew
Kerrigan, Colm. *Father Mathew and the Irish Temperance Movement,
  1849–1938.* Cork, 1992.
Lysaght, Moira. *Fr. Theobald Mathew.* Dublin, 1983.

81. Turlough Carolan
O'Sullivan, Donal. *Carolan.* London, 1958.
Rimmer, Joan. *The Irish Harp.* Cork, 1969.

82. Charles Gavan Duffy
Doyle, Eugene J. *Victoria Through Irish Eyes: Sir Charles Gavan Duffy in
  Victoria.* Dublin, 1983.
O'Broin, Leon. *Charles Gavan Duffy: Patriot and Statesman.* Dublin,
  1967.

83. Archbishop John Joseph Hughes
Brann, H. A. *Most Reverend John Hughes: First Archbishop of New York.* New York, 1912.
Hassard, J. R. *Life of the Most Rev. John Hughes, D. D. First Archbishop of New York.* New York, 1866.

84. William R. Grace
Albion, R. G. "William Russell Grace." In *Dictionary of American Biography.* Vol. 7:463.
Grace, J. P. Jr. *W. R. Grace, 1832–1904, and the Enterprises He Created.* New York, 1953.

85. Joe McGrath
Boylan, Harry. "Joseph MacGrath." In *A Dictionary of Irish Biography.* 4th ed. Dublin, 1998.
Farmar, Tony. *Ordinary Lives: Three Generations of Irish Middle-Class Experience.* Dublin, 1991.

86. Thomas Francis Meagher
Athearn, Robert G. *Thomas Francis Meagher: A Irish Revolutionary in America.* Boulder, Col., 1949.
Gwynn, Denis. *Thomas Francis Meagher.* Dublin, 1967.

87. Richard Martin
Lyman, Shevawn. *Humanity Dick: Richard Martin, King of Connemara.* Dublin, 1975.

88. James T. Farrell
Branch, Edgar M. *James T. Farrell.* New York, 1971.
Wald, Alan M. *James T. Farrell.* New York, 1978.

89. F. Scott Fitzgerald
Bruccoli, Matthew J. *Some Sort of Epic Grandeur: The Life of F. Scott Fitzgerald.* Revised ed. London, 1991.
Milford, Nancy. *Zelda.* New York, 1970.

90. Mother Mary Aikenhead
Butler, M. B. *A Candle Was Lit: The Life of Mother Mary Aikenhead.* Dublin, 1953.

91. Maria Edgeworth
Kowalski-Wallace, Elizabeth. *Their Father's Daughter: Hannah More, Maria Edgeworth, and Patriarchal Complicity.* New York, 1991.

92. John Barry
Clark, W. B. *Gallant John Barry.* New York, 1938.
Meany, William Barry. *Commodore John Barry, The Father of the American Navy.* New York and London, 1911.

93. John Ford
Anderson, Lindsay. *About John Ford.* London, 1981.
Ford, Dan. *Pappy: The Life of John Ford.* Englewood Cliffs, N.J., 1979.

94. Sir Roger Casement
Casement, Sir Roger. *The Black Diaries.* Edited by Peter Singleton-Gates and Maurice Girodias. Paris, 1959.
Inglis, Brian. *Roger Casement.* Belfast, 1993.
Sayer, Roger. *Sir Roger Casement: The 1911 Diaries, the Black and the White.* London, 1997.

95. Ned Kelly
Brown, Max. *Australian Son.* Adelaide, 1948.
Keneally, J. J. *The Complete Inner History of the Kelly Gang.* Melbourne, 1955.

96. William Brown
Ireland, John de Courcy. *The Admiral from Mayo.* Dublin, 1995.
Ratts, Hector R. *Alminente Guillermo Brown.* Buenos Aires, 1998.

97. Oscar Wilde
Ellmann, Richard. *Oscar Wilde.* London, 1988.
Julien, Philippe. *Oscar Wilde.* London, 1994.

98. T. K. Whitaker
McCarthy, John F. *Planning Ireland's Future.* Dublin, 1990.

99. John O'Hara
McShane, Frank. *John O'Hara.* New York, 1975.

100. Gerry Adams
Keena, Colm. *Gerry Adams, A Biography.* Cork, 1990.
Sharracok, David. and Devonport, Mark. *Man of War, Man of Peace? The Unauthorized Biography of Gerry Adams.* London, 1997.

The Irish in Ireland

Cullen, L. M. *Emergence of Modern Ireland, 1600–1900.* London, 1981.
Curtis, Edmund. *A History of Ireland.* London, 1936.
de Paor, Liam. *The Peoples of Ireland.* Notre Dame and London, 1986.
Foster, R. F. *Modern Ireland, 1600–1972.* New York and London, 1988.
Harbison, Peter. *The Archaeology of Ireland.* London, 1976.
Lee, Joe. *Ireland, 1912–1985, Politics and Society.* Cambridge, 1989.
Lyons, F. S. L. *The History of Modern Ireland.* New York, 1976.

The Irish in the Americas

Davin, N. F. *The Irishman in Canada.* Toronto, 1877.
Miller, Kirby. *Emigrants and Exiles.* New York, 1986.
Shannon, William B. *The American Irish.* Boston, 1967.

The Irish in Australia

Cleary, P. S. *Australia's Debt to Irish Nation Builders.* Melbourne, 1933.
Kiernan, T. J. *The Irish Exiles in Australia.* Melbourne, 1954.
O'Ferrall, Patrick. *The Irish in Australia.* Adelaide, 1987.

INDEX